STUDIES IN THE HISTORY
OF CHRISTIAN MISSIONS

R. E. Frykenberg
Brian Stanley
General Editors

STUDIES IN THE HISTORY OF CHRISTIAN MISSIONS

Alvyn Austin
China's Millions: The China Inland Mission and Late Qing Society, 1832-1905

Michael Bergunder
The South Indian Pentecostal Movement in the Twentieth Century

Judith M. Brown and Robert Eric Frykenberg, *Editors*
Christians, Cultural Interactions, and India's Religious Traditions

Robert Eric Frykenberg
*Christians and Missionaries in India:
Cross-Cultural Communication Since 1500*

Susan Billington Harper
*In the Shadow of the Mahatma: Bishop V. S. Azariah
and the Travails of Christianity in British India*

D. Dennis Hudson
Protestant Origins in India: Tamil Evangelical Christians, 1706-1835

Ogbu U. Kalu, *Editor*, and Alaine M. Low, *Associate Editor*
*Interpreting Contemporary Christianity:
Global Processes and Local Identities*

Donald M. Lewis, *Editor*
*Christianity Reborn: The Global Expansion of Evangelicalism
in the Twentieth Century*

Jon Miller
*Missionary Zeal and Institutional Control: Organizational Contradictions
in the Basel Mission on the Gold Coast, 1828-1917*

Andrew Porter, *Editor*
The Imperial Horizons of British Protestant Missions, 1880-1914

Dana L. Robert, *Editor*
Converting Colonialism: Visions and Realities in Mission History, 1709-1914

Wilbert R. Shenk, *Editor*
North American Foreign Missions, 1810-1914: Theology, Theory, and Policy

Brian Stanley
The World Missionary Conference: Edinburgh 1910

Brian Stanley, *Editor*
Christian Missions and the Enlightenment

Brian Stanley, *Editor*
Missions, Nationalism, and the End of Empire

John Stuart
British Missionaries and the End of Empire:
East, Central, and Southern Africa, 1939-64

Kevin Ward and Brian Stanley, *Editors*
The Church Mission Society and World Christianity, 1799-1999

Richard Fox Young, *Editor*
India and the Indianness of Christianity: Essays on Understanding—Historical,
Theological, and Bibliographical—in Honor of Robert Eric Frykenberg

British Missionaries
and the End of Empire

East, Central, and Southern Africa,

1939-64

John Stuart

WILLIAM B. EERDMANS PUBLISHING COMPANY

GRAND RAPIDS, MICHIGAN / CAMBRIDGE, U.K.

Published 2011 by
Wm. B. Eerdmans Publishing Co.
2140 Oak Industrial Drive N.E., Grand Rapids, Michigan 49505 /
P.O. Box 163, Cambridge CB3 9PU U.K.

Printed in the United States of America

17 16 15 14 13 12 11   7 6 5 4 3 2 1

Library of Congress Cataloging-in-Publication Data

Stuart, John.
British missionaries and the end of empire: East, Central,
and Southern Africa, 1939-64 / John Stuart.
p.   cm.   — (Studies in the history of Christian missions)
Includes bibliographical references (p.   ) and index.
ISBN 978-0-8028-6633-2 (pbk.: alk. paper)
1. Missions, British — Africa, Sub-Saharan — History — 20th century.
2. Africa, Sub-Saharan — Church history — 20th century.   I. Title.
BV3520.S78   2011
266′.023410670904 — dc22

2011005877

www.eerdmans.com

To Lesley McNeil Park

Contents

Acknowledgements

I am grateful to the many people upon whose advice and assistance I have relied in researching and writing this book. I thank especially Professor Andrew Porter for his research supervision and his encouragement, support and friendship. Thanks are due also, for their helpful comments, to the examiners of the doctoral dissertation on which this book is partly based: Professor John Peel and Professor John Wolffe. Professor David Killingray commented on the draft manuscript of the book, for which I am very grateful.

I am fortunate to have had the opportunity of working at the Department of History, King's College London, and at the Faculty of Arts and Social Sciences, Kingston University, London. At both places I have learned a great deal, from colleagues and students alike. I have also been able to draw on the expertise of conveners and participants at two seminars at the Institute of Historical Research, London: on Imperial and World History, and on Christian Missions in Global History.

I acknowledge with thanks financial assistance provided by the School of Humanities, King's College London, in the form of a three-year research studentship and a travel grant. I am grateful also to Professor Peter Marshall and to the Royal Historical Society for the award of a fellowship at the Institute of Historical Research. The Society also assisted with conference attendance and travel expenses. The Faculty of Arts and Social Sciences at Kingston University provided teaching relief, which facilitated the writing of the book. The period of my research coincided with two notable initiatives in the field of mission studies: the North Atlantic Missiology Project, and the Currents in World Christianity Project. I thank Professor Brian Stanley for facilitating my participation in these initiatives.

Acknowledgements

Research has entailed visits to many archive repositories, where I have benefitted greatly from the expertise and helpfulness of staff. My thanks to those at the following institutions: the Archives and Special Collections Department at the Library of the School of Oriental and African Studies, London; the Special Collections Department at the Library of the University of Birmingham; the National Archives of the UK; the National Archives of Scotland; the National Library of Scotland; the Centre for Research Collections at the Library of the University of Edinburgh; the Bodleian Library of Commonwealth and African Studies at Rhodes House, Oxford; Lambeth Palace Library, London; the Church of England Record Centre, London; the Mission Studies Library at Partnership House, London (now Crowther Mission Education Centre Library, Oxford); the Institute of Commonwealth Studies Library, London.

I also wish to thank for their assistance: Church of Scotland World Mission Council; Churches Together in Britain and Ireland; the Methodist Church; the Trustees of Lambeth Palace Library.

I am grateful to Lord Steel of Aikwood for allowing me to read private papers of his late father, Rev. David Steel.

Many other people have spoken or corresponded with me, to share their knowledge of missions, the church and colonialism in Africa. This has been extremely helpful to me, and I thank them all, particularly Rt Rev. Donald Arden, Professor Colin Baker, the late Professor Richard Gray, James Foster, Rt Rev. Dr. Graham Kings, Dr. Gordon Mungeam, the late Dr. Andrew Ross, Professor George Shepperson, and Rev. Vernon Stone.

My thanks to the editorial staff at Eerdmans for their help.

I acknowledge with thanks permission to draw on material previously published, as follows.

- From Taylor & Francis, for John Stuart, 'Overseas Mission: Voluntary Service and Aid to Africa: Max Warren, the Church Missionary Society and Kenya, 1945-63', *Journal of Imperial and Commonweath History* 36, no. 3 (2008): 527-43, accessible at http://www.informaworld.com
- From Palgrave Macmillan, for John Stuart, 'Empire, Religion and Colonial Botswana: The Seretse Khama Controversy, 1948-56', in Hilary M. Carey, ed., *Empires of Religion* (Basingstoke, 2008), pp. 311-32.

Throughout the period of researching and writing this book, family and friends have never been other than extremely encouraging and supportive. I'm especially grateful to Mary and John Wallace. My wife Lesley and our children Robyn and Miles have lived a long time with this project: I am indebted to them for their love and support.

Abbreviations

AA	*African Affairs*
AMU	African Mineworkers' Union
BCC	British Council of Churches
BMS	Berlin Missionary Society
CBMS	Conference of British Missionary Societies
CCAP	Church of Central Africa Presbyterian
CCAR	Church of Central Africa Rhodesia
CCK	Christian Council of Kenya
CERC	Church of England Record Centre, London
CMS	Church Missionary Society
CNC	Church and Nation Committee, General Assembly of the Church of Scotland
CPSA	Church of the Province of South Africa
CRO	Commonwealth Relations Office
CWM	Council for World Mission
DCP	Devlin Commission (1959) Papers
FMC	Foreign Missions Committee, General Assembly of the Church of Scotland
FP	(Geoffrey Francis) Fisher Papers
HJ	*The Historical Journal*
ICA	Inter-Church Aid
IJAHS	*International Journal of African Historical Studies*
IMC	International Missionary Council
IRM	*International Review of Missions*
JAH	*Journal of African History*

JCS	*Journal of Church and State*
JICH	*Journal of Imperial and Commonwealth History*
JRA	*Journal of Religion in Africa*
KAU	Kenya African Union
LCP	League of Coloured Peoples
LMS	London Missionary Society
LP	(Cosmo Gordon) Lang Papers
LPL	Lambeth Palace Library, London
MCP	Malawi Congress Party
MEF	Mindolo Ecumenical Foundation
MMS	Methodist Missionary Society
MOI	Ministry of Information
MRA	Moral Re-armament
NAS	National Archives of Scotland
NLS	National Library of Scotland
ODI	Overseas Development Institute
'PI'	'Prohibited Immigrant'
RHL	Rhodes House Library, Oxford
RNC	Rhodesia and Nyasaland Committee
RP	(Michael) Ramsey Papers
SOAS	School of Oriental and African Studies, London
SPG	Society for the Propagation of the Gospel
TNA: PRO	The National Archives of the UK: Public Record Office
TP	(William) Temple Papers
UBL	University of Birmingham Library
UCAA	United Central Africa Association
UDI	(Rhodesian) Unilateral Declaration of Independence, 1965
UMCA	Universities' Mission to Central Africa
UMCB	United Missions in the Copper Belt
USPG	United Society for the Propagation of the Gospel
VSO	Voluntary Service Overseas
WASU	West African Students' Union
WCC	World Council of Churches
YMCA	Young Men's Christian Association
YWCA	Young Women's Christian Association

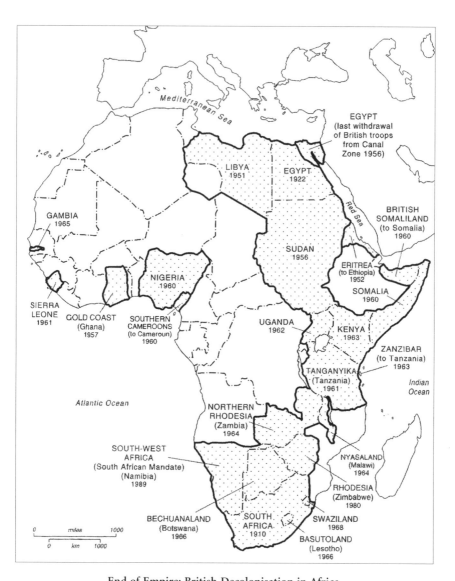

End of Empire: British Decolonisation in Africa

Oxford History of the British Empire, volume IV: *The Twentieth Century,* edited by Brown and Louis
(1999) Map 14.1, p. 349. By permission of Oxford University Press.

Nyasaland, 1960-61

Likoma Island in Lake Malawi is a relatively isolated place. In the twenty-first century that isolation is sometimes perceived as an advantage: the island is sufficiently accessible by boat and chartered plane to sustain an 'eco-friendly' tourist resort of some importance not only to the local economy but also to that of the republic of Malawi, formerly the British colony of Nyasaland. Tour operators invariably remind potential visitors that the island is also the site of St Peter's Anglican Cathedral, constructed during the first decade of the twentieth century from imported steel and locally fired bricks. Consecrated in 1911, St Peter's is still an active church as well as a tourist attraction. It is an imposing structure, twenty-five metres tall at its highest point, with a floor area roughly equal in size (it is claimed) to that of ancient Winchester Cathedral. Distance from areas of European settlement was an important factor in the decision of the Universities' Mission to Central Africa (UMCA) to establish in 1885 an island mission base on what Europeans knew then as Lake Nyasa. Missionaries were suspicious of the harmful effect that western civilisation was likely to have upon African life; yet complete isolation would have been contrary to the spirit and practise of mission, and over the course of time the UMCA commissioned two wood-burning steamships of British manufacture, one being named after the ill-fated first Bishop of Likoma Chauncy Maples, who drowned in the lake. The island thus became a viable base for Anglican mission work in central Africa as well as an official place of residence for bishops of Nyasaland (the diocese was formed in 1892). But the *Chauncy Maples* was eventually laid up for lack of funds in 1953. At the same time the then bishop, Frank Thorne, decided to move his residence from the island. His successor, appointed eight years later, certainly saw little merit in it as an administrative base. Isolation no longer seemed an advantage. It had indeed become a problem, part of a wider malaise affecting the UMCA in Nyasaland and beyond.

The new appointee, from 1961, was Rev. Donald Arden, and he had reasons of his own for not following episcopal precedent. Within a year of his arrival he would astonish the diocese by announcing his intention to marry. Previous bishops had been celibate in the Anglo-Catholic UMCA tradition. A High Churchman, Arden was not, however, a product of the UMCA. Born in 1916, he studied at the University of Leeds and then at nearby Mirfield, home of the monastic Community of the Resurrection. At Mirfield he became interested in overseas mission; then, after ordination and parish work in London, he sought the advice of another Anglican mission agency, the Society for the Propagation of the Gospel (SPG). It was 1942. Missionary recruits were scarce and overseas travel difficult and dangerous. Arden nonetheless managed to reach South Africa, where he spent eight years in diocesan work before moving on to similar activities in Swaziland. There he remained until offered a bishopric in a diocese about which he knew almost nothing. On arrival he found those affairs, as he related more than four decades later, in a parlous state.[1] There was almost no money. The European clergy appeared in need of rejuvenation. Thorne was an honourable and holy man about to retire after a quarter of a century's service as bishop; but he seemed out of touch and unable to fully comprehend the implications for the church of militant African nationalism in the local shape of Dr. Hastings Banda and the Malawi Congress Party (MCP). To Arden the contrast with the Presbyterian Church in Nyasaland appeared startling. In 1960 the missionaries of the Church of Scotland had handed over their ecclesiastical responsibilities to the Church of Central Africa Presbyterian (CCAP), becoming in effect ministers of the local church. Church and synod affairs were currently in the joint hands of Africans and Europeans, but under indigenous authority. Within another year the synod of the CCAP would have its first African general secretary, Rev. Jonathan Sangaya. Anglicans were a small minority among Nyasaland Christians compared with Presbyterians and Roman Catholics, and the future of their church, in the centenary year of the consecration of the first UMCA missionary bishop, Charles Frederick Mackenzie, did not seem promising.

Thorne's succession had been the subject of much discussion, not only in Nyasaland but also eight thousand kilometres away in London SW1, at UMCA headquarters in Great Peter Street and at nearby Lambeth Palace, official residence of the Archbishop of Canterbury. The appointment of a new

---

1. Author's interview with Rt Rev. D. S. Arden, 19 Aug. 2004.

bishop should have been a matter for the diocesan synod in consultation with the Archbishop of Central Africa, who was based in Southern Rhodesia (now Zimbabwe). But the Archbishop of Central Africa was also about to retire and there were other pressing considerations besides. All of central Africa was in turmoil, with Africans in Nyasaland and in the neighbouring British colony of Northern Rhodesia (now Zambia) demanding release from the imperial straitjacket of the Central African Federation into which they had been forced in 1953 with white-dominated Southern Rhodesia. As if that was not enough, UMCA headquarters had been informed that a campaign, possibly inspired by the MCP, was currently being waged in Nyasaland to have the radical English priest Rev. Michael Scott ('a sort of ecclesiastical Dr. Banda') appointed to succeed Thorne.[2] The most senior African clergyman in the diocese, Habil Chipembere, had only recently been made archdeacon. He would not be considered for the post. Arden was chosen to be the new bishop because he was the best candidate, and unlike African clergymen he had a university education. But the UMCA, mindful of a possible African reaction upon the church in Nyasaland, was keen to ensure that the new appointee, if European, should have no connections with Southern Rhodesia, long notorious for its antipathy to racial equality. The same considerations were duly taken into account when filling the archiepiscopal vacancy.

Arden felt that his immediate priority was to consolidate the church, financially and otherwise. He had to act quickly in order to secure the support of African clergy and congregations. It appeared that Thorne had recently allowed things to drift. The poverty of both mission and diocese compelled Arden to use international Anglican and interdenominational ecumenical contacts to secure funds for the church. On a visit to the United States in early 1963 he developed valuable links to this end with dioceses of the American Episcopal Church. By this time he had also begun to reconfigure diocesan affairs with a view towards increasing the level of African lay involvement in the church and sharing theological education resources with other Protestant denominations. All this activity took place within a troubled and uncertain political environment.

Sangaya's difficulties paralleled in some respects those of his Anglican counterpart. So limited were the finances of the CCAP that the salaries of its European ministers continued to be paid by the Church of Scotland. This was an arrangement irksome to members of the 'younger' church; it might too readily imply the retention of some sort of lien by the 'parent' in Britain. In

---

2. Lambeth Palace Library, London, Ramsey papers, 10, Canon G. W. Broomfield to Most Rev. A. M. Ramsey, 27 Oct. 1961.

1968, following Arden's example, Sangaya would journey to the United States in search of fellowship and disinterested financial support, especially from American Presbyterians. International contacts of this nature would assume considerable importance for cash-strapped church representatives in Africa during the 1960s. In certain respects, however, Sangaya's difficulties were unique, especially as they related to the political situation in Nyasaland. The transition of ecclesiastical authority from Church of Scotland missions to CCAP had not been smooth. Seven years after his ordination at the age of 45 (following a career as a teacher) Sangaya had in 1959 been appointed assistant general secretary of the Blantyre synod of the CCAP in preparation for the more senior role that he would undertake following the 'integration' (as the Scots insisted on describing it) of overseas missions into local church. But because of their outspoken support for Banda, some missionaries had by 1959 brought the wrath of the colonial authorities down upon missions and church alike. Not only that, numerically tiny but extremely vocal sections of the European Presbyterian congregations in the towns of Blantyre and the colonial capital, Zomba, were refusing to participate in the process of 'integration'. Grudgingly prepared to accept African leadership of the church, they remained intensely suspicious of links between the CCAP and Congress. In Scotland their cause was being taken up by influential members of the Kirk, worried that their compatriots in Africa might become the object of unwanted attention from Banda. The doctor had after all been detained without trial in March 1959 on suspicion of plotting the murder of the colony's European and Asian inhabitants. No one was certain what might ensue following his release from detention by order of Britain's Secretary of State for Colonies on 1 April 1960.

In the event, Banda's release did trigger some disorder, but not of a magnitude anticipated by Europeans. Some Anglican missionaries and the hapless Bishop Thorne were subjected by senior Congress officials to merely verbal assault. The party's supporters would have expected no less; in an independent Malawi, they were now being assured by Congress, Europeans would be retained only to dig latrines. Such rhetoric was intended both to muster support among Africans and to mock European pretensions, and it was incidental to Banda's main aim — to secure from Britain a commitment to self-government for Nyasaland. This he duly achieved at an official conference held in London during July and August 1960. Electoral success the following year confirmed Banda as, in effect, chief minister of the colony. Missions and churches now had to ready themselves for unprecedented local political change, and, subsequently, for the ending of the Central African Federation in December 1963. From 1964 they would also have to contend with new, independent national governments in Malawi and in Zambia. This situation was replicated in British colonial territories across Africa with the ominous, fateful exception of Southern Rhodesia: not until 1980 would it acquire majority African rule, as independent Zimbabwe.

Introduction

In its effects upon Protestant missions and churches the political situation in Nyasaland in the late 1950s and early 1960s was neither entirely typical of nor unique among Britain's colonies in east, central and southern Africa. Why then begin this history of British Protestant missionaries and the end of empire in Nyasaland? There are many reasons, one being the particularly vivid nature of events there. But the main reason is the complex nature of mission-state relations in the colony. By the time of its absorption into the British Empire in 1894, Nyasaland was already an important location for missionary activity, much of it (Anglican as well as Scottish Presbyterian) stimulated and inspired by David Livingstone. Church of Scotland and Free Church missionaries were fearful of Arab slave-traders, neighbouring Portuguese (in what is now Mozambique) and British chartered company interests alike. They argued in the late 1880s and early 1890s for the extension of British imperial influence. Thereafter, relations between Scottish missions and the colonial state proceeded amicably enough, if at times uneasily. Following the abortive African uprising against colonial rule led by John Chilembwe in 1915 the activities of the Scots became the subject of official enquiry. In the late 1920s and again in the late 1930s Scottish missionaries made known to government the extent of African anxiety about white settler ambitions for territorial aggrandisement, or 'closer union' in east and central Africa. This concern for African interests was scripturally based and paternalistic. It influenced missionary representation of African interests to colonial authority in many routine, informal ways but also in 'official' terms; missionaries served as nominated members of Nyasaland's Legislative Council. While the formation of the CCAP in 1924 ostensibly demonstrated the commitment of the Scottish missions to a self-governing indigenous church, control of ecclesiastical affairs remained until the late 1950s largely in European missionary hands. The growth of African nationalism during and after the Second World War, specifically in the form of the Nyasaland African Congress (formed in 1944, and renamed as the Malawi Congress Party in 1959), thus constituted a challenge not merely to the colonial state but to Scottish missions and African church also.

The challenge posed to churches and missions by African nationalist political parties was not of course unique to Nyasaland. But the almost proprietorial interest of Scots in the colony's affairs lent debate on its church-state relations a peculiar intensity. Debate was also informed by controversy about the future of the Central African Federation and about government efforts to quell the threat of African unrest. An official commission of enquiry into the 1959 disturbances headed by British High Court judge Sir Patrick Devlin had concluded that Nyasaland was currently, if only temporarily, 'a police state'. British Methodist missionaries had privately used the same phrase a year earlier, to communicate to colleagues in London their unease at the censorious and repressive tendencies of the colonial authorities in Northern Rhodesia.[1] Government action was not only radicalising African nationalists, it was having a similar effect upon certain British missionaries sympathetic to African nationalist aims. To these missionaries, the authorities seemed hostile to criticism and unwilling to come to terms with nationalist demands. In turn, those authorities were unduly ready to regard missionaries as agitators, with the Scots being the object of particular suspicion.

How influenced were British missionaries by African nationalism in the two decades after the Second World War? The effect was varied and subject to change over time. During this period there were things other than nationalism that worried missionaries. Communism was a matter of no little concern, as communist China's expulsion of western missionaries demonstrated. Of equal if not greater worry at times was the prospect of nuclear war. So likely did intercontinental conflict between the West and the Soviet Union appear in 1948 that at least one British missionary society drew up contingency plans for the abandonment of its London headquarters.[2] But in the late colonial period nationalism remained *the* constant, pressing factor in mission and church affairs.

1. School of Oriental and African Studies, London (hereafter SOAS), Methodist Missionary Society papers (hereafter MMS), T187, '1956-60' file, Rev. C. M. Morris to Rev. T. A. Beetham, 11 July, cited in Beetham to Rev. J. A. R. Watt, 28 July 1958.

2. University of Birmingham Library Special Collections (hereafter UBL), Church Missionary Society papers (hereafter CMS), G/AP10, Canon M. A. C. Warren to Home Secretary, 3 Dec. 1948. The CMS considered moving its secretariat to Ireland, or even Australia.

Many African nationalist leaders had received a mission education. But the influence of that education should not be overestimated. Mission education mattered, but nationalists were of diverse background and experience, and receptive to myriad other influences ranging from Pan-Africanism to Marxism.[3] Conversely, increasing numbers of British missionaries were by the late 1950s seeking to learn from African nationalism, as, also, from African religions, the better to enable the church to continue its work in an Africa under local, indigenous rather than white, colonial rule.[4] Young, recently ordained Scottish missionaries arriving in central Africa in the 1950s often considered evangelism 'a useful auxiliary to political action'.[5] They were more likely as a result to find common cause with African nationalists, mission-educated or not, than with older, more conservative mission colleagues. This was equally true of certain English clergymen such as the Methodists Colin Morris and Merfyn Temple, befriended by the Zambian nationalist leader Kenneth Kaunda. They also engaged personally in political activity in Northern Rhodesia.[6] Such recourse to politics was far from typical. But it signified a more widespread unease and even disgust among missionaries at the colonial state's intolerance of opposition. It was indicative also of growing missionary belief in the legitimacy of majority African rule.

For the Scots, active support for African nationalism was not an end in itself; it was essential to the vitality and relevance of the church in Africa. There was, too, another consideration. Support for nationalism might help invigorate the church in Scotland. For all its reputation for social awareness, and notwithstanding the impact of a mid-1950s home-grown evangelistic campaign with the slogan 'Tell Scotland', the Scottish Kirk remained a conservative institution in certain respects, hidebound by implicit obeisance to landed Tory values.[7] The activism of the Nyasaland missions, underpinned in part by the 'radical' ethos of another Scottish-based Christian organisation, Rev. Dr George MacLeod's Iona Community, conversely offered the prospect of church revitalisation, in part through support for the African nationalist

---

3. Adrian Hastings, *The Construction of Nationhood: Ethnicity, Religion and Nationalism* (Cambridge, 1997), pp. 148-66.

4. For example, John V. Taylor, *The Primal Vision: Christian Presence amid African Religion* (London, 1963).

5. National Library of Scotland, Accession 7548, General Assembly of the Church of Scotland Foreign Missions Committee papers (hereafter NLS), B395, Watt to Rev. N. C. Bernard, 24 Feb. 1954.

6. Kenneth Kaunda and Colin Morris, *Black Government?* (Lusaka, 1960).

7. Callum G. Brown, *The Social History of Religion in Scotland since 1730* (London and New York, 1987), pp. 218-19.

cause. Many younger male Scots missionaries in late-1950s Africa were members of the Community (which did not admit women at this time). For some Methodists in Britain, meanwhile, Colin Morris's ministry in the Copperbelt town of Chingola had about it a strong element of the prophetic: requests from Morris's unsympathetic European colleagues that he be censured for 'political' utterances caused Methodist Missionary Society headquarters to respond that it was '... loth to ask the Methodist Church with all its traditions for social righteousness to curb a possible reformer'.[8] Morris, those in London believed, was carrying out work vital to the church and to the people of Africa. Nor was British missionary awareness of Africa's importance to the worldwide church confined to English nonconformists or Scots. The Anglican missionary and author Rev. John V. Taylor of the Church Missionary Society (CMS) was a strong advocate of African church leadership and of the use of African languages and music in the liturgy. Taylor argued publicly for African Christian involvement in politics.[9] He was meanwhile privately critical of the UMCA for its unwillingness to support Africans agitating peacefully against the colonial state.[10]

Missionaries in British colonies were influenced also by certain 'political' priests in South Africa such as Michael Scott and his fellow-Anglican Father Trevor Huddleston. Yet none appears to have aspired to politics as vocation, believing instead that leadership of African states as of churches should pass to Africans. Notwithstanding developments in relation to the CCAP in Nyasaland, however, British missions had been slow to plan for this eventuality. The UMCA, which was excessively reliant upon episcopal authority and which remained determinedly aloof from the 'political' world, had virtually eschewed such planning. Its bishops and missionaries took the view that western mission, like British colonialism, remained a viable presence in Africa, 'wind of change' notwithstanding. Yet 1960 — the year of British Prime Minister Harold Macmillan's invocation of that phrase — was momentous for British missions in Africa. A state of emergency that had existed in Kenya since 1952 was ended. Constitutional conferences on Nyasaland and on Kenya convened in London. A Royal Commission investigated and reported on the future of the Central African Federation. It was by no means clear that the end of empire in British colonial Africa was imminent in 1960, but change of unprecedented magnitude now seemed not only possible but likely. Many

8. SOAS, MMS, T187, '1956-60' file, Beetham to Rev. E. G. Nightingale, 24 July 1958.

9. J. V. Taylor, *Christianity and Politics in Africa* (Harmondsworth, 1957).

10. Bodleian Library of Commonwealth and African Studies at Rhodes House, Oxford, Universities' Mission to Central Africa papers, SF139, Rev. J. V. Taylor to Canon G. W. Broomfield, 20 April 1959.

missionaries acknowledged publicly as well as privately that the church in Africa could not remain either unaffected or indifferent.[11]

In Nyasaland were to be found many of the salient characteristics of the British Protestant missionary experience of end of empire in Africa. Not the least of these characteristics was the missionary effort to come to terms with political change. African nationalism disrupted and yet also invigorated the church. Missionaries welcomed it and were alarmed by it, and they responded to it in many different ways. Yet missionaries' experience of end of empire was not solely shaped by political transition in the colonies; broader religious influences were also at work on the church in Africa. These took many forms, not least that of independent churches, often in secession from churches of mission origin. Conversely, while UMCA officials desired a European bishop for the diocese of Nyasaland they were mortified by the possibility of African preference for Michael Scott. Scott had no ambitions in this respect. But his activism against colonialism and racism seemed to demonstrate how the church might engage meaningfully with issues of concern to Christians of *any* race or nationality. At the beginning of the 1960s African Christians were arguably more alert to such possibilities than were many of their European counterparts.

Writing Missionary Histories

African Christianity has changed a great deal since the formal ending of British colonial rule. It is possible that with its range and adaptability it may in the long term exert a truly transformative effect upon western Christianity.[12] Recently, African Christianity has been growing at an unprecedented rate. That growth owes something both to churches of mission origin and also to the effects of what Paul Gifford has termed the 'Pentecostal explosion'.[13] And the effect has been felt well beyond Africa. Christian evangelism is now very likely to be undertaken by Africans, not merely within the continent but also far beyond it, in the United Kingdom and elsewhere.[14] Migration from Africa

11. J. W. C. Dougall, *Christians in the African Revolution: The Duff Missionary Lectures, 1962* (Edinburgh, 1963).

12. Philip Jenkins, *The Next Christendom: The Coming of Global Christianity* (New York, 2002).

13. Paul Gifford, 'Some Recent Developments in African Christianity', *African Affairs* 93, no. 373 (1994): 524-8.

14. John Clark, 'CMS and Mission in Britain: The Evolution of a Policy', in Kevin Ward and Brian Stanley, eds., *The Church Mission Society and World Christianity, 1799-1999* (Grand Rapids, MI, and Richmond, Surrey, 2000), pp. 330-43.

currently provides an important stimulus to church growth throughout Europe.[15] The influence of the African episcopate is increasingly felt. This is as evident from the 2005 appointment of the black Ugandan John Sentamu to the archbishopric of York as from the contemporaneous agonising of the Anglican Communion about homosexuality in the ministry.[16] Much has indeed changed since the mid-1970s when African and Asian church leaders called unsuccessfully for a moratorium on western missions.[17] Western missions have themselves undergone a great deal of change; their work in Africa is now as likely to focus on developmental and human rights issues as on evangelism. And rather than being primarily British, missions are most likely to be of American nationality and of theological orientation that is largely conservative and evangelical.[18]

What of the many British missionary societies of the imperial era, whether Anglican, such as the CMS, SPG or UMCA, or nonconformist, such as the London Missionary Society (LMS), or the (Presbyterian) missions of the Church of Scotland? Not all have survived, and the passage of time together with changes in personnel, in policy, even in nomenclature has all but relieved the remainder of any burden of association with empire. The subject of missions' links with empire remains, nevertheless, the subject of considerable historical debate.

This book examines the impact upon British Protestant missions of developments in and relating to parts of British colonial Africa. I have not attempted to cover sub-Saharan British Africa in its entirety even though every colony may be said to have had some kind of 'missionary history'. I have chosen instead to focus on certain events in east, central and southern Africa. There, to an extent much greater than in west Africa, missionaries had to contend with white settler opinion (including that in South Africa) as well as with African nationalism and colonial authority. Missionaries' ability to influence events was limited: the dramatic events of late colonial Africa offer a contrast therefore to 'the drama of imperial expansion' during the nineteenth century, in which missionaries undoubtedly played a more influential role.[19]

In his book *Religion versus Empire?* Andrew Porter has surveyed the rela-

---

15. Gerrie Ter Haar, *Halfway to Paradise: African Christians in Europe* (Cardiff, 1998).

16. Stephen Bates, *A Church at War: Anglicans and Homosexuality* (London, 2004).

17. Elliott Kendall, *The End of an Era: Africa and the Missionary* (London, 1978), pp. 86-107.

18. Julie Hearn, 'The "Invisible" NGO: US Evangelical Missions in Kenya', *Journal of Religion in Africa* 32, no. 1 (2002): 32-59.

19. John H. Darch, *Missionary Imperialists? Missionaries, Government and the Growth of the British Empire in the Tropics, 1860-85* (Eugene, OR, 2009), p. 236.

tionship between missions and overseas expansion from Britain in the period 1700-1914. While acknowledging that missionaries may indeed have identified with empire, Porter concludes that mission theology was more typically characterised by a kind of 'anti-imperialism'. He argues that 'in so far as they were beginning before 1914 to provoke, equip and even sympathise with the first stirrings of indigenous political nationalisms — in Egypt or India — [missionaries] were nurturing seeds of empire's twentieth century demise'.[20] Complementing this argument is Porter's emphasis not on Protestant missions' strength, but on their relative weakness in certain respects: 'highly effective as missions were in promoting cultural change', he suggests, 'they were among the weakest agents of "cultural imperialism"'.[21] Indigenous peoples, according to Porter, proved readily capable of shaping mission to their own ends — or of discarding it entirely.[22] Such assertions accord with those of some historians of empire, such as A. G. Hopkins.[23] Yet they run contrary to arguments advanced by other historians, most notably perhaps Jean and John Comaroff, who in the early 1990s influentially argued that missionaries were especially effective agents of empire and colonialism.[24] More recently Jeffrey Cox has argued, with particular reference to the work both of the Comaroffs and of Edward Said, that 'if missionaries are to be interpreted it is through the rhetoric of unmasking'. To this end, Cox identifies three distinct, overlapping master narratives of mission history: 'the imperialist/nationalist with its presumption of marginality, the Saidian with its unmasking of imperial complicity, and the providentialist with its difficulties in confronting the imperial character of the missionary enterprise'.[25] Yet it undoubtedly remains difficult, as Cox acknowledges, to identify a 'key' that might unlock all the secrets of the missionary encounter either with African peoples or with colonial states.[26] Those encounters were of an extremely complicated nature. They were informed on the missionaries'

20. Andrew Porter, *Religion versus Empire? British Protestant Missionaries and Overseas Expansion, 1700-1914* (Manchester, 2004), pp. 322-3.

21. Andrew Porter, '"Cultural Imperialism" and Protestant Missionary Enterprise, 1780-1914', *Journal of Imperial and Commonwealth History* (hereafter *JICH*) 25, no. 3 (1997): 388.

22. Richard Gray, *Black Christians and White Missionaries* (New Haven, CT, 1990).

23. A. G. Hopkins, 'Back to the Future: From National History to Imperial History', *Past & Present* 164 (1999): 198-243.

24. Jean and John Comaroff, *Of Revelation and Revolution: Christianity, Colonialism and Consciousness in South Africa* (Chicago, 1991).

25. Jeffrey Cox, *Imperial Fault Lines: Christianity and Colonial Power in India, 1818-1940* (Stanford, CA, 2002), pp. 10-14.

26. Cox, *Imperial Fault Lines*, p. 16.

side not merely by theology but also by contemporary ideas and assumptions about race and empire.

In studying and writing about missionaries it is certainly necessary to confront the racial and imperial aspects of their activities. Yet according to Hopkins, an important objective in writing imperial history is *not* to 'unmask' European racism but to 'acquire a better grasp of the basis and purpose of colonial rule, and to relate both to the indigenous history of subject peoples'.[27] This is a problematic assertion for the historian of missions, especially those in late colonial Africa. Missionaries may at times have been as capable of racism as of 'anti-imperialism'. There is evidence of both characteristics. There was no single missionary response to the end of empire in Africa. Missionary responses were too varied and too complex for this to have been the case.

That variety, with all its tensions and contradictions, is readily apparent in the material located in missionary archives and upon which this book is substantially based. Cox has written that 'interpreting missionary records requires constant attention to the multiple levels of exclusion in the narratives'.[28] The levels of such exclusion, notably in terms of race, can indeed appear both remarkable and remarkably persistent in source material from the mid-twentieth century. Also, and as Peggy Brock reminds us in relation to those local evangelists upon whom the spread of Christianity ultimately depended, a 'hidden history' of mission and of empire exists beyond the missionary archive.[29] That cannot be gainsaid, least of all in relation to Africa.[30] Yet for what it reveals both wittingly and unwittingly of missionary attitudes, the material in that archive is of great importance in enabling us to understand better the missionary encounter with African nationalism, with imperialism and with the end of empire.

The history of mission has in any case altered a great deal during the last three decades, and only partly in response to the influence of Said and the Comaroffs.[31] The work of many other historians during that period has typi-

---

27. Hopkins, 'Back to the Future', p. 230.

28. Cox, *Imperial Fault Lines*, p. 5.

29. Peggy Brock, 'New Christians as Evangelists', in Norman Etherington, ed., *Missions and Empire* (Oxford, 2005), p. 150.

30. On the limitations of the archive, see Derek R. Peterson and Giacomo Macola, eds., *Recasting the Past: History Writing and Political Works in Modern Africa* (Athens, OH, 2009).

31. Andrew Porter, 'Church History, History of Christianity, Religious History: Some Reflections on British Missionary Enterprise since the Late Eighteenth Century', *Church History* 71, no. 3 (2002): 555-84.

cally been characterised by concern for the complexity of mission's relationship with empire.[32] As for denominational mission histories, once a record of achievement and an aid (of perhaps doubtful utility) to recruitment, they now typically eschew master narratives for reflection on a range of diverse issues, including theology, gender and race.[33] Increasingly, historians of mission tackle questions of race, gender, empire and also (albeit still to a relatively small extent) postcolonialism.[34] Four decades after the formal ending of British rule in Africa the history of missions during the period from the 1940s to the 1960s is gradually beginning to undergo reconsideration and re-evaluation. This book aims to contribute to that process by critically examining British Protestant missionary experiences in detail across a wide denominational and geographical range. It focuses variously and for the most part on the London Missionary Society, the Church Missionary Society, the foreign missions of the Church of Scotland and the Universities' Mission to Central Africa. In terms of colonial territories it focuses primarily on Bechuanaland, Nyasaland, Northern Rhodesia and Kenya. It argues for diversity and ambiguity as key factors in missionaries' relationship both with empire and with African nationalism during the period 1939-64. Missionaries were suspicious of nationalism, yet for the most part they eventually welcomed it. As for empire, missionaries sometimes supported it, sometimes drew comfort from it, sometimes criticised it and finally learned to live with its formal demise. They would continue to undertake overseas work in Africa after the formal ending of empire. Missions had links with empire, but their work did not ultimately depend upon the continuation of British imperial rule. African nationalists might decry missions as imperialistic, but after the formal ending of empire, mission and church organisations would continue to work in African independent states.

---

32. Porter, *Religion versus Empire?*; Gray, *Black Christians;* Brian Stanley, *The Bible and the Flag: Protestant Missions and British Imperialism in the Nineteenth and Twentieth Centuries* (Leicester, 1990); Adrian Hastings, 'The Clash of Nationalism and Universalism within Twentieth Century Missionary Christianity', in Brian Stanley, ed., *Missions, Nationalism, and the End of Empire* (Grand Rapids, MI, and Cambridge, 2003), pp. 15-33.

33. For example, Ward and Stanley, eds., *The Church Mission Society.*

34. Anna Johnson, *Missionary Writing and Empire, 1800-1860* (Cambridge, 2003), pp. 30-37; Robert S. Heaney, 'Coloniality and Theological Method in Africa', *Journal of Anglican Studies* 7, no. 1 (2009): 1-11.

Histories of Christianity in Africa and beyond Africa

Africans responded to mission in many different ways. As John Lonsdale has written, 'there were many Christianities to choose from'.[35] In terms of the expansion of those Christianities what happened outside Africa might often be as important as what happened within. This is as true for missions and churches in Africa as for African economies, cultures and societies. And for all its emphasis upon Africa, this book also considers how mission in the colonies was influenced by developments elsewhere, especially in Britain, the country of origin for so many missionaries in Africa.

The effect of empire upon Britain and upon other western societies continues to provoke much debate.[36] The term 'end of empire' is itself contested. By no means did decolonisation mean the end of unequal relationships between Africa and the West. Some continuity was evident all the same, and historians have noted the importance of certain 'networks' of communication, influence, patronage and resistance to empire.[37] Others have meanwhile examined the implications for empire and 'post-imperial' Britain alike of old and new 'transnational' flows of people, of commerce and of ideas.[38] For much of the twentieth century British Protestant missionaries were mainstays of international, interdenominational and ecumenical networks of communication and support that have outlasted empire.[39] No wide-ranging, comparative history of Protestant mission activity in the mid-twentieth century would be complete without mention of organisations such as the International Missionary Council (IMC) and the World Council of Churches (WCC), founded in 1921 and 1948 respectively. They shared a commitment to the worldwide unity of Protestant churches. Arguably, they have not fulfilled either western missionary or African church expectations of such unity.[40] In transcending the colonial period the WCC (into which the IMC was integrated in 1961) provides an example of continuity; but its role and that of the

---

35. Bruce Berman and John Lonsdale, *Unhappy Valley: Conflict in Kenya and Africa: Book Two* (Oxford, 1992), p. 367.

36. Andrew Thompson, *The Empire Strikes Back? The Impact of Imperialism on Britain from the Mid-Nineteenth Century* (Harlow, 2005); Martin Shipway, *Decolonization and Its Impact: A Comparative Approach to the End of the Colonial Empires* (Malden, MA, and Oxford, 2008).

37. Alan Lester, *Imperial Networks: Creating Identities in Nineteenth Century South Africa and Britain* (London and New York, 2001).

38. Antoinette Burton, ed., *After the Imperial Turn: Thinking With and Through the Nation* (Durham, NC, 2003).

39. Timothy Yates, *Christian Mission in the Twentieth Century* (Cambridge, 1994).

40. Jeffrey Cox, *The British Missionary Enterprise since 1700* (London, 2006), pp. 245-7.

IMC should be kept in perspective: discontinuity was a salient characteristic of mission and church affairs in late colonial and early independent Africa. Nevertheless, those organisations mattered to missionaries, and this book makes due reference to them and to their British national equivalents: the Conference of British Missionary Societies (CBMS) and the British Council of Churches (BCC).[41] Denominationalism was an important aspect of Protestant mission activity, but so also was ecumenism. In emphasising its ostensibly transnational and interracial characteristics, Protestant ecumenical networks may have helped overseas mission adapt to a 'post-imperial' world.[42]

Writing in 1979, Hastings suggested that the formal ending of European empires rescued mission churches, 'in the nick of time', from possible oblivion. Political change did indeed hasten the indigenisation of church leadership.[43] But that process was extremely protracted: missions' underinvestment in the training of local clergy meant that the church in Africa continued to rely heavily upon European-born leaders until the end of the 1960s. The outlook of those leaders was neither exclusively 'African' nor 'European'; rather was it most often interracial, as may be seen in the 'post-imperial' careers of church leaders such as Huddleston (from 1960 to 1968, Bishop of Masasi, in Tanganyika, now Tanzania). The decolonisation of the church in Africa, like that of the colonial state, was no straightforward, planned affair.

John McCracken has pointedly noted how Scottish missionary attitudes to African political affairs lurched during the 1950s and 1960s from the politically quiescent to the prophetic and then back to the politically quiescent.[44] We should not be too surprised by this. There were theological factors, such as that identified by David Maxwell: notably, 'a simplistic recognition of the secular authority of the state grounded on Romans 13'.[45] With some notable individual exceptions such as Colin Morris, British missionaries tended not to be very politically aware. Their main wish for the state, be it colonial or African independent, was that it should allow them to work unhindered. To be

41. The CBMS was formed in 1912, the BCC in 1942.

42. John Stuart, 'Beyond Sovereignty? British Protestant Missions, Empire and Transnationalism, 1890-1950', in Kevin Grant, Philippa Levine and Frank Trentmann, eds., *Beyond Sovereignty: Britain, Empire and Transnationalism, c. 1860-1950* (Basingstoke and New York, 2007), pp. 103-25.

43. Adrian Hastings, *A History of African Christianity, 1950-75* (Cambridge, 1979), p. 259.

44. John McCracken, 'Church and State in Malawi: The Scottish Presbyterian Missions, 1875-1965', in Holger Bernt Hansen and Michael Twaddle, eds., *Christian Missionaries and the State in the Third World* (Oxford and Athens, OH, 2002), pp. 176-93.

45. David Maxwell, 'Decolonization', in Norman Etherington, ed., *Missions and Empire* (Oxford, 2005), p. 291.

sure, they had since the 1920s become increasingly dependent upon government funding, especially in the sphere of African education. Such largesse came at a heavy price, as many missionaries realised even by 1939; it meant the gradual but insidious attenuation of mission influence over education policy. This process would continue during the Second World War and after. Even before Christian voluntary organisations in Britain began to realise the implications for their work of the postwar welfare state, British missionaries anticipated that the 1940 Colonial Welfare and Development Act would be characterised not by concern for the spiritual well-being of colonial peoples but instead by remorseless 'technical efficiency'.[46] Missionaries rarely regarded the interventionist, omnicompetent imperial state with anything other than suspicion. They were appalled by the societal and environmental effects of the massive groundnuts scheme undertaken by the state in Tanganyika in the late 1940s. Nevertheless, they were at times unduly preoccupied by their own affairs, notably by the extent to which control over African education was ceded to local educational authorities.[47] They were often insufficiently mindful of the larger iniquities of empire. Individual missionaries had long been sceptical and even critical of colonial authority, but wide acceptance of and support for African majority rule took much longer to develop. Missionaries made remarkably little demur in 1953 when the Central African Federation was brought into being, against African wishes. They were for a considerable time divided among themselves as to the government of Kenya's anti-Mau Mau policies. They were slow to criticise openly the government of South Africa for its policies in support of apartheid.

This book is not directly concerned with South African affairs. Church and mission attitudes to apartheid have been the subject of several recent studies.[48] But the experience of British missionaries in much of colonial Africa during the period 1939-64 cannot be fully understood without reference to events in South Africa. The controversy surrounding the marriage in 1948 of Seretse Khama, regent-elect of the Bangwato people of the Bechuanaland

---

46. Rev. H. D. Hooper, 'The Church and Colonial Development', CBMS *Report for the Year 1939-40* (London, 1940), p. 62.

47. David H. S. Lyon, *In Pursuit of a Vision: The Story of the Church of Scotland's Developing Relationship with the Churches Emerging from the Missionary Movement in the Twenty-Five Years from 1947 to 1972* (Edinburgh, 1998), pp. 154-6.

48. Neil Overy, '"These Difficult Days": Mission Church Reactions to Bantu Education in South Africa' (University of London PhD thesis, 2002); Robert Skinner, 'Christian Reconstruction, Secular Politics: Michael Scott and the Campaign for Right and Justice, 1943-45', in Saul Dubow and Alan Jeeves, eds., *South Africa's 1940s: Worlds of Possibilities* (Cape Town, 2005), pp. 246-66.

Protectorate (now Botswana), to Ruth Williams, a white English woman, demonstrated how ill-equipped was the ostensibly influential LMS to handle the implications for the church of political and racial controversy: the government in Pretoria successfully pressured its counterpart in London to banish Seretse from the Protectorate.[49] Fear of Afrikaner expansion into British colonies in central Africa after 1948 overrode missionary concerns about the imposition of the Central African Federation. Only with the coming into effect of the Bantu Education Act in South Africa in January 1954 did British missionaries begin to reconsider their previous unwillingness to criticise apartheid publicly. They remained, though, hesitant about subjecting empire to criticism. They considered Britain's colonial policy in east and central Africa, with its emphasis on racial 'partnership', the very antithesis of apartheid. Only with the increasing recourse of the colonial state to violence in central Africa as in Kenya did they fully comprehend, and finally acknowledge, that 'partnership' could not mean racial equality.

Reluctance to criticise government was widespread but was most apparent within the UMCA. Charles M. Good, Jr, in a detailed study of the mission's medical work in Nyasaland, describes the UMCA position on the Central African Federation controversy as one of 'cowardice'.[50] That is a harsh verdict. The affairs of the UMCA for much of the period 1939-64 were characterised less by cowardice than by naïve management and leadership. UMCA missionaries saw themselves as custodians in certain ways of African life. They were not unsympathetic to African grievances, but few understood much less sympathised with militant nationalism. The mission's idealised vision of African church and society was out of step with changing political and social developments.[51]

The contrast between the UMCA and the much larger CMS was notable, and not merely for theological reasons. In Canon Max Warren, the CMS had from 1942 until 1963 a general secretary often acknowledged as unusually farseeing and influential. Less often noted are the constraints upon Warren's influencing ability. Having nonetheless a keen sense of history, Warren considered that the CMS had good reason to feel embarrassed by its past relationship with empire; the Society had lobbied in the early 1890s for imperial expansion

---

49. Susan Williams, *Colour Bar: The Triumph of Seretse Khama and His Nation* (London, 2006).

50. Charles M. Good, Jr, *The Steamer Parish: The Rise and Fall of Missionary Medicine on an African Frontier* (Chicago and London, 2004), p. 417.

51. Andrew Porter, 'The Universities' Mission to Central Africa: Anglo-Catholicism and the Twentieth Century Colonial Encounter', in Brian Stanley, ed., *Missions, Nationalism, and the End of Empire* (Grand Rapids, MI, and Cambridge, 2003), pp. 79-107.

into Uganda. In the mid-1950s the CMS aimed to mobilise support not at all for empire but for the overseas church. Since the time of Warren's nineteenth-century predecessor Henry Venn, the CMS, like other Protestant bodies, had ostensibly been committed to the 'euthanasia' of mission and the development of self-governing, self-supporting and self-propagating churches.[52] Personally committed to the indigenisation of the church in Africa, Warren nevertheless envisaged in the 1950s a continuing role for British missions in recruiting, training and fundraising on behalf of the overseas church. Warren strongly believed that British Christians were still needed and wanted overseas. But mission as religious vocation was already in decline by this time.

In his book *The Death of Christian Britain,* Callum Brown has emphasised the apparently uneven path taken by secularisation in Britain during the mid-twentieth century. From 1945 to the end of the 1950s, there appears to have been, according to Brown, a short-lived resurgence in British Christian belief.[53] This interpretation has been much debated.[54] It is not clear what effect such a phenomenon may have had on overseas mission from Britain. The decline of twentieth-century Anglo-Catholicism from its interwar highpoint certainly affected the UMCA. The decline of English (and Welsh) Congregationalism affected the mission agency with which it was most closely associated, the nominally interdenominational LMS. All Protestant missions experienced a dearth of new British recruits in the two decades after the Second World War. At the war's end mission officials of every denomination hoped that ranks might be swollen by demobilised military personnel. Such an influx never materialised, and it is impossible to gauge the number of potential mission recruits who opted instead for other careers, such as government service in the colonies. In that respect at least, British missions did not constitute an important part of what has been described as the 'second colonial occupation' of Africa in the late 1940s and early 1950s.[55] Meanwhile, the context not only of mission service but also of support in Britain for missions was changing, for a variety of reasons.

British missionary societies relied heavily upon denominational giving by supporters 'at home'. The formation after the war of new, non-religious aid

52. C. Peter Williams, *The Ideal of the Self-Governing Church: A Study in Victorian Missionary Strategy* (Leiden, 1990).

53. Callum G. Brown, *The Death of Christian Britain: Understanding Secularisation, 1800-2000* (New York, 2001), pp. 170-92.

54. For example, in Jane Garnett, Matthew Grimley, Alana Harris, William Whyte and Sarah Williams, eds., *Redefining Christian Britain: Post-1945 Perspectives* (London, 2007).

55. D. A. Low and J. M. Lonsdale, 'Introduction: Towards the New Order, 1945-63', in D. A. Low and A. Smith, eds., *History of East Africa: Vol. III* (Oxford, 1976), pp. 12-16.

organisations such as the Oxford Committee for Famine Relief (later OXFAM) introduced a complicating factor. Frank Prochaska has noted the tendency of British Christians to support activities overseas rather than at home after 1945.[56] Increasingly, this found expression less in denominational than in interdenominational (and even non-denominational) terms. Agencies such as the World Council of Churches and the churches' Inter-Church Aid and Refugee Service (from 1964, Christian Aid) began to assume larger roles. Overseas mission work required volunteers with professional expertise beyond the educational, medical and theological spheres. Something else changed also: the expectation that mission should necessarily entail a lifetime vocation. Missions increasingly competed with secular non-governmental organisations for suitable staff and volunteers.

All these developments were in train by the early 1960s. They were both influenced by and in turn impacted upon mission theology. Mission, long regarded by those in the West as an indispensable aspect of the church's work, became the subject of intense and often critical theological reappraisal. Of itself this was hardly a new development: missionaries constantly re-examined their faith and their vocation. But they increasingly faced questioning and criticism of mission by indigenous leaders of the 'younger' churches and by African nationalists also.[57] By the mid-1950s the word 'missionary' seemed to carry unacceptable overtones of western domination.

Indigenous criticism of missions took varied form. Of tremendous influence during this period were the stimuli — or more often shocks — caused to missions by the continuing growth of independent African church movements. The failure to invest greater resources in African clergy and lay leadership and to plan for devolution of ecclesiastical authority inevitably led to African dissatisfaction. Sometimes this failure was compounded by rumour and by missionaries' inability or unwillingness to comprehend the extent of African hostility to imperial political initiatives such as the Central African Federation.[58] One of many consequences might be church fragmentation. Perhaps the most notable and even at the time well-publicised manifestations of this tendency was the breakaway Lumpa Church of Alice Lenshina in Northern Rhodesia.[59] The Lenshina phenomenon caused bafflement and even

---

56. Frank Prochaska, *Christianity and Social Service in Modern Britain: The Disinherited Spirit* (Oxford, 2006), p. 160.

57. David J. Bosch, *Witness to the World: The Christian Mission in Theological Perspective* (London, 1980), pp. 159-81.

58. Luise White, *Speaking with Vampires: Rumor and History in Colonial Africa* (Berkeley and Los Angeles, 2000), pp. 296-305.

59. Andrew D. Roberts, *The Lumpa Church of Alice Lenshina* (Lusaka, 1972), originally

alarm among Scottish missionaries. Yet many were intrigued by and not un-admiring of its success; its vitality encouraged optimism for the future of African churches under African leadership. Nevertheless, what to some missionaries were signs of vitality could seem to others evidence of unpredictability, or worse. The East African Revival (or Balokole), which originated and developed in Rwanda, Uganda and parts of Kenya in the 1930s, was an indigenous Christian movement of great spiritual power and influence; yet while some Anglican missionaries welcomed its invigorating effect upon the church, to others its message encompassing religious and racial equality could appear dangerously 'anarchical'.[60] But Revival would come to be appreciated and even revered by missionaries, for underpinning Kikuyu Christian witness in the face of Mau Mau persecution in 1950s Kenya.[61] Ultimately, missionaries concluded, the church in Africa must be a truly African church. This meant more than a previously nominal commitment to African ecclesiastical training and leadership; it also meant confronting, however belatedly in some cases, the reality of racially segregated churches.[62]

Notwithstanding the dedication of individual men and women from Britain, only with difficulty could missions claim in a period of intense African nationalism to be immune either from racial discrimination or from association with empire. Mirroring wider African dissatisfaction with empire and colonialism, African clergy became increasingly reluctant to accept stipends and working conditions grossly inferior to those of their European counterparts. During the course of the period 1945-64 such income differentials grew. Colonial economies were hit hard by monetary inflation in the years immediately following the Second World War, and missionaries indefatigably (and with some success) lobbied their headquarters for increases in pay and allowances. In consequence, mission administrators could not help but query the extent to which overseas commitments could be maintained. Priorities were reconsidered. Cutbacks ensued. And yet missionary societies, albeit on a scale smaller than before, still managed to recruit, train and send overseas for Christian service men and women from Britain.

During and after the Second World War overseas voluntary service contin-

---

published in Robert I. Rotberg and Ali A. Mazrui, eds., *Protest and Power in Black Africa* (New York, 1970), pp. 513-68.

60. UBL, CMS, G/AP11, Warren to Rev. F. H. West, 13 Feb. 1946. On Revival, Catherine E. Robins, 'Tukutendereza: A Study of Social Change and Sectarian Revival in the Balokole Revival of Uganda' (Columbia University PhD thesis, 1975).

61. Max Warren, *Revival — an Enquiry* (London, 1954).

62. Colin Morris, *The Hour after Midnight: A Missionary's Experiences of the Racial and Political Struggle in Northern Rhodesia* (London, 1961).

ued to appeal (as it still does) to a small but notable number of British Christians. Historians of mission have noted the appeal of such service to sectors of British society at certain periods in history: the last two decades of the nineteenth century saw a huge increase in women's participation in mission.[63] Women continued to play a major role in mission in the late colonial period; they accounted for 313 of the 1054 western staff on the books of the CMS in 1946. The smaller SPG had 261 missionaries at this time, of which approximately 70 per cent were women. Missions continued to place great emphasis upon what was still regarded as 'women's work' — teaching and nursing. At certain times demand for women missionaries increased; their work among Kikuyu women and children was regarded as vitally important by both missions and government in Kenya. At missionary societies' headquarters in Britain there was always likely to be a female women's secretary, but as Ruth Compton Brouwer has noted in respect of the IMC, the upper echelons were typically dominated by men; women held only 'important secondary roles'.[64] This did not necessarily mean that women connected with mission lacked assertiveness. As they had before 1939, some women missionaries rejected the UMCA's continuing insistence on celibacy, 'marrying out' to the sometimes grievous loss of the mission.[65] In the late 1950s LMS missionaries' wives successfully protested the Society's refusal to permit them to retain for their personal use income earned from non-mission work.

By the early 1960s British missionaries accepted virtually without question that their work in Africa should be carried on under the aegis of the church. This eventuality, with all its administrative and financial as well as theological implications, could not readily have been foreseen in 1939, or even 1945. Then, with the LMS and the CMS either celebrating or about to celebrate a century and a half of overseas evangelistic endeavour, many missionaries had believed that the ending of a world war would somehow herald a new era of mission from Britain. Some missionaries thought differently, believing that the churches of the West must instead learn from those in Africa. In 1945 Dr. Joe Church, a CMS missionary in Rwanda who had pledged support to the Revival movement, was already making plans for a 'missionary deputation' from east Africa to Europe, with the aim of instituting a revival of the Christian spirit in

63. Rhonda Semple, *Missionary Women: Gender, Professionalism and the Victorian Idea of Christian Mission* (Woodbridge, 2002).

64. Ruth Compton Brouwer, *Modern Women Modernizing Men: The Changing Missions of Three Professional Women in Asia and Africa, 1902-69* (Vancouver, BC, 2002), pp. 30-33.

65. Linda Kumwenda, 'Healing, Conflict and Conversion: Medical Missions in Northern Rhodesia, 1880s-1954' (University of London PhD thesis, 2005), pp. 120-30.

the war-damaged West. The deputation's visit to Britain in 1947 was a small but significant event, anticipating by many decades the greater influence that African Christianity would in time exert on the world church.[66]

Missionaries and the End of Empire

Famously, 1947 was also the year in which India and Pakistan achieved independence. What of the end of empire in Africa? There seemed no prospect of this eventuality in the late 1940s. Whatever the causes of empire's formal end in Africa they were many and varied, and too complex to go into in a book concerned primarily with missions and missionaries. Economic and other important factors undoubtedly predate the Second World War. Nevertheless, for a history of missions and late colonial empire 1939 provides a convenient start date. The 1930s had been a decade of gloom for missionaries. There was in 1939 expectation of better times ahead, once the war was won. Chapter One examines how missionaries responded to the pressures of war. Government demands forced missionaries to re-evaluate the relationship between missions and the state. Reluctantly conceding the necessity of greater state involvement in colonial Africa during wartime, missionaries fretted about the possible consequences for education and evangelism. This anxiety was compounded by fears that white settler communities in Southern Rhodesia and South Africa would extract territorial concessions from the imperial government in London, at the expense of Africans. The possibility of large-scale racial unrest caused alarm. Missionaries of various denominations combined with sympathetic church-based and secular interest groups and launched, in 1945 and with the backing of the Archbishop of Canterbury, a public campaign against racial discrimination in the colonies. This made little impact, but its planning reveals much about missionary attitudes and preoccupations. The chapter also examines other notable aspects of wartime mission affairs, such as the role played by the English Presbyterian clergyman, William Paton, secretary of the IMC and of the provisional committee of the WCC.

Paton died in 1943 as did, a year later, his friend and ecumenical collaborator William Temple, Archbishop of Canterbury, 1942-44. Paton had continually stressed to colleagues the need for continuing emphasis upon evangelism and development of the 'younger' churches. But the immediate postwar period was one of indecision and uncertainty. African affairs proved especially

66. J. E. Church, *Quest for the Highest: An Autobiographical Account of the East African Revival* (Exeter, 1981), pp. 214-34.

difficult and controversial. Chapter Two focuses on the diverse ways in which matters relating to South Africa impinged damagingly upon British missionary interests. The marriage of Seretse Khama to Ruth Williams became intertwined with debate on the future of the High Commission Territories of Bechuanaland (now Botswana), Basutoland (now Lesotho) and Swaziland. The LMS, with a long tradition of involvement in Bangwato society, could not help but become involved. The controversy demonstrated how difficult it had now become for missionaries to argue on behalf of African interests.

Chapter Three considers missionary attitudes to the Central African Federation. Responding to the accession of the National Party to power in South Africa in 1948, the British government planned a territorial bulwark against northward Afrikaner expansion. The idea of federating the colonies of Southern Rhodesia, Northern Rhodesia and Nyasaland was pursued vigorously by white settlers. Despite African opposition the scheme was finalised in 1953. Missionaries were divided on this issue as on no other during the period. Some individual missionaries and some missionary societies protested against the imposition of federation against African wishes. But there was no consensus, and for the most part missionaries tacitly accepted the necessity of the scheme, believing that it would facilitate the development of racial and religious 'partnership' in central Africa, in contrast to the situation in the Union of South Africa.

Government failure to implement policies in support of 'partnership' along with settler aggrandisement and arrogance nurtured African anger in Nyasaland and Northern Rhodesia. Meanwhile, in west Africa, the Gold Coast proceeded to independence, as Ghana, in 1957. Chapter Four focuses upon developments in central Africa, with particular emphasis on Northern Rhodesia and Nyasaland during the period 1954-60. It examines the disputes that arose within the Church of Scotland on whether or not to support African nationalism and, by implication, the dismantling of the Federation. The chapter also considers the impact upon the Scottish missions of African Christian independency, in the form of the Lumpa Church of Alice Lenshina.

Events in Kenya, which are the subject of Chapter Five, followed a somewhat different course from those in Nyasaland and Northern Rhodesia. A state of emergency was declared in Kenya in October 1952 and remained in effect until January 1960. The emergency complicated church-state relations to an unprecedented degree. It also exposed tensions between the missions of the CMS and the bishop and diocese of Mombasa. Missions (Scottish Presbyterian as well as Anglican) participated in government-sponsored schemes for the rehabilitation of Mau Mau suspects. The launch in February 1955 of an international ecumenical appeal for funds for rehabilitation and for detainees' dependents ultimately proved influential in facilitating church, mission and wider Christian involvement in Kenyan education and social services during and after the emergency period.

Chapter Six draws together developments relating to the end of empire in east, central and southern Africa, from 1954 to 1964. In addition it examines the changing nature of the missionary vocation during that time. It also considers the implications for missions and churches of secular interest group, NGO and state involvement in aid and development schemes for Africa at the end of the colonial period and after.

CHAPTER 1

Missions, War and the 'Colour Bar', 1939-45

Britain's declaration of war against Germany on 3 September 1939 brought to an end one period of uncertainty in international affairs, just as it instigated another. Like most British people, missionaries had for some time anticipated the outbreak of hostilities. Now Britain and its empire were threatened. But for several years past Christianity had seemed under threat — notably from militarism, communism and fascism. Missions had also struggled to cope with adverse economic and financial conditions in every part of the world. Some British missionaries were extremely pessimistic. In June 1934, the general secretary of the Church of Scotland's Foreign Mission Committee had wondered whether 'Christian idealism' would any longer suffice to equip new recruits for the disillusion that undoubtedly awaited them in service overseas.[1] Contemporaries spoke repeatedly of 'crisis' and of western — and Christian — prestige lost, perhaps by now irretrievably in the world outside Europe. The First World War had been a disaster in this, as in almost every other respect. But Europe continued to mistreat Africa, as Italy's 1935 invasion of Abyssinia showed only too clearly. Neither did developments relating to Britain's African empire give cause for optimism. In the mid- to late-1930s it seemed possible that the government in London might support Germany's claim for the return of her former colonies in Africa. In Northern Rhodesia labour unrest in the copper industry exploded into violence in 1935. In London, meanwhile, mission representatives wondered how to respond to the latest in a series of attempts by South Africa to incorporate within its borders

1. A. S. Kydd, 'The Missionary Situation and the Need of Revival', *International Review of Missions* (hereafter *IRM*) 23, no. 92 (1934): 559.

26

the disputed High Commission Territories of Swaziland, Basutoland and the Bechuanaland Protectorate.

Despite — indeed because of — their difficulties, missionary societies preferred not to contemplate large-scale retrenchment of institutions that had been built up over time. Little thought was given to the devolution of ecclesiastical authority in Africa. In late 1933 a CMS commission had considered the possibility of 'a native episcopate', to be trained in Africa and Britain. Nothing came of this idea. Unsettled social and racial conditions in Africa continued nevertheless to prompt thoughts of change in church leadership. Writing in 1937 Rev. Dr. Robert Shepherd, principal of Lovedale College in the Eastern Cape, argued that 'a large and real measure of freedom and self-government' for African churches might be necessary to offset the danger of separatism.[2] But British missions in Africa were not yet ready to take such a step. Uncertainty stifled initiative and reinforced conservatism.

Fresh thinking was more apparent in European theological circles but took time to feed into mission practice. Karl Barth and Hendrik Kraemer each made notable contributions to the theology of mission during the 1930s. The Oxford conference of the Universal Christian Council for Life and Work in 1937 and the IMC conference at Tambaram, Madras (now Chennai), in 1938 (in preparation for which Kraemer wrote *The Christian Message in a Non-Christian World*) proved influential in the decision to form, provisionally, a World Council of Churches. Debates at Tambaram showed missionaries moving in theological terms at least beyond the distinction between 'older' western and 'younger' non-western churches to a point where the whole world, including 'the West', might properly be regarded as a mission field.[3] Still, political developments continued to intrude and threaten, both within and outside Europe: the Tambaram conference had originally been scheduled to take place in China, but it was relocated because of Sino-Japanese hostilities.

Arguably, following the outbreak of war and the subsequent Nazi occupation of Europe, London's importance (along with that of neutral Geneva's) as a free centre of western European Protestantism increased enormously. London, for that reason, must feature strongly in any account of missions during the Second World War. Religious leaders such as William Temple, Bishop of Chichester George Bell and William Paton together exerted from London a strong influence on British life and also on ecumenical affairs. Paton, as secre-

2. R. H. W. Shepherd, 'The Separatist Churches of South Africa', *IRM* 26, no. 104 (1937): 453.

3. William Paton, 'The International Missionary Council and the Future', *IRM* 35, no. 97 (1936): 106-11.

tary of the IMC (until his death in August 1943), could not but be interested in imperial and colonial matters. But he viewed these in a broader context: of global politics, as well as of global Christianity. Conversely, many colleagues were preoccupied by colonial Africa's potential for unrest during and after the war. They feared that white settler racialism might provoke serious African unrest, which might in turn threaten missions and empire alike. Events in wartime Africa and the question of the 'colour bar' thus compelled the attention of missionaries whether in the 'mission field' or at the 'home base' in Britain.

Missionary Fears of Racial Unrest

Unlike their colleagues in parts of east and southeast Asia, British Protestant missionaries in colonial Africa were not directly endangered by the Second World War. For some, war provided opportunity. Rev. Alexander Sandilands temporarily forsook mission work with the LMS in southern Africa to become chaplain to the African Auxiliary Pioneer Corps, stationed in the Middle East.[4] For others, war seemed hardly to intrude at all on church and mission life. From Likoma Island, Bishop of Nyasaland Frank Thorne (1892-1981) confessed himself 'half-ashamed' in January 1940 to be 'sitting in inglorious ease and security in Africa' while the people of England lived daily with anxiety, danger and the possibility of death. 'It is you at home, not we out here', he wrote, 'who are enduring hardness as good soldiers of Jesus Christ'.[5]

A comprehensive history of missions in Africa during the Second World War remains to be written. Such a study may reveal either that responsibility for church affairs was increasingly devolved to African clergy and lay workers or that such clergy and lay workers had greater opportunity to take initiative. Such devolution as did occur is likely to have been small in scale and temporary in effect. At this time missionaries remained vital to the western idea of mission in Africa. Thorne noted with satisfaction in 1939 that following a spate of recent ordinations, African clergy in his diocese now outnumbered their European counterparts. Ten years later the racial balance had become badly skewed due to a shortage of missionaries: twenty-eight African priests as against a mere eighteen European. This was a matter for concern in a dio-

4. School of Oriental and African Studies, London (hereafter SOAS), Council for World Mission archive, London Missionary Society papers (hereafter CWM), AF/13, Rev. A. Sandilands, report, 1945.

5. Lambeth Palace Library, London (hereafter LPL), MS 3122, Rt Rev. F. O. Thorne, diocesan report, 6 Jan. 1940.

cese of racially segregated church congregations: European worshippers, small in number as they were, would not accept being ministered to by Africans. 'The outstanding need is for European priests', Thorne informed UMCA headquarters in August 1949.[6] In the context of the time, his request was entirely unremarkable. It was indeed fairly typical.

Racial segregation was the norm in British tropical Africa. Accepting of this, missionaries nonetheless drew a distinction between the protection ostensibly afforded Africans by British colonialism and the lack of such protection within the Union of South Africa, a self-governing Dominion. Missions supported the idea of imperial 'trusteeship', which, in its interwar incarnation, owed much to the ideas of Sir Frederick Lugard, author of *The Dual Mandate in British Tropical Africa* (1922).[7] During the 1920s Joseph Oldham (1874-1969), secretary of the IMC from 1921 to 1937, exerted considerable influence upon African colonial and educational policy. But Oldham was now less directly involved with mission than with other initiatives such as the ecumenical Life and Work movement and the embryonic WCC. The upheavals and violence of the 1930s in the Copperbelt and the subsequent pressures of war on all the African colonies caused missionaries to question the value of 'trusteeship' to indigenous peoples. William Paton concluded in 1941 that it had become a term of 'doubtful value'.[8] This was evident from continuing unrest in Northern Rhodesia. Furthermore, missionaries believed that South Africa and virtually self-governing Southern Rhodesia were both likely to be rewarded by the imperial authorities with territorial concessions for their part in the war. Preoccupied with the war, the government in London might prove susceptible to the blandishments of Jan Smuts and Sir Godfrey Huggins, Prime Ministers of South Africa and Southern Rhodesia respectively. Mission secretaries believed it vital therefore that government and public attention be focussed on colonial 'race relations'. Racial inequality, they thought, might lead to large-scale violence.

Yet missionary worries about settlers in Africa were complicated by suspi-

6. LPL, MS 3122, Thorne to Canon J. Macleod Campbell, 21 Feb. 1939, and 20 Aug. 1949. The African population in Nyasaland in 1949 was about 2 million, the European population about 2,000.

7. Kevin Grant, 'Trust and Self-Determination: Anglo-American Ethics of Empire and International Government', in Mark Bevir and Frank Trentmann, eds., *Critiques of Capital in Modern Britain and America: Transatlantic Exchanges, 1800 to the Present Day* (Basingstoke, 2002), pp. 151-73.

8. SOAS, International Missionary Council/Conference of British Missionary Societies papers (hereafter IMC/CBMS), 202, 'Colonial Settlement' file, Rev. W. Paton to C. W. Judd, 4 June 1941.

cion about government plans for the colonies. This suspicion focussed primarily on the Colonial Welfare and Development Act, which came into effect in 1940 and which promised to the colonies the unprecedented sum of £5 million per annum for a period of five years. The British government had been unsettled by the colonial unrest of the 1930s; it hoped that this promise of investment would stave off further trouble and also deter the growth of nationalist sentiment. The legislation also had considerable propaganda value at a time of war: Secretary of State for Colonies Malcolm MacDonald emphasised Britain's continuing commitment to 'the physical, mental [and] moral development of the colonial peoples of whom we are trustees'.[9] MacDonald had not considered it necessary to consult with religious organisations, and missionaries were uncertain as to the implications for their work of his legislation. Consequently, they invited his successor, Lord Lloyd, to address the 1940 annual general meeting of the CBMS. Lloyd was an ardent Anglo-Catholic who believed with equal fervour in Christianity and the British Empire. He was alone among the five wartime secretaries of state for colonies in having a personal interest in missions. In his address Lloyd emphasised the 'spiritual foundations' upon which the Empire rested, and praised unreservedly the work of the missions.[10] But this was a personal, not an official endorsement. It counted for very little in practical terms, and Lloyd, following the advice of his officials, failed to reveal anything meaningful of government intentions. The Colonial Office had neither the time nor the inclination to provide reassurance to worried missionaries, and this lack of official interest exacerbated their unease about Africa.

Mission officials in Britain now became increasingly preoccupied by the possibility of racial conflict, with the Copperbelt seeming its most likely location. They regarded the copper industry as a cause of enormous social dislocation, contributing to African 'detribalization' and moral and spiritual decay. In 1932 the IMC had commissioned a study of the region.[11] It prompted the establishment under IMC auspices of the United Missions in the Copperbelt, to which the LMS, the UMCA and the Church of Scotland missions contributed funds and staff. The violence of 1935 had provoked alarm, but worse was to follow in 1940. On 3 April riots broke out once more with, again, fatal consequences for Africans: local troops killed 17 striking miners. Of little interest in Britain, these deaths seemed to missionaries a harbinger of

9. UK House of Commons Debates, 361, 47, 21 May 1940.

10. The National Archives of the UK: Public Record Office, London (hereafter TNA: PRO), INF/1/408, Lord Lloyd, address to CBMS general meeting, 14 June 1940.

11. J. Merle Davis, ed., *Modern Industry and the African* (London, 1933).

greater unrest. They awaited with interest the response of the authorities. A commission of enquiry reported, clearing the police and the military of blame. The commission did recommend improvements to African workers' pay and conditions, but the government of Northern Rhodesia refused to countenance this with the war in progress.

Missionaries considered the colonial authorities as in thrall to the mining industry and its discriminatory 'South African'-style labour practices. They were not alone in this presumption. Secular humanitarian organisations such as the Anti-Slavery Society took a similar view. Margery Perham, an authority on colonial administration and a perceptive but friendly critic of official policy, publicly noted that the situation in the Copperbelt was 'inconsistent with the speeches which our leaders have made distinguishing the spirit and racial policy of our Empire from that of the Nazis'.[12] To missionary uncertainty regarding development and welfare policy was now added exasperation at official indifference to African grievances. What made this harder for those in London to bear was the perception that colleagues in central Africa were insufficiently aware of the implications for the church.

Co-operation was the byword of ecumenism. It had characterised the World Missionary Conference of 1910 and the subsequent founding of co-operative organisations such as the CBMS and IMC. The establishment of regional or national Christian Councils during the 1920s represented an attempt to take ecumenism further, by involving representatives of the 'younger' churches as well as of missions in co-operative Christian ventures. The National Christian Council of India, set up partly at Oldham's instigation in 1922 and with indigenous and western members, provided a template. In central Africa, however, Christian Councils formed in Nyasaland (in 1942) and in Northern Rhodesia (in 1944) conformed to prevailing racial norms: their committees' membership was entirely European. Mission officials in Britain were uneasy about their overseas colleagues' reluctance to involve African clergy or laypeople in the Christian Councils.[13] Rev. James Dougall, the Edinburgh-based general secretary of the Church of Scotland missions, urged his compatriots in Nyasaland to act:

> we cannot carry African Churches with us in co-operation if they are not represented in all co-operative Christian bodies . . . we are on a

---

12. *The Times,* 3 March 1941.

13. National Library of Scotland, Accession 7548, General Assembly of the Church of Scotland Foreign Missions Committee Papers (hereafter NLS), B332, Rev. J. W. C. Dougall to Rev. P. H. Borrowman, 18 Nov. 1942.

shaky footing if Africans are not qualifying for leadership in all questions of Christian co-operation. . . . The question is whether Council is not going to lose the tide and realise some day with a shock that leadership has passed from the Church and the Mission to non-Church political or community movements.[14]

James Dougall (1896-1980) was a fair-minded man and unusually sympathetic to African aspirations. His experience of Africa was long and varied. At age 27 he had been secretary to the 1923 Phelps-Stokes Commission on African education. He subsequently worked in Kenya, as a school principal and later as official educational adviser to Protestant missions in east Africa. In the late 1930s he worked for the CBMS in London. Dougall was only too aware of the pressures on missionaries in Africa to conform to local norms. As he informed the Scottish chairman of the Nyasaland Christian Council: 'You need not tell me that there is no paternalism among missionaries because I have seen plenty of it and have myself been guilty of it'.[15] But his pleas had little effect. Scottish missionaries in wartime Nyasaland were engaged in their own struggle, as they saw it, against the 'aggressive' evangelising tactics of Roman Catholics and Seventh Day Adventists. They were wary of advice from home as to the merits of closer interdenominational co-operation. These merits seemed nebulous at best; according to one Scot, 'nobody at home worries about co-operation between say the Presbytery of Inverness and the London Presbytery of the Presbyterian Church of England'.[16] With little interest in committee work, missionaries preferred to support African grievances through private petitioning of government officials and mining companies.[17]

William Paton and Missionary Responses
to African Affairs in Wartime

Mission officials in Britain were more nervous than colleagues in the colonies about what Dougall perceived as the 'rising conscience of nationality' among Africans. But the actions of white settlers had an even greater jolting effect. In August 1941 Huggins floated the idea of an official conference to discuss the

14. NLS, B298, Dougall to Rev. Dr. W. Y. Turner, 6 Nov. 1942, and 11 Jan. 1943.
15. NLS, B298, Dougall to Turner, 11 Jan. 1943.
16. NLS, B299, Rev. D. Campbell to Dougall, 6 Sept. 1945.
17. SOAS, IMC/CBMS, 1216, 'UMCB/Mining Companies' file, Secretary, Roan Antelope Copper Mines, London, to Secretary, UMCB London Committee, 4 Aug. 1943.

amalgamation of Northern and Southern Rhodesia. He had merely been test-ing the political waters and quickly dropped the idea, but it induced panic among mission secretaries fearful of a violent African reaction. They consid-ered making representations to government. But the Colonial Office (Lord Lloyd having left office and dying soon after, in February 1941) was indifferent to their concerns. Frustration ensued. Inspiration for alternative action then came from an unexpected source — the Malvern Conference, held in January 1941. A meeting of Anglican clergy and laypeople convened and chaired by William Temple, then Archbishop of York, Malvern represented an attempt to plot in theological terms a course for postwar British society.[18] Although a CMS delegate attended, the conference was not in any way concerned with overseas mission. Nevertheless, to some Anglicans the idea of a missionary conference based on events at Malvern appealed strongly.[19] The year 1940 had after all been one of missed opportunity for asserting the importance of mis-sion. There was to have been a Lambeth Conference. Ostensibly the 1940 event would have 'reaffirm[ed] the missionary purpose of the Church with deepened understanding and consecration . . . for working a spiritual revolu-tion in the Church throughout this country and beyond . . .'[20] Inspired by Malvern, senior Anglican clergy such as Bishop Noel Hudson of the SPG, Rev. William Wilson Cash of the CMS and Cyril Garbett, Bishop of Winchester, discussed the possibility of a similar, missionary event.[21] So productive were informal discussions that in May 1941 Cash decided to contact IMC secretary Paton with the intention of broadening the scope of the project, to include other Protestant denominations.[22] In so doing he came up against Paton's strong and stubborn ideas of what constituted appropriate ecumenical activ-ism in a time of war.

Born in London in 1886, William Paton had a temperament (if not a tem-per) that has been described as 'volcanic'. A man of almost indefatigable en-ergy, he was resolute, dogged, sometimes insensitive to others — and pro-

18. John Kent, *William Temple: Church, State and Society in Britain, 1880-1950* (Cam-bridge, 1992), pp. 148-67.

19. University of Birmingham Library Special Collections (hereafter UBL), Church Missionary Society Papers (hereafter CMS), G/O 2/6, Rt Rev. N. B. Hudson to Rev. W. W. Cash, 9 April 1941.

20. LPL, Missionary Council of the Church Assembly (hereafter MCCA), MC/COU/M/2, minutes, 16 May 1939; MC/COU/D/3, McLeod Campbell, memo, 'The Preparations for Lambeth 1940', n.d.

21. UBL, CMS, G/O 2/6, Cash, notes, 30 April 1941.

22. One nonconformist was involved in the discussions, Hugh Martin, the Baptist cler-gyman who was director of the religions division at the Ministry of Information.

foundly religious. Pembroke College, Oxford, had worked a transformative effect upon him: there he had become involved in the work of the Student Christian Movement. Following theological studies at Westminster College Cambridge he worked with the Young Men's Christian Association in India, and was the first secretary of the National Christian Council of India. He was ordained as a Presbyterian minister in 1917. Paton was married, and his six children were to him a source of pride, pleasure and some financial difficulty. His belief was underpinned by a theology essentially 'orthodox' yet in some ways more eclectic: six years in India had imbued in him a strong respect for other, non-Christian faiths.[23] He was respectful also of his wife, Grace's, conversion to Anglicanism, informing her that 'If it is God's will for you, it is His Will that you face the whole thing . . . it will not be I who hinders you . . .'[24] In 1939 Paton combined his IMC duties with responsibilities for the nascent WCC and also for the CBMS. By 1940 he had also become involved in an ecumenical 'peace aims' group, intended to consider postwar issues from a Christian perspective.[25] Paton's ubiquity made him the most important and influential (and overworked) British Protestant missionary of the war period.

The First World War had posed Paton a theological dilemma, for which pacifism offered at the time a kind of resolution. Subsequently convinced that the churches had been seduced by war in 1914, he was determined in 1939 that they should remain above 'national' interests. Yet good relations with government were vital to mission and church. Only with its help might overseas work including that of German missions whose staff had been interned continue under missionary aegis. Paton worked hard to establish a *modus vivendi* with the government. The government, for its part, was keen to maintain good relations with all missions, whether Protestant or Roman Catholic. The Ministry of Information (MOI) set up a dedicated religions division, initially comprised of three departments, for Protestant, Roman Catholic and Orthodox and Old Catholic affairs (it added a Jewish department in July 1941). Many clergymen worked for the division as temporary civil servants. On 14 September 1939 representatives of Protestant missions discussed wartime arrangements with senior ministers. They expressed unease at the possibility of being used for propaganda purposes, but were assured that this would not occur. The MOI also made a provisional commitment (later honoured by the Ministry of Labour and National Service) that serving missionaries and those

23. Eleanor M. Jackson, *Red Tape and the Gospel: A Study of the Significance of the Ecumenical Missionary Struggle of William Paton (1886-1943)* (Birmingham, 1980), pp. 82-100.

24. Jackson, *Red Tape and the Gospel*, p. 26. Grace Paton subsequently converted again, to Roman Catholicism.

25. Jackson, *Red Tape and the Gospel*, pp. 265-71.

in training for mission would be exempted from National Service.[26] Given the religious and racial diversity of Britain's empire, government for the most part refrained from publicly equating the national and imperial struggle against fascism with Christianity. But the Foreign Office well knew the value of cultivating neutral Christian opinion overseas — and also the risk of alienating that opinion. The First World War had been a failure in that latter respect, with colonial and imperial authorities interning, in some cases without question, German-speaking Swiss missionaries. Now, from late 1939, the MOI and the Foreign Office facilitated overseas travel by missionaries such as Paton to neutral and allied territories, the United States being the most important destination.[27]

Government was undoubtedly using Paton, to some extent. But he derived some benefit from the arrangement. Paton's visits to the United States in 1940 and 1942 convinced him that Americans would exert enormous influence on postwar world affairs. By 1943 he was considering the implications for missions of issues such as 'international supervision' of colonial and mandated territories.[28] The breadth of Paton's interest in and knowledge of international affairs exceeded that of British colleagues such as Hudson and Cash. Wrote Hudson wonderingly, 'I do think that the dear man wants watching . . . otherwise, before we know where we are we shall be raked into every conceivable movement and campaign, political and international!'[29] Paton thought about mission in broad, strategic terms. He was therefore unimpressed by the idea of a Malvern-style missionary conference, and was alarmed by Cash's proposal that the conference have as its theme a 'Christian Conception of Empire'.[30] This might make missions appear too closely aligned with the state. It would be sufficient, Paton advised the Anglicans, for the missionary societies to make known their concerns to him; he would personally make the necessary representations to the government.[31] He had no intention of delegating that particular task.

Certainly, in their recent representations to the government, missionaries had done themselves few favours. The Colonial Office was dismissive of the

26. TNA: PRO, INF/1/401, minutes of meeting, 14 Sept. 1939.

27. TNA: PRO, INF/1/777, Rev. R. R. Williams, 'Religious Visitors to America', memo, 13 April 1945.

28. SOAS, IMC/CBMS, 202, 'Needs of Colonies' file, Paton to C. W. W. Greenidge, 26 Feb. 1943.

29. UBL, CMS, G/APf6, Hudson to Cash, 23 Jan. 1940.

30. SOAS, IMC/CBMS, 202, 'Christian Conception of Empire' file, Paton to Cash, 27 May, and 4 June 1941.

31. SOAS, IMC/CBMS, 202, 'Christian Conception of Empire' file, Cash, notes on meeting with Paton and others, 6 July 1941.

suggestion (made by the CBMS in an extremely wordy memorandum) that 'revolution' might ensue in central Africa as a result of government inaction in the sphere of 'race relations'.[32] For all that, missionaries were far from alone in their concern about the potentially corrosive effects of racial inequality upon Empire and upon Britain. One of the most notable activists against racial discrimination in Britain as well as in the colonies was Harold Moody, founder and president of the League of Coloured Peoples (LCP). As Anne Spry Rush has argued, the League invoked a 'colonial' version of British national and imperial identity that abhorred racial distinctions.[33] Its reformist rather than radical agenda attracted support from some white Britons as well as from people of African and Asian origin and descent. Jamaican-born and of African descent, Moody was a medical doctor by profession. He was a devout Christian and active in the Congregational Church and also in the LMS, for which he was chairman for 1943. Moody campaigned against the 'colour bar' in Britain's armed services and for legislative action against racial discrimination in British society. He believed that development and welfare schemes would improve the lives of colonial peoples — and lessen the likelihood of racial conflict. In 1940 he personally lobbied British church leaders, Anglican, Nonconformist, Roman Catholic and Scottish, persuading them to endorse an LCP statement welcoming the Colonial Development and Welfare Act.[34] He would go on to propound a 'Charter for Coloured Peoples' in 1944. This document was modelled in part on the Atlantic Charter, agreed between British Prime Minister Winston Churchill and US President Franklin Roosevelt in August 1941. Distracted by imperial affairs, missionaries appear to have paid little attention to the Atlantic Charter; but they perceived Moody's activism as both indicative and representative of wider British public interest in and concern about the harmful effects of racial discrimination, 'at home' and in the colonies. The ongoing activities of the LCP and the Anti-Slavery Society reinforced this view, as also did the formation of the Fabian Colonial Bureau, in October 1940. It appeared that support for a 'colour bar' campaign would not be restricted to religious organisations.

32. *Conference of Missionary Societies in Great Britain and Ireland to Lord Lloyd, Secretary of State for the Colonies: A Memorandum Inspired by a Statement of Policy on Colonial Development and Welfare, Cmd. 6175* (London, 1941); TNA: PRO, CO 859/74/6, J. L. Keith, minutes, 20 May 1941.

33. Anne Spry Rush, 'Imperial Identity in Colonial Minds: Harold Moody and the League of Coloured Peoples, 1931-50', *20th Century British History* 13, no. 4 (2002): 356-83.

34. LPL, Lang papers, 176, Dr. H. A. Moody to Most Rev. C. G. Lang, 8 June 1940; *The Times*, 12 September 1940.

Missionaries and Their Collaborators in Wartime London

The war progressed unpredictably. In early 1942 its course altered in dramatic as well as unpredicted fashion. Military defeat at Singapore in February had catastrophic consequences for British and imperial prestige. In August the Indian National Congress instigated an anti-imperial 'Quit India' movement. Missionaries in central Africa considered that they too might now have to face 'with much heart-searching the principles of our own relationship with the African people . . .'[35] That relationship seemed by no means secure: 'Africans are losing faith in the so-called Christian Groups whose racial prejudices seem to be as strong as those of the man in the street . . .', they reported; 'the Christian mission in Africa is at present linked far too strongly with white domination'.[36] In such circumstances it seemed imperative that missionaries display more openly their concern for non-western peoples.

Canon Harold Grace was already giving a great deal of thought to that task. In order to appease Anglican concern about Africa, Paton had asked him to conduct a study of racial discrimination in the colonies. This enabled Paton to focus on other things. Secretary of the CBMS Africa committee, Grace (1888-1967) was a career missionary. He had worked in Uganda, for the CMS and as principal of King's College, Budo, before moving in 1935 to the Gold Coast, to become principal of Achimota College. He returned to Britain in 1939, to take up a post at CBMS headquarters, Edinburgh House, in Eaton Place, London SW1. The CBMS was a representative institution, funded for the most part by contributions from its member societies. It was a constituent body of the IMC (with which it shared offices). It had a small secretarial team. It did not make policy, but facilitated, through a number of committees, cooperation between Protestant missions especially in terms of relations with government. Grace was energetic and well suited to the committee-driven world that he now inhabited. He proved adept at forging new relationships between the CBMS and other organisations. He even overcame suspicion that the Fabian Colonial Bureau might be a haven for 'leftists', and exchanged ideas with its secretary, Rita Hinden.

In truth, the hothouse conditions of wartime London provided an environment in which the most unlikely partners might develop an irresistible, if often only brief, mutual attraction. A shared interest in racial matters drew missions to the attention of academics such as George Keeton, professor of

---

35. SOAS, CWM, AF21/11B, Rev. A. J. Haile and Miss J. Bryson to Rev. T. Cocker Brown, 2 May 1942.

36. SOAS, CWM, AF44, Haile, report to LMS board of directors, 1942.

English law at the University of London, and Kenneth Little, researching his book *Negroes in Britain* (1948). Shared mistrust of the overarching, interventionist state would also facilitate wartime collaboration between missionaries, the educationist A. D. Lindsay and the political scientist Sir Ernest Barker. Grace's membership in a church-based Anglo-African Committee also made possible further personal and institutional contacts. This committee had been set up at a meeting of the (Anglican) Missionary Council of the Church Assembly, held two days after the fall of Singapore.[37] The committee would raise funds for the welfare of African students in London. At that same meeting was a guest speaker on the subject of the 'colour bar': this was Lord Hailey, who, since the publication of his magisterial *An African Survey* (1938), had become Britain's most eminent and most esteemed expert on colonial affairs.[38] Hailey seems to have taken from his encounter with the Council a strong appreciation of the church's avowed commitment to 'partnership', between mission and church and between European and non-European races. Long a staple of missionary rhetoric, the term 'partnership' was deployed insistently by Anglican clergy during 1941. Cash used it to promote a missionary version of Malvern, in terms of his 'Christian Conception of Empire'.[39] For other clergy 'partnership' might both encapsulate and be used to extol the wartime relationship between the Church of England and the Episcopal Church in the United States.[40] Ultimately, it is impossible to gauge accurately Hailey's debt to church and mission espousal of 'partnership'. But, entrusted by government with the task of reformulating, in the aftermath of Singapore, the outdated, discredited doctrine of 'trusteeship', he duly adopted the term 'partnership', using it to considerable public effect during 1942 in Britain and in the United States.[41]

Hailey was an expert on Africa, and he was not involved in party politics. Americans trusted him. So did missionaries. But even his reassuring pronouncements about imperial 'partnership' proved insufficient to quell further unease about central African affairs. This was now being fed by Bishop Thorne's reports from Nyasaland, which described intensification of anti-

---

37. The Missionary Council, formed in 1921, was an advisory body on Anglican overseas mission.

38. LPL, MCCA, MC/COU/M/2, minutes, 17 Feb. 1942.

39. UBL, CMS, G/O 2/6, Cash, notes, 30 April; Williams to Cash, 27 March, and 16 April 1941.

40. Canon J. McLeod Campbell, *Our American Partners: The Life and Activities of the Episcopal Church in America* (London, 1941).

41. Suke Wolton, *Lord Hailey, the Colonial Office and the Politics of Race and Empire in the Second World War: The Loss of White Prestige* (Basingstoke, 2000), pp. 119-48.

European and anti-church sentiment among Africans.[42] Simultaneously, the widening of the war began to exert unanticipated pressures on the home front. The American military 'occupation' of Britain began. The arrival during 1942 of thousands of black American servicemen focussed public attention on racial discrimination in Britain. The authorities were uncertain how to respond.[43] Some clergymen took a stand against the US Army's segregationist practices, but the Protestant churches, wary of antagonising American opinion, refrained from open criticism.[44] For missionaries, meanwhile, the black Americans' arrival constituted nothing less than a challenge to Britain's reputation for racial tolerance.[45]

In June 1942 Canon Gerald Broomfield, general secretary of the UMCA (who had been present at Hailey's address to the Missionary Council) publicly announced that 'colour discrimination is as great an evil as slavery' and that the churches should 'play a big and well-informed share in the struggle to abolish it'.[46] 'Our job', he asserted, 'is to create informed public opinion which will help our leaders in their fight for better conditions . . .'[47] Broomfield (1895-1976) was an unlikely activist. A theologian, with an Oxford DD, he had been an educational missionary and for a time a canon at Christ Church cathedral, Zanzibar. Destined probably for an episcopal appointment in Africa, he had instead taken up an unexpected request from the mission to become its general secretary in 1936. He and Grace now began to work together. The two men were quite different in temperament. Grace was ebullient, even mercurial, whereas Broomfield, although given to flashes of dry humour, was generally reserved and methodical at work. The two men differed but slightly in their attitude to non-Europeans. Grace tended to cheerfully disparage, irrespective of race, those with whom he disagreed, be they Africans, settlers or even other missionaries; for Broomfield Africans and people of African descent were still as 'children', in need of European assis-

42. Bodleian Library of Commonwealth and African Studies at Rhodes House, Oxford (hereafter RHL), Universities' Mission to Central Africa Papers (hereafter UMCA), SF29xi, Thorne to Canon G. W. Broomfield, 2 May 1942.

43. Sonya O. Rose, *Which People's War? National Identity and Citizenship in Britain, 1939-45* (Oxford, 2003), pp. 245-63.

44. Graham Smith, *When Jim Crow Met John Bull: Black American Soldiers in World War II Britain* (London, 1987), pp. 89-92.

45. SOAS, Conference of British Missionary Societies papers (hereafter CBMS), 260, 'Colour Bar, 1940-43' file, Canon H. M. Grace to J. P. Fletcher, 12 Oct. 1942.

46. CBMS, *Report for the Year 1941-42* (London, 1942), p. 18.

47. CBMS, *Report for the Year 1941-42*, G. W. Broomfield, address, 'Christianity and the Colour Bar', pp. 61-3.

tance.[48] They both believed that missionary societies were uniquely well equipped to alert public opinion to the evils of race discrimination in Britain and in the colonies, as more than a century earlier religious groups had in relation to slavery and the slave trade. With the support of the CBMS, Broomfield wrote, and published in spring 1943, a book with this aim in mind. Its title was *Colour Conflict.*

The book dwelt only in passing on religious matters and pursued no explicit theological argument. Broomfield praised the British Empire, as the antithesis of Nazi Germany. But he warned against white settler expectation of gaining from the war at the expense of Africans. Drawing on the work of Hailey and others, Broomfield provided examples of discrimination against Africans in matters of land and labour. He also considered the subject of interracial marriage, concluding that it was inadvisable. He was in no way critical of Smuts or Huggins; indeed, he considered that economic conditions in South Africa might necessitate continued 'separation' of the races for some time to come.[49] His main concern, however, was for the racial situation in the colonies: Britain should continue to reform its colonial policy with the aim of asserting African interests over those of Europeans. Colonial development and welfare represented merely a 'good beginning' in this respect. The people of Britain, he argued, had a duty to ensure that their empire discharged its 'sacred trust' to the people of the colonies.[50]

By the time of their publication these sentiments were already anachronistic, as was Broomfield's earlier equation of the 'struggle' against racial discrimination with that against slavery. Broomfield had no desire to stimulate public criticism of an empire in peril from both Nazi Germany and Japan. Only by reforming its attitudes to race in the colonies, he believed, could the Empire endure. And if the Empire could reform its colonies it would set the best possible example to Europeans in the Dominion of South Africa. Essentially, Broomfield believed in British colonial rule. Equally, he had no wish to compromise, through overt criticism of government in Pretoria, the work of white South African liberals such as Edgar Brookes and Alfred Hoernle. His concerns in this respect mirrored those of the churches in Britain, anxious not to offend American sensibilities about race by drawing attention to the discriminatory practises of the US Army.

To Anglican colleagues Broomfield's book was both remarkably impres-

48. SOAS, CBMS, 254, 'Sub-Committee' file, Broomfield to Grace, 4 Feb.; Grace to Broomfield, 5 Feb. 1943.

49. Gerald Webb Broomfield, *Colour Conflict: Race Relations in Africa* (London, 1943), p. 134.

50. Broomfield, *Colour Conflict,* pp. 98-102.

sive and propitious in its timing. Rev. John McLeod Campbell, secretary of the Missionary Council of the Church Assembly, contacted Temple, now Archbishop of Canterbury and author of the recently published *Christianity and Social Order* (1942). The churches, Campbell suggested, might now plan a public campaign against racial discrimination, infused (if given Temple's imprimatur and participation) with 'all the intensity and challenge of Wilberforce's, Buxton's [and] Livingstone's campaigns . . .'[51] Sympathetic though he was to Campbell's suggestion, Temple had other, more pressing concerns. Campbell, Broomfield and the others would have to bide their time.

Planning a Campaign against the 'Colour Bar'

By 1943 it had become apparent that the war would not end in victory for the Axis powers. Official thoughts turned to postwar planning, for Britain and the colonies. In July Oliver Stanley, the fifth (and final) wartime Secretary of State for Colonies, made an important policy statement. Stanley announced a range of initiatives intended to demonstrate the extent of Britain's commitment to imperial 'partnership'. In so doing he also reaffirmed Britain's intention to retain authority over its colonies after the war and to decide what was best for their peoples, of whatever race.[52] Stanley espoused education as one of the 'pillars' of 'partnership', yet his vision of education in the colonies differed in many ways from that of the missions. For one thing, the Colonial Office wished to neutralise African colonial disaffection through the provision of higher-level education, of which missions had no experience. Also, the Colonial Office was increasingly interested in new ideas about social engineering; and this interest would find expression in schemes for 'mass education', 'community development' and the like. Missionaries thought these ideas spiritually impoverished. Although government still relied upon missions for the provision of African primary education, its interventionist tendencies now seemed increasingly to represent a potential threat to Christian education in the colonies.[53]

Involvement with the official Advisory Committee on Education in the Colonies being among his many responsibilities, Grace argued the case for mission education with the Colonial Office and its educational adviser,

---

51. LPL, Temple papers (hereafter TP), 42, McLeod Campbell to Most Rev. W. Temple, 1 Feb. 1943.

52. J. M. Lee and Martin Petter, *The Colonial Office, War and Development Policy: Organisation and the Planning of a Metropolitan Initiative, 1939-45* (London, 1982), pp. 156-63.

53. SOAS, CBMS, 254, 'Field' file, Grace, circular letter, 2 Nov. 1943.

Christopher Cox.[54] Grace had also become involved (through the Missionary Council's Anglo-African Committee) with the West African Students' Union (WASU) and its co-founder Ladipo Solanke. To Solanke the CBMS offered the prospect of links to other groups sympathetic to the interests of Africans in Britain.[55] But war increased the WASU's interest in political matters, and from 1942 its members lobbied for self-government in Britain's west African territories, utilising whatever contacts they thought useful — including missionaries. In response to this lobbying, the Colonial Office tried to channel African enthusiasm into support for official- and church-based campaigns for student hostels in London.[56] Given Grace's experience of life in the Gold Coast, it was understandable that Solanke saw him as a potentially helpful contact. But Grace, like Broomfield, was less interested in supporting African claims for self-government than in campaigning for changes in British colonial attitudes.

By mid-1943 Broomfield and Grace had made little or no progress on plans for a public campaign. They knew that the idea was anathema to Paton. He continued to regard a discreet, well-timed word in the ear of a government minister or senior civil servant as the best means of advancing missions' interests where contentious issues were concerned. Public campaigns were an unpredictable business, and liable to be counterproductive. But on 21 August 1943, Paton, who had recently been hospitalised in Kendal, Cumbria, with an inflamed ulcer, died of post-operative complications. He was 56 years old, and his death was a huge loss to Protestant missions and ecumenism. In 1941 Paton had entrusted to Grace the task of investigating racial discrimination in the colonies, for the CBMS. This was partly intended to divert Grace away from planning for a public campaign. Following Paton's death Grace, with Broomfield, now decided once again to approach Temple, to seek his support for their plans.

By early 1944 Temple was desperately unwell, from the gout that had troubled him throughout his adult life. But he proved receptive to the entreaty now coming from Broomfield, that he formally endorse a campaign against the 'colour bar'.[57] The previous November, Temple had spoken on the subject, informally (and ineffectually), with none other than Smuts, who was visiting

54. SOAS, CBMS, 254, 'Colonial Office' file, Grace to C. W. M. Cox, 10 May 1944.

55. SOAS, CBMS, 261, 'WASU Correspondence' file, O. F. Solanke to Grace, 30 Dec. 1942.

56. Hakim Adi, *West Africans in Britain, 1900-60: Nationalism, Pan-Africanism and Communism* (London, 1998), pp. 112-14; LPL, MCCA, MC/COU/M/2, minutes, 13 July 1943, and 19 March 1946.

57. LPL, TP, 42, Broomfield to Temple, 11 Feb. 1944.

London.[58] A campaign, Temple now finally acknowledged, might indeed provide an 'admirable opportunity' for co-operation between the churches at home and the missions with their interests overseas.[59] Grace and Broomfield set to work with alacrity, secure in the knowledge of archiepiscopal support and finally confident of realising their hopes. They instigated discussion with colleagues of many other denominations under the aegis of the CBMS. It was decided that a manifesto be devised, with a public campaign to follow. In the event, it would take more than ten months to agree on the wording of the manifesto.

At the time of its eventual completion, in January 1945, the manifesto consisted of 444 carefully chosen words. Missionaries had consulted extensively, with each other and with representatives of other religious and secular organisations. They had sought the opinion of the Colonial Office, and of Joseph Oldham. Their deliberations were characterised above all by intense, almost paralysing, concern to avoid offending British authorities and, for fear of repercussions against local churches, to avoid offending also the government of South Africa. Theological concerns were also a source of delay, as committees debated whether the wording might contain or even imply troublesome religious doctrine. One mission secretary caustically remarked of the process being 'a rather bad illustration of the incredible slowness' of Christian organisations.[60] There was no consultation with missions in Africa. This, it was thought, would cause even further delay.

The manifesto's title was 'The Colour Bar and Race: Policy of British Missionary Societies'.[61] In its opening paragraph it cited a recent declaration by Allied political leaders in support of 'equal rights' for all peoples, irrespective of race. The manifesto then addressed the people of Britain directly, appealing to their sense of 'fair play' and urging them not to tolerate 'artificial barriers' to the progress and prosperity of indigenous peoples in Northern Rhodesia, Southern Rhodesia and Kenya, but instead to support a colonial policy based on 'the spirit of true partnership'. Unwilling to refer openly to South Africa or to the disputed High Commission Territories, missionaries concluded with an ambiguously worded assertion that they would 'view with grave misgivings any changes in the existing political status of African territories at present under British control'. Any 'abdication of responsibility by the

58. LPL, TP, 42, Temple to Rev. F. H. Hulme, 16 June 1944.

59. LPL, TP, 42, Temple to Broomfield, 12 Feb. 1944.

60. SOAS, CBMS, 260, 'Colour Bar Campaign, 1943-46' file, Canon M. A. C. Warren to Grace, 9 Jan. 1945.

61. The manifesto also carried the endorsement of a number of other religious organisations including the Friends Service Council and the Young Women's Christian Association.

British people would seem to be a breach of trust. It would delay indefinitely the fulfilment of the just hopes of the native people, and as a result would accelerate the growth of racial bitterness'.[62]

The manifesto was in essence an assertion of watchfulness and a reminder to the government and to the British public of missionary concern for the interests of indigenous peoples in the colonies. Apart from its wording, much thought was also given to the publicising of the manifesto, and to the form that the subsequent public campaign might take. Temple's Christian activism provided a model; missionaries particularly wished to emulate the success (if not the controversy) of his contribution to a large-scale public meeting organised by the Industrial Christian Fellowship, and held at the Albert Hall, London, in September 1942.[63] But Temple would take no part in any event on the subject of the 'colour bar'. He had died, in October 1944. An interregnum of several months' duration followed. The CBMS approached his nominated successor, Geoffrey Fisher, Bishop of London, uncertain if he would agree to be associated with a potentially controversial matter. Fisher agreed to chair the press conference in Edinburgh House at which the manifesto was announced, on 15 March 1945. It was an uncomfortable experience for the archbishop-in-waiting, who was ill at ease in the presence of newspaper reporters; he reacted badly to a question on the manifesto's lack of reference to Australian aboriginal peoples. Broomfield rescued the occasion, by reiterating the missions' particular concern with Africa.[64] Broomfield subsequently prevailed upon Fisher to take the lead at the public meeting to launch the 'colour bar' campaign. This would be held at Westminster Central Hall on 12 June. Fisher ensured in advance that he would not be required to answer questions and risk possible misrepresentation in the press.

CBMS officials made strenuous efforts through missionary societies and other organisations to drum up interest in the meeting. This frantic activity was stimulated by fears that the event would be a flop. The war in Europe was ending. How much public interest was there likely to be in colonial affairs and race relations? As it happened, the meeting was a sell-out. Almost three thousand people attended (the CBMS even made a small profit). They heard Fisher urge support for the missions, in their efforts to eradicate racial dis-

62. SOAS, CBMS, 260, manifesto, 'The Colour Bar and Race: Policy of British Missionary Societies' (1945).

63. SOAS, CBMS, 260, 'Colour Bar, 1940-43' file, Rev. A. M. Chirgwin to Grace, 16 Dec. 1942. On the Albert Hall meeting, see Stephen Spencer, *William Temple: A Calling to Prophecy* (London, 2001), pp. 98-105.

64. LPL, Fisher papers, 3, unsigned notes on press conference, 15 March 1945.

crimination. Broomfield spoke on the situation in central Africa, with particular reference to the Copperbelt. Two MPs also addressed the meeting: Labour's Arthur Creech Jones (chairman of the Fabian Colonial Bureau), and the Conservative Leonard Gammans, who was similarly interested and involved in colonial matters. They endorsed the manifesto and expressed their personal support for the work of the missions.[65]

These events instilled in Broomfield an untypical mood of euphoria. 'Nothing quite like it has happened before', he had declared at the press conference, with reference to the manifesto. Later in 1945 he would write: 'there never was an occasion when it was more appropriate or more urgent that the Churches . . . should speak clearly on this subject. We had heard so much of the ideals for which the war was being fought, of the human rights of all men, and of the iniquity of the *herrenvolk* idea'.[66] To Broomfield it was possible to believe in 1945 that an empire committed to 'partnership' and benefiting also from the evangelising presence of missionaries might indeed enhance the material *and* spiritual welfare of African peoples.

Mission, Empire and the Uncertainties of Peace, 1945

Launched at Westminster Central Hall in June 1945, the missionary and humanitarian campaign against the 'colour bar' proved impossible to sustain. Like so many other organisations, missionary societies became preoccupied with the process of adjusting to the end of the war. Due to wartime travel restrictions, overseas mission staff had been unable to take furlough. Arrangements had to be made for them and also for those missionaries and their families interned and imprisoned by the Japanese in Asia. Recruitment had been hampered by the war. The financial outlook appeared uncertain. A mood of anticipation and expectation that the cessation of hostilities might facilitate the expansion of overseas evangelistic activity was accompanied by apprehension, and even anxiety. What would be the postwar situation in India, in colonial Africa and in South Africa? What would be the effect on missions of further, recent legislation for colonial welfare and development?

For all the disruption and damage it caused to overseas mission activities, wartime had appeared to missionaries and their sympathisers an opportune moment to mobilise British public opinion on the subject of racial discrimi-

65. SOAS, CBMS, 260, 'Statement and Meeting' file, texts of addresses, 12 June 1945.
66. RHL, UMCA, SF115, Broomfield, notes for bishops of east and central Africa, 5 Sept. 1945.

nation in the colonies. It is notable that this belief appeared particularly strong among Anglicans. This may have been partly due to a desire to compensate for the cancellation of the Lambeth Conference and partly also to a desire to contribute to the public discourse on social issues set in train at Malvern. It was undoubtedly due in large measure to the unsettled situation in central Africa, where the UMCA had a strong presence. Yet missionaries of all Protestant denominations, not merely Anglican, perceived that racial violence posed a threat to the church in Africa and to British colonial rule. The Scots were alive to the possibility of African unrest in Nyasaland. The LMS, running what was in effect a state church in the Bechuanaland Protectorate, maintained a wary eye on South Africa's intentions towards the High Commission Territories. All accepted the necessity of a public statement and campaign on the subject of the 'colour bar'.

Certain missionaries regarded this focus upon racial discrimination as excessive, and even misguided. As we have seen, Paton did not favour a public campaign. Neither, for that matter, did Oldham: better, he had suggested, for missions to equip Africans through education to fight their own battles (but he too thought it foolish to antagonise Pretoria).[67] Paton insisted that all missions retain focus on their primary task of evangelism. His address to the LMS board of directors in April 1943 on that subject had been typically forthright. Allowing for the 'growth of national feeling in the countries of the East and an increasing sense of racial self-consciousness in Africa', he reminded his audience of the imperative to 'marshal our total Christian forces round the centre of an increasingly self-governing indigenous church'.[68] Paton realised that British missions and British Empire alike might have limited scope for manoeuvre at the end of the war. American power seemed likely to predominate. The world would not revert to its prewar state. An internationalist in his thinking and in his work, Paton envisaged a kind of 'world government' organisation to ensure that the economic and political conditions that had led to war would not recur. He envisaged missions and churches contributing through representative agencies such as the IMC and a World Council of Churches. These ideas owed much to his contact with American Protestants who strongly favoured the idea of a 'world government'.[69] Few other British missionaries thought about political organisations in such expansive terms.

67. SOAS, CBMS, 260, 'Colour Bar Campaign, 1943-46' file, J. H. Oldham to Grace, 19 Dec. 1944.

68. SOAS, CWM, BM/1, Paton, 'Missions after the War', address to LMS board, 21 April 1943.

69. John Nurser, *For All Peoples and All Nations: Christian Churches and Human Rights* (Geneva, 2005).

Max Warren, who had become CMS general secretary in June 1942, was something of an exception. Like Paton, Warren benefitted from a wartime visit to the United States (and Canada), in the winter of 1943-44. He was particularly enthused by the work of the American mission strategist John Merle Davis.[70] Warren returned to Britain with a clearer appreciation of the likely influence of the US on the postwar world.[71] Warren also discerned that American mission preoccupation with the Far East and Latin America might actually be to the advantage of British missions in Africa. In that continent, he thought, lay opportunity not for thoughtless expansion but rather for the consolidation by British missions of existing work and the encouragement of indigenous church leadership.[72] In 1945 he instigated a programme of retrenchment of CMS overseas activities, the better to retain focus on evangelism and church growth. Although he contributed to discussion of its wording, Warren was sceptical of the manifesto's value. He acknowledged all the same that racial discrimination was indeed an important matter, on which missionaries could not be silent, or inactive. Indeed, as Warren saw it, by asserting the view from Britain, missions on the 'home front' might help facilitate a clearer perspective on African affairs than that obtainable from within Africa itself.[73]

The idea of a mission-sponsored manifesto and public campaign against the 'colour bar' was unusual to the extent of being almost an aberration. It was a product of wartime conditions. For much of the 1920s and into the 1930s, British missions had been able to rely upon Joseph Oldham to represent their interests to imperial authority. Paton's approach similarly relied upon personal contact with government ministers and civil servants. Such contact constituted only part of Paton's work of course and, like Oldham, he was wary of missions becoming identified with the state. Paton accomplished a great deal during the war, but at the expense of his health. He encountered tremendous difficulties in advancing the interests of mission and ecumenism. Yet he was not preoccupied with African colonial affairs to the exclusion of much else, as were some other British missionaries at this time. His concerns also encompassed Indian (as well as African) nationalism and the fate of the Jews in Europe. Ultimately it is impossible to gauge what influence Paton might have been able to exert on postwar imperial affairs, had he lived. Imperial and international affairs underwent a great deal of change during the war. Britain had promised independence to India, but there was no urge to 'decolonise' more generally; the Empire meant

70. J. Merle Davis, *New Buildings on Old Foundations* (New York and London, 1945).

71. UBL, CMS, G/AD1/9, Warren, report of visit to US and Canada, Dec. 1943-Feb. 1944.

72. UBL, CMS, G/AP1, Warren, address to CMS secretaries, 3 April 1944.

73. UBL, CMS, G/01/3, Warren to Ven. L. J. Beecher, 13 June 1945.

too much to Britain in terms of economy, security and prestige. The growth of nationalism in Asia and Africa and the founding in 1945 of the United Nations meant, however, that British colonial affairs would become increasingly subject to African protest as well as to international scrutiny and criticism. This marked a change from the prewar period. Changing too were official attitudes towards missions. Neither imperial nor colonial authorities wished missionaries ill. Some government ministers were sympathetic to their aims. But after 1945 it would prove impossible to recreate the kind of informal, influential relationships that Oldham had maintained with members of the governing elite. In the aftermath of the Second World War some missionaries would hanker for what seemed in retrospect the certainties of the 'Oldham era'.

Mission officials in wartime Britain were keen to influence government policy and public opinion on African colonial affairs. They were themselves influenced by perceptions of African susceptibility to unrest, and revolt. In that respect missionary attitudes towards African peoples differed remarkably little from those of many other Europeans.[74] Missionaries were not yet ready to advocate African advancement; instead they offered suggestions as to how deficiencies in colonial rule might be remedied or repaired, to the advantage of Africans. But missionary efforts at activism in relation to the 'colour bar' were characterised by hesitancy and uncertainty at a time when British church leaders were contributing to debate on education policy and postwar reconstruction. The hesitancy and uncertainty contrasted with the activism of two as yet unknown Anglican priests working in Johannesburg. There, Michael Scott and Trevor Huddleston were redefining the purpose and practice of mission. Their names would become well known soon enough, in South Africa and beyond. So too would the name of Seretse Khama, the 24-year-old regent-in-waiting of the Bangwato people of the Bechuanaland Protectorate. In August 1945 Seretse arrived in Britain, intending to study law at the University of Oxford. He was welcomed by senior officials of the LMS, which was celebrating its triple jubilee that year. To missionaries, officials and supporters of the Society, Seretse seemed to represent the past, the present and also hopes for the future of mission and church in Africa. His presence enhanced their festivities. Seretse dutifully and publicly acknowledged the benefits that the Society had bestowed upon him, his family and the Bangwato.[75] Within three years his marriage to Ruth Williams would envelop the couple and the LMS in racial and political controversy.

74. Frank Furedi, *The Silent War: Imperialism and the Changing Perception of Race* (London, 1998).

75. SOAS, CWM, BM/1, LMS board of directors' minutes, 19 Sept. 1945.

CHAPTER 2

Tshekedi Khama, Seretse Khama and the South African Factor in Missionary Affairs, 1948-52

The interracial conflict that missionaries feared might erupt in Africa during the Second World War did not materialise. Their campaign in Britain against the 'colour bar' did not endure beyond the initial public meeting, held in London in June 1945. War's end brought new problems requiring immediate attention. There was a rush of applications for furlough, many from missionaries in Africa. Not all were viewed sympathetically. 'Now that the war is over and people are anxious to get home, breakdowns in health are becoming somewhat fashionable', one Scot wrote sardonically from Nyasaland.[1] But missionaries' sense of deprivation and weariness was real enough: some who returned to Britain on furlough chose not to resume their missionary careers. How might they be replaced? The London Missionary Society had instigated ambitious schemes for postwar evangelistic advance. Eligible men and women had seemed ready enough to declare a personal interest in mission, but few followed through with a formal offer to serve. The Society appointed only ten new missionaries in 1945, well below the number needed to fill vacant posts. Its officials clung to the need for at least 250 active overseas staff. They put into effect contingency plans: suitable 'older' recruits (aged over 30) would be accepted; and long-serving missionaries would be asked to defer retirement. These measures proved to be of limited use. Financial reserves, built up during wartime (when it had been difficult to spend funds), evaporated as costs soared. The National Insurance Act of 1946 made new financial de-

---

1. National Library of Scotland, Accession 7548, General Assembly of the Church of Scotland Foreign Missions Committee Papers (hereafter NLS), B299, Rev. D. Campbell to Rev. J. W. C. Dougall, 14 June 1945.

mands on missionary societies as employers. Because of the global spread of their activities, missions were hard hit by a 30 per cent devaluation of sterling in 1949. Monetary inflation in overseas economies eroded the value of missionary incomes. This had a negative impact upon morale. Its effect was exacerbated by missionaries' perception that Roman Catholic 'rivals', celibate, ascetic and ostensibly dedicated to 'the downfall of Protestantism', would take advantage.[2]

Government initiatives seemed unlikely to favour missions. The 1945 Colonial Welfare and Development Act authorised increases in expenditure on the colonies. But missions found it difficult to supply suitably qualified Christian staff for educational projects funded on a grant-aided basis. Teacher-training facilities were underdeveloped, and the Colonial Office gave little specific direction on educational policy; after 1945 this was increasingly left to educational authorities in the colonies.[3] Missions were in any case often too intent on retaining denominational control of educational facilities and failed to adequately foresee much less prepare for burgeoning African demand for education. African disenchantment with missions was linked to dissatisfaction with empire.

Their active participation in the war on behalf of the Empire stimulated among some Africans at least the expectation of greater educational opportunity and political change.[4] The founding of the United Nations in 1945 meanwhile seemed to signify a new internationally agreed emphasis upon sovereign national states, at the expense of western empires. Britain was determined to retain control of its African colonies, and also to blunt African nationalism. Political concession to Africans was considered possible only in west African colonies with negligible European populations, such as the Gold Coast. In east and central Africa Britain had to contend with assertive white settler communities. None were more assertive than the communities in the Union of South Africa, especially those of Afrikaner stock. Afrikaner political leaders would exert great influence upon postwar British policy for Africa with important consequences, not only for indigenous peoples but also for missions, in South Africa and in nearby colonial territories. Amid upheaval in mission activities after the ending of the war, South Africa's racial policies and its influence on

2. School of Oriental and African Studies, London (hereafter SOAS), Council for World Mission Archive, London Missionary Society Papers (hereafter CWM), AF/44, R. J. F. Phillips, report, 1948.

3. Clive Whitehead, 'The Historiography of British Imperial Education Policy, Part II: Africa and the Rest of the Colonial Empire', *History of Education* 34, no. 4 (2005): 448.

4. David Killingray, *Fighting for Britain: African Soldiers in the Second World War* (Woodbridge, 2010).

British imperial affairs ensured that matters relating to race discrimination would continue to preoccupy missionary minds. In no missionary society was this preoccupation more profound than the LMS.

Because it operated within South Africa the LMS was susceptible to the effects of Pretoria's legislation on matters such as African education: it maintained an important educational and teacher-training facility at Tiger Kloof in the Northern Cape. But South African influence stretched even farther, to affect the neighbouring British-controlled Bechuanaland Protectorate, one of the contested High Commission Territories, along with Basutoland and Swaziland. Here since the late nineteenth century the LMS had built up a close, complex relationship with the indigenous Bangwato people. For missionaries, that relationship meant serving the church and also helping to defend the Bangwato against predatory white settler interests in the tradition of notable nineteenth-century antecedents such as John Mackenzie. The ending of the Second World War was therefore a time for both evangelistic advance and increased vigilance in case South Africa renewed its efforts to incorporate the Bechuanaland Protectorate.

Postwar events in Africa did not follow their expected course. Notwithstanding the shock to missionaries caused by the coming to power of the National Party in 1948 and the introduction of laws in support of apartheid, it was the actions of the Bangwato rather than of the South African government that most confounded LMS expectations, above all in relation to the Bangwato leader Tshekedi Khama and to the 1948 marriage of his nephew Seretse Khama to Ruth Williams.

South Africa, Michael Scott, Tshekedi Khama and the LMS

Given their other preoccupations in 1945 British missionaries were hardly aware of new developments in African nationalism. They took little heed of the Pan-African Congress, held in Manchester in October that year.[5] Although Harold Moody of the League of Coloured Peoples had been involved in the planning of the Congress he took no part in its proceedings, and the League went into decline after his death in 1947. Missionaries mourned the loss of Moody; but they remained unclear as to the implications of nationalism for their work and for the church in Africa. Nationalism was after all merely one of many challenges that the church faced. And there was little that seemed truly 'Pan-African' about

5. Hakim Adi and Marika Sherwood, *The 1945 Manchester Pan-African Conference Revisited* (London, 1995), pp. 41-50.

nationalist sentiment in the 1940s: levels of African dissatisfaction with colonialism and with European authority seemed to vary within and between region and colony, depending upon social and economic conditions. Arguably, though, it was in South Africa that the situation was most unsettled.

During the war the South African state had imposed great hardships on its African and Indian populations. These prompted a reciprocal increase in African political and trade union activism. Legislation against peoples of South Asian origin meanwhile drew a sharp response from local political groups and also from the government of India. 1946 became a year of protest and of violence: a strike by 70,000 African mineworkers was forcibly put down by police. Indians in Natal engaged in a campaign of passive resistance. The problems facing the country appeared to demand a response from the churches. In 1943 a diocesan commission appointed by the Anglican Bishop of Johannesburg Geoffrey Clayton made recommendations in a report to the government on the subject of political representation and race relations.[6] This moderately worded document was of particular significance to Anglicans in Britain. It satisfied them as to the good intentions of the 'local' Anglican Church: the Church of the Province of South Africa (CPSA). The report also seemed to demonstrate the effectiveness of Clayton's leadership. Effectively, it enabled British Protestant churches and missionary societies to refrain in good conscience from overt criticism of South African internal affairs. The Society for the Propagation of the Gospel, with close links to the CPSA, let it be known to other British Protestant missionary societies that any such criticism would likely prejudice relations between the government and religious institutions, be they missions, churches or ecumenical agencies such as the Christian Council of South Africa, which had been formed in 1936.[7] Missionaries agreed that their attitude to South African affairs, whether ecclesiastical or political, would be one of non-intervention from Britain.

Meanwhile, also during 1943, Michael Scott and Trevor Huddleston had arrived separately in Johannesburg. Their views on race, society and the responsibilities of the church differed from those of Clayton and the Anglican hierarchy. Scott (who had lived briefly in India) participated in the Natal passive resistance campaign. As a result he was imprisoned, incurring the displeasure of Clayton for whom disobedience to the law was inconsistent with priestly vocation. Uneasy with the government's racial policies, the church

6. Michael E. Worsnip, *Between the Two Fires: The Anglican Church and Apartheid, 1948-57* (Pietermaritzburg, 1991), pp. 22-7.

7. SOAS, Conference of British Missionary Societies Papers (hereafter CBMS), 260, 'Colour Bar Campaign, 1943-46' file, Canon G. W. Broomfield to Canon H. M. Grace, 10 Aug. 1944.

had little inclination to criticise those policies, much less protest against them. Its view of the state was benign. Scott challenged this view, as did Huddleston; but their thinking was too radical to be anything other than a source of discomfort, embarrassment and suspicion not only to their Anglican superiors and colleagues but also to the clergy of other Protestant churches of British origin. Huddleston (1913-98) was a member of the Community of the Resurrection, which since 1903 had maintained a presence in South Africa nominally linked with the CPSA. Scott (1907-83) differed from Huddleston in his indifference to institutional ties of almost any sort; but the two men shared a hatred of injustice and an active compassion for the oppressed. That compassion was not limited to black South Africans. In 1946 Scott became interested in developments relating to neighbouring South West Africa. Pretoria had long coveted this former German colony, now a United Nations 'trust' territory, administered by South Africa. The UN rejected in 1946 a South African request that it incorporate South West Africa within its borders.[8] The request had alarmed South Africa's black African and Indian populations. African National Congress president Alfred B. Xuma travelled to New York to argue personally to the UN against the incorporation of South West Africa into the Union. Xuma also contacted other African leaders, including Tshekedi Khama, acting regent of the Bangwato. It was through Tshekedi that the controversy over South West Africa came to the attention first of Scott, and then of British missionaries.

Tshekedi had temporarily acceded to the regency of the Bangwato in 1926, at the age of 20. The nominal regent, his nephew Seretse, was a young child. Tshekedi became a successful, if exacting leader. He was shrewd and manipulative. Such attributes were useful, not least in view of South Africa's intentions towards the Protectorate. Tshekedi opposed South Africa resolutely, and in doing so acquired a reputation as a defender of African interests. The South West Africa question was of more than passing interest to him. There lived in the protectorate some 15,000 Herero, one of the indigenous peoples of South West Africa who in 1907 had fled the depredations of German colonial rule. The leaders of the effectively stateless Herero now appealed to Tshekedi for assistance; their country was technically under international supervision by the UN, and they had no wish to see it pass under South African control. Convinced that Pretoria's interest in South West Africa might presage a fresh attempt to incorporate the High Commission Territories, Tshekedi

8. Peter J. Henshaw, 'Britain and South Africa at the United Nations: South West Africa, "Treatment of Indians" and "Race Conflict", 1946-61', *South African Historical Journal* 31 (1994): 82-9.

embarked upon a vigorous campaign on behalf of the Herero, lobbying his fellow Chiefs in the Protectorate for support and firing off letters to unofficial agencies in London, among them the LMS.[9]

The history of the LMS in Africa since the late nineteenth century was closely intertwined with that of the Bangwato, one of eight tribes (or nations) in the Protectorate. One of the Society's most notable missionaries, John Mackenzie, had during the 1860s formed a close bond with Tshekedi's father, Khama the Great. Mackenzie subsequently influenced the extension of imperial rule over Bechuanaland, for the protection of its peoples from South African business and political interests. The Bechuanaland Protectorate was instituted in 1885. By this time Khama, as kgosi (or king) of the Bangwato, had decreed that the LMS should be the sole Christian institution of the kingdom, located within the Protectorate in what became officially known as the Bangwato Reserve. The LMS became in effect the state church of the Bangwato, occupying a position arguably unique in British colonial Africa.[10]

The LMS supported Tshekedi as acting regent. Its officials lobbied the imperial authorities on his behalf, and they also collaborated with other British religious groups to argue to government in London that South Africa should not be allowed to obtain control of the Protectorate. Although they admired him for his tenacity and his devout Christian faith, missionaries found exasperating Tshekedi's penchant for politicking. Unprepared for any entreaty on behalf of the Herero (about whom they had little knowledge, or concern), the Society's headquarters officials were baffled by Tshekedi's request for assistance for them, in 1946. Nevertheless, they made a desultory approach to the Dominions Office, responsible for official matters relating to the High Commission Territories (because of their proximity to South Africa). This had no effect. Tshekedi's other supporters in Britain such as the Anti-Slavery Society fared no better in their representations on his behalf. In late 1946, alerted by Xuma and other friends in South Africa to Scott's activities, Tshekedi invited him to Serowe, the Bangwato capital. Scott agreed to take up the Herero cause. He subsequently travelled to South West Africa to help the Herero draw up a petition to be presented to the UN.[11] As far as the LMS was concerned, a matter of merely local difficulty had occurred, and had not affected the Society unduly. Before long, however, Scott's activities and also those of Tshekedi would become very problematic indeed.

9. SOAS, CWM, AF30/47A, T. Khama to LMS, 21 May 1946.

10. Paul S. Landau, *The Realm of the Word: Language, Gender and Christianity in a Southern African Kingdom* (London, 1995).

11. Michael Crowder, 'Tshekedi Khama, Smuts and South West Africa', *Journal of Modern African Studies* 25, no. 1 (1987): 26-30.

In early 1948 British missionary attitudes towards South African racial affairs were characterised by a mixture of complacency and concern. Although they did not entirely trust South African Prime Minister Jan Smuts, British missionaries grudgingly respected him: he had not after all seemed to wish them undue harm. His successor from May 1948, National Party leader D. F. Malan, conversely wore antipathy to all things British on his sleeve, as his supporters expected. The shift in official attitudes to race (which was more apparent than real) in the aftermath of the National Party's unexpected electoral success in 1948 took missionaries almost completely by surprise. They had mistakenly assumed that local church leaders such as Clayton, the Christian Council, and other unofficial bodies such as the South African Institute of Race Relations had quietly been exerting a 'liberalising' influence on government.[12] So profound appeared the change that missionaries struggled even to express the extent of their disquiet. For IMC secretary Norman Goodall (1896-1985), 'the very word *apartheid* ha[d] shifted discussion of the old problem of race relations to a more dynamic plane . . . the explosive word intensifying fears and quickening apprehension'.[13]

Missionaries were wary of pronouncing publicly on South African affairs, not wishing to compromise local churches. Nor did they wish to offend Afrikaner opinion. Church leaders such as Clayton, now Archbishop of Cape Town, were meanwhile adamant to the point of vehemence that British churches should not interfere in matters of local church concern.[14] Senior Anglican clergy in England accorded with Clayton's wishes, albeit reluctantly. They would not protest publicly about racial matters in South Africa. Neither would senior colleagues of other Protestant denominations. But in choosing to be publicly silent on apartheid, churches and missions effectively left Scott and Huddleston as the lone British religious critics of the South African state. In November 1949 Scott made his first personal appearance, on behalf of the Herero, before the trusteeship committee of the UN General Assembly.

By this time Scott's activities had aroused a great deal of attention. He was helping to internationalise discourse on human rights just as the UN was securing agreement from the majority of its members on a Universal Declaration of Human Rights. British missionaries were both bemused and irritated by Scott. To them he was a curious mixture of zealot and naïf, likely suscepti-

---

12. On the shortcomings of these organisations, see David Thomas, *Christ Divided: Liberalism, Ecumenism and Race in South Africa* (Pretoria, 2002).

13. Norman Goodall, 'Editorial', *International Review of Missions* (hereafter *IRM*) 38, no. 151 (1949): 273. Goodall was William Paton's successor at the IMC.

14. Lambeth Palace Library, London (hereafter LPL), Fisher Papers (hereafter FP), 65, Most Rev. G. H. Clayton to Most Rev. G. F. Fisher, 4 March 1949.

ble to manipulation, they thought, by others with an overtly political agenda.[15] As Ann Yates and Lewis Chester have emphasised in their biography of Scott, he *was* a complex, troubled and extremely difficult person.[16] Mission officials distrusted him. And they preferred to publicly express their concern for African affairs in ways that would not antagonise political authority, whether British or South African. In August 1949 the Conference of British Missionary Societies published a statement on African nationalism, modelled on its 'colour bar' manifesto issued four years previously. This latest document had originally been prompted by a meeting in London in 1947 between CBMS representatives and two West African political activists, Kwame Nkrumah and Bankole Awoonor-Renner of the West African National Secretariat. Published after lengthy deliberation and discussion, the statement expressed 'deep sympathy and understanding' for those African national movements that aimed 'at freedom, self-determination by constitutional methods and the removal of all forms of racial discrimination'.[17]

The statement made no impact. Only gradually did missionaries acknowledge that the best solution to the church's ills might lie within the church in Africa itself, primarily in an indigenous ministry that might help to win and hold for the church those urban Africans upon which the continent's political future might in time most likely depend. LMS and other mission officials drew sombre conclusions from the work of the Swedish missionary and theologian Bengt Sundkler, who published his influential book *Bantu Prophets in South Africa* in 1948. Sundkler disarmingly admitted that by his very presence as a western missionary he may have been 'part of the problem' facing the church in Africa.[18] He identified many reasons for African disillusion: reluctance to invest in theological education for local clergy, and thence to devolve ecclesiastical authority; willingness, on the other hand, to maintain huge differentials in pay.[19] The IMC subsequently commissioned the Anglican bishop Stephen Neill to undertake a survey of theological education in Africa, completed in 1950. Three years previously, at Whitby, Ontario, Canada, missionaries of many denominations and nationalities had discussed the implications for churches and missions of current

---

15. SOAS, CBMS, 296, 'South West Africa/Scott' file, Grace to Rev. N. Goodall, 21 Dec. 1948.

16. Ann Yates and Lewis Chester, *The Troublemaker: Michael Scott and His Lonely Struggle against Injustice* (London, 2006).

17. SOAS, CBMS, 257, 'Statement on African National Movements' file, CBMS statement, Aug. 1949.

18. Bengt G. M. Sundkler, *Bantu Prophets in South Africa* (London, 1948), p. 16.

19. Sundkler, *Bantu Prophets in South Africa*, p. 32.

'revolutionary' change in the world.[20] Some British missionaries subsequently argued for immediate reappraisal of the evangelistic task, and even of mission as vocation. Contemplating the strained relationship between the West and other parts of the world, and its likely impact upon both 'younger' and 'older' churches, Norman Goodall questioned the value even of 'a distinctive vocation' justifying 'Societies' or 'Orders' of missionaries'. The 'familiar geographical conception of missions as a sending activity (largely from West to East)', he argued, called for immediate re-examination.[21] Conversely, other British missionaries such as Max Warren continued to strongly espouse mission from the West. By such efforts, Warren argued, missionaries could facilitate a more 'international' perception of world affairs, and even a more critical view of imperialism, in the West and beyond.[22]

Such views were indicative of diverse opinions and slowly changing ideas. But if certain British missionaries exhibited a capacity for self-appraisal and self-criticism, there remained a perceptible gap between rhetoric and reality in the late 1940s, not least where the church in Africa was concerned. Ostensibly committed to the development of African church leadership, missionaries remained as wary of expressing support for African nationalism as of criticising the government of South Africa. Scott was setting a public agenda that missionaries, for all their distaste of his methods, could not ignore. Yet their efforts seemed in comparison not only tentative but also unsuccessful. With the assistance of the British Council of Churches the CBMS recruited William Wand, Bishop of London, to head an interdenominational deputation to the Commonwealth Relations Office, or CRO (as the Dominions Office had been renamed), in November 1949. This had two aims: to lobby for increased colonial welfare and development funding for the High Commission Territories; and to request that the Territories not be handed over to South Africa. In this way British churches and missions hoped to draw public attention to the problems of southern Africa without offending the authorities in Pretoria. But Philip Noel-Baker, Labour Secretary of State for Commonwealth Relations, refused either to make any commitment on funding or to discuss the political future of the Territories.[23] Frustrated, mission and church representatives tried, again without success, to forge temporary, informal alliances with others interested in South Africa. These included: Canon

20. C. W. Ranson, ed., *Renewal and Advance: Christian Witness in a Revolutionary World* (London, 1948).

21. Norman Goodall, 'First Principles', *IRM* 39, no. 155 (1950): 259-60.

22. Max Warren, 'The Missionary Obligation of the Church in the Present Historical Situation', *IRM* 39, no. 155 (1950): 395-7.

23. SOAS, CWM, AF30/47D, Rev. R. K. Orchard to Rev. A. J. Haile, 5 Dec. 1949.

John Collins, founder of Christian Action; the trade union and political activists Margaret and William Ballinger; and John Fletcher of the Society of Friends, through whom a fruitless attempt was made to recruit the novelist Alan Paton (whose *Cry, the Beloved Country* had recently been published, to great acclaim) for a series of speaking engagements in Britain.[24] In December 1949 British ecumenists decided to form, under the auspices of the BCC, a new committee, to be known as the Race Relations Group. This was intended to facilitate public debate in Britain on race in the African colonies and in South Africa. It was to provide a forum for British Christians who were interested in Africa but wary of the 'political' methods being used by Scott. The Race Relations Group was not a success, and was wound up in 1953. It was not completely without influence, however; its activities can be seen as presaging the decision of the Royal Institute of International Affairs to form in 1952 what would become the Institute of Race Relations.

The LMS and Seretse and Ruth Khama

The person who put most effort into the formation of a church-based Race Relations Group was the Congregationalist clergyman Ronald Orchard (1911-89). Born in Liverpool, Orchard for family reasons had to forgo the opportunity of a missionary career with the LMS in China. Instead he worked in the Society's offices in Leeds and later in London, becoming secretary and LMS committee chairman for Africa (and also China) in 1946. Orchard's sole direct experience of Africa by 1948 was gleaned from an official visit to LMS missions there during 1946-47. This at least enabled him to appreciate that the unsettled economic and political situation was likely to exert a major influence on mission and church affairs. The racial discrimination that he observed in central and southern Africa certainly troubled him; but he believed that the church could be a force for good, encouraging tolerance and understanding between races.[25] Orchard was a committed ecumenist, and would later become secretary of the IMC. He was not a controversialist. His main task as LMS secretary was to support work in Africa in the context of the Society's commitment to world mission. As was usually the case with mission headquarters officials, Orchard relied for information about local issues less

24. SOAS, CBMS, 573, 'Race Relations Group, 1949-52' file, Rev. R. D. Rees, notes on meeting with Canon L. J. Collins, 14 Oct., and with the Ballingers, 21 Dec.; Goodall to J. P. Fletcher, 21 Nov. 1949.
25. SOAS, CWM, AF32, Orchard, secretarial report, March 1948.

on black African contacts than on locally based missionaries, notably the veteran Rev. Alfred Haile (1882-1982), former principal of Tiger Kloof, friend of both Tshekedi and Seretse, and now based at Bulawayo, Southern Rhodesia. Orchard's main contact within the Bangwato reserve was a more recent LMS recruit, Rev. Alan Seager, who, with his wife Ruth, was based at Serowe. Notwithstanding the information provided him by these colleagues, Orchard by late 1949 found it ever more difficult to fulfil his secretarial responsibilities. African affairs were becoming more complicated and troublesome, for him and his committee. It was partly for that reason and partly because of Scott's activities that Orchard saw the Race Relations Group as a worthwhile vehicle for closer Christian engagement with matters in South Africa and the African colonies.

During the latter half of 1949 fresh complications arose in the Bechuanaland Protectorate that would have a considerable impact on the LMS. Following the death of Seretse's mother in 1930, Tshekedi had become guardian to his nephew Seretse. With his second wife Ella Moshoela (whom he married in 1938), Tshekedi had five children. But he paid particular attention to Seretse, as heir apparent. In 1944 Seretse concluded his studies at Fort Hare College in the Eastern Cape and seemed ready to succeed Tshekedi. Most of the Bangwato welcomed this prospect: Tshekedi's high-handedness had never endeared him to all the tribe. During the war Tshekedi had raised a Bangwato detachment of the African Pioneer Corps. Intended as a demonstration of loyalty to Crown and Empire, this action displeased Bangwato women, who saw their men folk sent off to North Africa and the Middle East.[26] Keen that Seretse, as their ruler-to-be, should further his education and prepare for leadership, the Bangwato decided that he should travel to England to study. He arrived in time to participate in the LMS triple jubilee celebrations. The Society took an active interest in his educational progress, which, for a variety of reasons, proceeded fitfully. Then in 1947 he met Ruth Williams, a clerk at a firm of Lloyd's underwriters. They fell in love and decided to marry.

The marriage, in September 1948, between an African prince and a white English woman caused an international sensation.[27] What was its impact on mission and church in Africa? LMS headquarters disapproved of the marriage, and made strenuous but unsuccessful attempts to prevent it. The Society had no policy on interracial marriages, but its officials took the view that

26. Ashley Jackson, *Botswana, 1939-45: An African Country at War* (Oxford, 1999), pp. 115-20.

27. Williams, *Colour Bar*, pp. 14-26. What follows in this chapter is based in part on John Stuart, 'Empire and Religion in Colonial Botswana: The Seretse Khama Controversy, 1948-56', in Hilary Carey, ed., *Empires of Religion* (Basingstoke, 2008), pp. 311-32.

these should be entered into only after the most careful consideration and pastoral guidance. By this reckoning Ruth and Seretse had behaved rashly and Seretse foolishly, in light of his tribal responsibilities. Despite some sympathy for the situation in which the newlyweds now found themselves, this perception held within LMS headquarters, and affected the Society's handling of the ensuing controversy. Tshekedi undoubtedly had his faults, officials reasoned, but he was a strong leader. Seretse, conversely, seemed lacking in judgement. To missionaries and African clergy working in the Bangwato Reserve the situation was less clear cut. Opinion differed as to Seretse's merits. There was keen interest therefore, in his return, alone, to the reserve in November 1948. A kgotla (tribal council) was convened to debate the marriage and the Bangwato succession. Seretse argued that in spite of marrying a white woman without the tribe's permission he was still ready and able to be their leader. Tshekedi described his disappointment at Seretse's decision to marry outside the tribe and without consulting his people. His mood was emotional: 'I am your father', he asserted, '. . . I have looked after the tribe for you'.[28] The outcome of the debate was inconclusive, as was that of a further kgotla in December. Alan Seager was in attendance throughout, such gatherings customarily being opened and closed with prayer. He noted presciently '. . . for the next few months at least, probably years, there is going to be so much intrigue that any reasonable progress in Tribal affairs will cease'.[29] Seager then solicited local opinion within the Reserve, as his colleague Alfred Haile did more widely in the Protectorate. There was discernible support for Tshekedi among the Bangwato, but many people and especially women (excluded from the kgotla, which was composed only of adult males at this time) confided that they would welcome Seretse as leader and Ruth as his wife. Haile saw in this situation potential for a split within the church, between factions in support of the two men. But the missionaries' enquiries caused rumour to circulate among the Bangwato that missionaries and African clergy alike favoured Seretse, and were collaborating with Tshekedi's opponents. An anxious Haile advised LMS headquarters against evincing open support for either man.[30] It would be best to adopt an attitude of neutrality and await developments.[31]

Orchard concurred with this advice. He had no intention of openly endorsing either Seretse or for that matter Tshekedi, who now began soliciting support from anyone in London who might assist him. In April 1949 Tshekedi

---

28. SOAS, CWM, AF37/79A, Rev. A. Seager to Orchard, 22 Nov. 1948.
29. SOAS, CWM, CWM, AF30/47C, Seager to Orchard, 30 Dec. 1948.
30. SOAS, CWM, AF37/79A, Haile to Orchard, 17 May 1949.
31. SOAS, CWM, AF37/79B, Haile, memo, 22 Feb. 1950.

wrote to Orchard, asking him to intercede with the CRO. Orchard did meet informally with a CRO official, but balked at Tshekedi's request that he also liaise with the Fabian Colonial Bureau and with Michael Scott.[32] Orchard did take care to keep Tshekedi informed of the contact he had made with the CRO official, in the hope that Tshekedi would continue to rely on the LMS rather than on secular interlocutors in Britain who might wish to make political capital out of his dispute with Seretse. To the Bangwato, however, it appeared that Tshekedi was intent on bolstering his own position, rather than advancing the interests of the tribe. Sentiment within the tribe began to move ever more strongly against him. Developments culminated in a kgotla decision of June 1949 in which the Bangwato finally acclaimed Seretse as their rightful leader. Hugely disappointed, Tshekedi, with members of his family and some supporters, went voluntarily into internal exile. All that remained now, it seemed, was for Seretse's chieftainship to receive the official imprimatur that it required from the British government.

For its part, the government was in no hurry to make a decision. In July it authorised a judicial enquiry into Seretse's fitness to rule. This was largely a means by which to buy time, because the governments of South Africa and of Southern Rhodesia had now begun to make representations to the CRO: official recognition of Seretse should be withheld, they argued, because his marriage was repugnant to Afrikaner and Rhodesian ideas of racial purity. Also, it might encourage greater African criticism of and perhaps even revolt against those ideas and the laws that upheld them. The judicial inquiry took place during November, and its report was passed to the government in early December. It did not prompt a conclusive decision on Seretse's right to accede to the kingship.

In Serowe, Seager worried about the impact on church life of Tshekedi's exile, and especially of the departure of his wife Ella and sister Bonyerile, active Christians both. What caused Seager additional worry, however, was to be personally accused, with his African colleague Rev. Joshua Danisa, of collaboration with Seretse. In response he convened a meeting of church members at which he and Haile strongly asserted the church's neutrality in political matters.[33] This was a fiction, as Seager well knew. The church had always sought to adapt to prevailing political circumstances within the Reserve. With the question of succession in abeyance, however, it seemed to Seager politic to espouse and maintain an uncommitted stance.

The government's continuing reluctance to announce a decision about

32. SOAS, CWM, AF30/47D, T. Khama to Orchard, 25 April 1949.
33. SOAS, CWM, AF37/79B, Haile, memo, 22 Feb. 1950.

Seretse made missionaries uneasy. What did they anticipate would be the response of the government and of the CRO in particular? Their expectations were conditioned by past experience. During the 1920s and 1930s the LMS, with representatives of other missions and of secular humanitarian organisations, had consistently lobbied against incorporation of the High Commission Territories. Joseph Oldham was often to the fore in these representations. Missionaries believed their efforts to have been influential in South Africa's continuing failure to attain its aim of incorporation. This was a not unreasonable assumption, reliant as it was on missionary belief in the commitment of the imperial authorities to the trusteeship of African peoples. To be sure, the High Commission Authorities occupied an anomalous position in terms of imperial authority, being the responsibility of the Dominions Office, and later the CRO, rather than of the Colonial Office. Yet for missionaries this was not a problematic state of affairs; its main consequence, as they saw it, was a need for increased vigilance on their part, to keep the CRO reminded of its obligations to the peoples of the High Commission Territories. But the 1948 electoral success of Malan's National Party had alarmed the CRO, which was suspicious of Afrikaner expansionist intentions, not only towards the High Commission Territories but towards the Rhodesias also. After prolonged deliberation of the Seretse case, the cabinet finally decided in late January 1950 that in order not to cause offence to South Africa, Seretse should renounce his right to rule. He was summoned to London. There, he refused to comply with CRO demands. On 8 March Patrick Gordon Walker, who was now Commonwealth Relations Secretary, made an announcement in the House of Commons: Seretse would be banished from the Protectorate for a period of five years (Tshekedi was to be banished also, but only from the Reserve). The government would instigate direct rule in the Reserve, through an officially nominated 'native authority'. The announcement confounded almost every expectation, not least that within the LMS.

Over the course of several months Orchard had tried in vain to discern government intentions, through discreet contact with the CRO.[34] He had hoped to be in some way prepared when the decision was announced. In the event, Seretse pre-empted Gordon Walker by making government intentions known to the press in advance of the official announcement. In response, well-meaning individuals and organisations and critics of the government all vied to express support for Seretse and declaim the decision to banish as appeasement of South Africa. The cricketer Learie Constantine helped form a Seretse Khama Fighting Committee. The Labour MP Fenner Brockway be-

34. SOAS, CWM, AF40/82A, Orchard, notes on visit to CRO, 5 July 1949.

came involved. Orchard was aghast, less at the actions of the CRO than at the clamour that now surrounded Seretse and Ruth and, by association, the LMS. 'The lid has blown well and truly off', he reflected ruefully.[35] How should he respond, especially given the history of LMS support for the Bangwato? LMS supporters and members of Congregational churches throughout the UK inundated the Society's headquarters with written requests that it make a public show of support for Seretse and Ruth. Newspaper reporters clamoured for a statement. This was not at all to Orchard's liking. With his Africa committee colleagues he deliberated carefully before devising a statement, which he released to the press on 31 March. He made no criticism of the government in the statement, but questioned the motives for the banishment and also requested that the decision be reconsidered. In addition, he affirmed the Society's concern for all the Bangwato equally, irrespective of whether they might support Seretse or Tshekedi.[36]

This affirmation was important. Orchard was determined on a publicly neutral stance. He had no wish for mission or church to be identified as supporting either Seretse or Tshekedi. Neither did he wish the LMS in Britain to be in any way drawn into political or parliamentary dispute between the government and its critics. Furthermore, Orchard intended that the statement should display the concern not merely of the LMS but also that of all British Protestant churches and missionary societies. It was partly with an eventuality such as the Bangwato succession crisis in mind that he had pressed so strongly during 1949 for a Race Relations Group to be formed within the British Council of Churches. Via the Group, Orchard was able to deploy the LMS statement to further use. It formed the basis both of a letter from Geoffrey Fisher, Archbishop of Canterbury, to the Prime Minister, Clement Attlee, and also of a further public pronouncement, by the BCC on the now highly topical subject of 'race relations' in the Empire and Commonwealth.[37]

If these initiatives gave evidence of Christian concern in Britain, they meant little or nothing to the Bangwato, the majority of whom desired from church and mission an open, unequivocal display of support for Seretse. They had been overwhelmingly dismayed by news of the banishing. In the Reserve disorder ensued, and there was a boycott of official activities. The hold of the church on its members suddenly began to seem fragile. Whole congregations expected African clergy such as Danisa to take a stance, for either Tshekedi or Seretse. These expectations of support fed into personal arguments among the

35. SOAS, CWM, AF37/79B, Orchard to Haile, 10 March 1950.
36. SOAS, CWM, AF38/79F, Orchard, statement for LMS, 31 March 1950.
37. LPL, FP, 67, Fisher to C. R. Attlee, with enclosure, 21 April 1950.

Bangwato over land and livestock, in which clergy were also expected to take sides. Missionaries feared that the unsettled situation might favour the evangelistic efforts of other, 'rival' Zionist and Pentecostal churches, threatening further the influence of the LMS on Bangwato Christianity.[38] In the circumstances the LMS statement was inadequate, and insufficient to distance the Society in the minds of the Bangwato from the actions of the government.[39] Direct efforts by the Bangwato to effect a change of public attitude by the LMS came to nothing. In June a group of women wrote to the Society's headquarters, imploring that it give a lead 'in this sad state of affairs'.[40] Orchard could not recommend such a step, in part because of a fresh complication: the Society now faced further threat, from the actions of the Department of Native Affairs in Pretoria. It was contemplating new legislation in support of apartheid, to include a ban on students from outside South Africa attending schools within its borders.[41] This would directly affect Tiger Kloof, which drew many of its students from the Bechuanaland Protectorate. Orchard now had greater reason not to authorise any public display of support for Seretse by the LMS: to do so might antagonise the South African authorities still further.

From personal meetings with Gordon Walker on the subject of Seretse, Orchard discerned that the secretary of state was genuinely concerned about the possible fate of Tiger Kloof.[42] He believed that Gordon Walker would reconsider his decision to banish Seretse. Gordon Walker had no intention of doing so. Yet the LMS secretary continued to lobby the CRO. Why was this? Did Orchard believe that he might be able to influence official policy? An intensely dutiful mission secretary, Orchard was attempting as best he could to be true to the history and tenets of the LMS as an organisation that represented African interests to imperial authority. In 1950 that authority still resided in the imperial capital, London. Consequently, dealings with the CRO, whether formal (in the shape of deputations) or informal, were for Orchard a fact of life. In any case, Orchard had strong doubts about Seretse's character and about his capacity for leadership. He thought that Brockway and other politicians were manipulating Seretse, for political reasons. Orchard did not entirely trust Seretse. He refrained from contacting him for fear of compromising LMS 'neutrality'. Conversely, he was sympathetic towards Gordon Walker, believing him to have the impossible task of negotiating with intransigent Afrikaners such as Malan who, it was by now widely believed in Lon-

38. SOAS, CWM, AF37/79D, Rev. A. Sandilands to Orchard, 5 Aug. 1950.
39. SOAS, CWM, AF37/79B, Haile to Orchard, 14 March 1950.
40. SOAS, CWM, AF37/79B, M. B. Mokgwathi to Orchard, n.d., but June 1950.
41. SOAS, CWM, AF40/82A, Haile to Orchard, 22 Nov. 1950.
42. SOAS, CWM, AF40/82A, Orchard to P. C. Gordon Walker, 21 July 1949.

don, had threatened to take South Africa out of the Commonwealth if Seretse became Chief.

The LMS maintained some informal contact with Seretse, through Seager. During 1950 Seager worked at effecting reconciliation between the two Khamas, still in dispute over the chieftainship.[43] Tshekedi expressed hope that he and Seretse might indeed 'join hands' and together challenge the CRO to reconsider their case.[44] Little came of this, and relations between the two men remained difficult. The same was true of Seretse's relationship with the LMS, such as it still was in 1950. Learie Constantine, Fenner Brockway and many others in Britain had offered open support, as well as criticism of government. They continued to do so following Seretse's arrival, in exile, in London in August 1950, accompanied by Ruth and their infant daughter Jacqueline. The LMS was conversely intent, as Orchard later put it, to remain 'emphatically neutral on the political issues'.[45] Seretse could not rely upon a show of support by the Society. This was of little consequence to him; he and Ruth had by now many other contacts in Britain upon whom they could rely.

By 1950, overworked, exhausted and ordered to rest by his doctor, Orchard (who, remarkably, also had secretarial responsibilities for missions in China) may have pondered the extent to which African affairs seemed to be diverting the LMS from its main task, evangelism. He could see no way out of his present difficulties. The Society was in a bind, trapped as it had perhaps never been before by its historical as well as religious obligations to an African tribe, the members of which stubbornly refused to conform to missionary expectations. As if that was not difficulty enough, the Commonwealth Relations Office was little interested in the travails of the LMS and its beleaguered secretary for Africa.

Seretse and Ruth: An Imperial Crisis and a Crisis for the LMS

Tshekedi was intent on making whatever use he could of the LMS. In March 1951, dissatisfied and frustrated by exile outside the Reserve, he undertook an extended visit to London to argue for his reinstatement as acting regent. He lobbied the LMS and other potentially sympathetic organisations. But he found it difficult to muster support of the kind being accorded Seretse. This was not for want of trying. In meetings with missionaries he strove to

---

43. SOAS, CWM, AF37/79C, Seager to T. Khama, 3 May, and to S. Khama, 4 May 1950.
44. SOAS, CWM, AF37/79D, T. Khama to Haile, 18 Aug. 1950.
45. SOAS, CWM, AF32/34A, Orchard to Haile, 16 March 1951.

emphasise his commitment to all the Bangwato. Orchard was not unimpressed by these arguments, which, he knew, owed much to Tshekedi's continuing desire to resist the threat of South African incorporation of the High Commission Territories. Although unwilling still to commit the LMS to open support for Tshekedi or Seretse, Orchard now had cause to ponder the consequences for the Society of its refusal to court controversy.

By mid-1951 it was apparent that the Bangwato succession controversy formed but one aspect of an increasingly complex set of imperial geopolitical problems relating to southern and central Africa. In June was published in London a White Paper, on the 'closer association' of three British colonies: Southern Rhodesia, Northern Rhodesia and Nyasaland. The idea of 'closer association' was stimulated by government anxieties about Afrikaner economic and territorial expansionism and by Rhodesian lobbying. Were it to become official policy, the consequences for Africans in the three territories might be serious. It was not in the Bangwato Reserve alone that the LMS maintained missions; it also operated in both Southern Rhodesia and Northern Rhodesia. It was therefore conceivable that the Society might have to make representations to the government on behalf of Africans in those territories. Might it also face pressure for public action, of the kind that the Seretse controversy had aroused? Having read the White Paper, and in the aftermath of a discussion with Tshekedi on the future of the High Commission Territories, Orchard wrote to Haile. 'I am just a little uneasy about our policy of neutrality in the Bamangwato dispute lest it should be interpreted as a lack of courage on the part of the Mission. . . . I am anxious to be sure that neither pressure of work nor fear of consequences lets us be false to the tradition of John Philip, John Mackenzie and all our other notable predecessors'.[46] Earlier in the year, Orchard had obtained from a CRO official an informal, private assurance: transfer of the High Commission Territories to South Africa was 'politically unthinkable'.[47] This may have induced in him greater sanguinity about the incorporation question. Yet despite his new-found unease about LMS neutrality, Orchard felt unable to argue to colleagues that the Society should be more openly critical of the authorities for their treatment of Seretse. Instead, he made further use of his ecumenical contacts, this time in an attempt to increase awareness within British churches of the perils that 'closer association' in central Africa might pose to indigenous peoples.[48]

46. SOAS, CWM, AF26/17A, Orchard to Haile, 25 July 1951. 'Bamangwato' was the contemporary term.

47. SOAS, CWM, AF26/17A, J. P. Gibson to Orchard, 10 March 1951.

48. SOAS, CWM, AF34/37A, Orchard, notes on CBMS Africa Committee meeting, 11 Sept. 1951.

Orchard continued to hold out hope that the CRO would reconsider its decision to banish Seretse. Doubtful of Seretse's leadership abilities, he nevertheless believed that some form of compromise arrangement between Seretse, Tshekedi and the imperial authorities would be in the best interests of the Bangwato: he thought it might prove possible for Seretse to be allowed to return to the Reserve, to occupy a position other than as Chief. Developments during 1951 gave some grounds for optimism. In response to Tshekedi's lobbying, the government sent to the Protectorate a team of unofficial observers, who were to report on the situation.[49] But their visit became a farce and the conclusions of the ensuing report were overshadowed by a general election in the UK. After six years in power, the Labour Party was succeeded in the government in October 1951 by a Conservative administration under Winston Churchill. Orchard was not alone in believing that this change might finally herald a resolution of the Bangwato succession crisis.

Sensing opportunity, Tshekedi, only recently returned to Africa, hastened to go to London. He secured from the new administration an apparent promise that his banishment would be rescinded. Alarmed about the possible consequences of Tshekedi's actions for the succession, supporters of Seretse among the Bangwato now organised a deputation, to go to London and plead Seretse's case with the CRO. Before they could conclude their preparations, the Conservative Secretary of State for Commonwealth Relations, Lord Salisbury, made a startling announcement in Parliament on 27 March 1952: rather than for a period of five years Seretse's banishment would instead be 'permanent and final'. The decision had been taken for imperial geopolitical reasons relating to the Bechuanaland Protectorate, to South Africa and to plans for 'closer association' of British colonial territories in central Africa.

Having recently hoped that action by the new Conservative government might help extricate the LMS from its predicament, the statement left Orchard flabbergasted. 'Why on earth', he raged, 'should they choose this particular moment to make such an announcement? Is not Southern and Central Africa in ferment enough? . . . There is such a blare of publicity . . . that I am sure to get questions. . . . I hardly think we can take refuge in silence'.[50] Such was the extent of concern in British religious circles that Orchard had little difficulty in organising, through the BCC, a deputation, led by Fisher, to meet with Salisbury at the CRO. The intention was not to protest as such, but to

49. Michael Crowder, 'Professor Macmillan Goes on Safari: The British Government Observer Team and the Crisis over the Seretse Khama Marriage, 1951', in Hugh Macmillan and Shula Marks, eds., *Africa and Empire: W. M. Macmillan: Historian and Social Critic* (Aldershot, 1989), pp. 254-78.

50. SOAS, CWM, AF32/34C, Orchard to Haile, 28 March 1952.

question the decision and to ascertain the extent of external pressure, from South Africa (what Fisher referred to as 'ulterior motives'). Salisbury gave nothing away. He merely reiterated what was now the official line: Seretse's return would threaten disorder in the Reserve.[51]

The decision had stunned the Bangwato, but it also gave fresh impetus to the organising of the six-man deputation to London. Seager provided the deputation with a message to LMS headquarters, devised by church members in Serowe. The delegates arrived in London on 9 April after a lengthy air journey and remained there for almost five weeks. They had two ultimately fruitless meetings with Salisbury, who refused their request that Seretse be allowed to return to the Reserve. The deputation's main spokesman, Moutlwatsi Mpotokwane, also visited the LMS head office on three occasions during the first week of May. At the first meeting, at which several LMS officials were present, Mpotokwane insisted that far from being disunited or in dispute as to the relative leadership merits of Tshekedi and Seretse, the Bangwato were all but unanimous in their support of Seretse and Ruth. The government, he asserted, was guilty of hypocrisy, in refusing to admit the reasons for Seretse's continuing exclusion. Only at two subsequent meetings did Mpotokwane speak more freely, being now alone with Orchard whom he had met previously on the latter's tour of Africa in 1947-48. It was not about government policy alone that the Bangwato were uneasy, Mpotokwane confided; the attitude of the LMS was a matter of no little confusion and concern. Why had its officials been so reticent about expressing open support for Seretse? Could they not have been more forthcoming, given the longstanding relationship between the LMS and the Bangwato? Orchard could not have found this questioning anything but difficult. He had recently been in touch again with his contacts at the CRO, and had no wish for this to be known by the Bangwato; it might cause them to suspect collusion. He reassured Mpotokwane of the sincerity of LMS intentions and its commitment to the well-being of all the Bangwato. Mpotokwane did not appear convinced and suggested to Orchard that the Society risked its motives being misinterpreted, at the very least.[52] A week later he and the other delegates left London, and returned to Africa. They were angry with the British government and uncertain of the attitude of the LMS.

Days after the arrival of the deputation back in the Reserve, Bangwato dissatisfaction with government, which until then had mostly taken the

---

51. SOAS, CBMS, 571, BCC press release, 9 May 1952.

52. SOAS, CWM, AF33/35D, Orchard, notes on meetings with M. Mpotokwane, 1, 5 and 7 May 1952.

form of non-co-operation, erupted into violence. Three African policemen were killed. Seager attempted without success to intervene, attracting only Bangwato criticism for his efforts. Responding to reports of the unrest, Orchard wearily acknowledged the difficulties. He informed Seager that reassurance might somehow be found '. . . in the fact that you are criticized from both sides. That certainly seems to suggest that you have been successful in pursuing a policy of neutrality even though it is not a very comfortable situation to be in'.[53] Orchard was prepared to concede that the violence might at least force the government to take more seriously its ostensible commitment to order, stability and 'good government' in the Reserve. This could only be to the benefit of the church. 'We have not only to be clear ourselves that the building up of the Church is a first priority', he wrote, 'we have also got to make it apparent that this is where our emphasis lies'.[54] This would not be easy to achieve, given the extent of the present furore. Gradually, the tension eased. In May 1953 the government authorised the installation of Rasebolai Kagamane as 'native authority'. He was not of the house of Khama and the decision did not meet with the approval of those Bangwato who longed for Seretse's return. As far as Seager and his African colleagues were concerned, however, the relative calm that now prevailed made possible greater attention to church rather than to political matters. The constitution of the courts of the local church was revised, to permit greater African participation. This coincided with changes made by the LMS to its regional administrative structures in southern Africa. Seager also renewed personal contact with Tshekedi, back in the Protectorate from August 1952 and residing at a new village created at Pilikwe, some 80 kilometres from Serowe. Although his relationship with Tshekedi was cordial enough, Seager had little success in effecting rapprochement between Tshekedi, his supporters and the church in Serowe. Keen to have the educational and medical benefits that other churches might provide, Tshekedi would later encourage Anglican and Roman Catholic missions to work in the Protectorate. Over time, independent African churches would acquire a greater presence, and influence also.[55]

The relative calm in the Reserve came as relief to Livingstone House, the LMS head office. Orchard had been out of his depth. He had been unable to devise on behalf of the Society a suitable response to a crisis of imperial proportions. This inability would be indicative of other difficulties still to come,

---

53. SOAS, CWM, AF33/35G, Orchard to Seager, 3 July 1952.
54. SOAS, CWM, AF10G, Orchard to Haile, 13 Aug. 1952.
55. Alan Seager, *In the Shadow of a Great Rock* (Connah's Quay, 2005), pp. 95-108.

for the LMS and other missionary societies, in relation to African colonial affairs during the 1950s. Orchard drew some comfort from his own religious faith. He informed Seager that '. . . the Almighty has a way of over-ruling our mistakes when we are trying to act in accordance with His will . . .' As for the church in the Bangwato Reserve, Orchard believed that if it could show '. . . that it derives its life from a higher source than the Tribe, and exercises an authority which is not dependent on Chief or administration, it may well begin a new chapter both in its own story and in the story of the Church in Bechuanaland as a whole'.[56]

After the Crisis: What Next for Missions?

As missionaries both in Africa and at headquarters in London well knew, relationships between LMS missions, church and the Bangwato had from their inception in the late nineteenth century never been less than fraught. Through many vicissitudes those relationships, along with the Bangwato chieftaincy, had nevertheless endured until the crisis precipitated by the marriage of Seretse and Ruth. The British government took away from Seretse — and from Tshekedi also — the right to rule. Seretse would return to his homeland only in 1956, having renounced his claim to be Chief. The crisis damaged the claim of the LMS to be regarded as a church of all the Bangwato, a claim that had always been contingent upon Bangwato acceptance and approval. Tshekedi manipulated the LMS, as had Bangwato leaders before him. But the LMS was far from being a passive instrument of Tshekedi's will in relation to Bangwato society. Its relationship with the Bangwato was more complicated than that. Mission and church played important roles in Bangwato life, and the Society's relationship with the tribe was of vital importance to its identity. What the LMS did not anticipate in the late 1940s, however, was the extent of apparent change in African attitudes to empire and also to mission, as represented most vividly by Seretse in his refusal to conform to LMS expectations. The crisis ultimately revealed how fragile in certain respects might be the church's hold on an African community.

Seretse's attitude to the LMS was characterised by coolness at best. He was not overtly religious, as was Tshekedi. He may have expected a show of support from the Society in regard to his marriage and his succession to the chieftainship. He did not receive one. He and Ruth turned to secular agencies for help, and from them they obtained unquestioning support. In 1952

56. SOAS, CWM, AF/18, 'Seager' file, Orchard to Seager, 22 Jan. 1951, and 23 April 1952.

Brockway and others set up the Council for the Defence of Seretse Khama and the Protectorates. That same year another supporter, Michael Scott, was among the founding members of a new organisation with still broader aims: the Africa Bureau.[57] Organisations such as these were both indicative of and a further stimulus to greater public interest in African colonial affairs.

Scott's petitioning of the UN, on behalf of Tshekedi and the Herero, had by this time demonstrated how representatives of colonial peoples could bypass networks of communication in Britain between humanitarian and religious organisations and imperial authority, and focus international attention on a South African government whose actions appeared in breach of human rights. Imperial problems thus became internationalised to a much greater extent than previously. Missionaries were far from unaware of these developments. They took a keen interest in UN discussion and debate on a Universal Declaration of Human Rights, which was finally agreed in December 1948.[58] They particularly valued the protection it might afford Christian minorities in newly independent, former imperial territories such as India and Pakistan.[59] One particular country occupied an anomalous position: South Africa (which had abstained in the UN vote on the Universal Declaration). Missionaries perceived South Africa's racial problems (and their impact on neighbouring British colonies) as having an imperial as well as an international aspect. During and after the Seretse Khama crisis of 1948-52 they continued to believe that the South African state might be susceptible to religious lobbying. Norman Goodall of the IMC engaged in a long-term diplomatic strategy. He attempted (ultimately with little success) to win the Dutch Reformed Church in South Africa round to the international, ecumenical mainstream in the hope of exerting some influence thereby on National Party racial policy.[60] In March 1949 Orchard wrote to Goodall. The case of South Africa might present certain difficulties, Orchard acknowledged; but missionary societies should speak out on matters in African colonies, under British jurisdiction. Accordingly,

57. Stephen Howe, *Anticolonialism in British Politics: The Left and the End of Empire* (Oxford, 1993), pp. 196-200.

58. In 1946 Protestant churches and missions formed a new agency, the Commission of the Churches on International Affairs, to lobby the UN. See O. F. Nolde, 'Ecumenical Action in World Affairs,' in Harold E. Fey, ed., *The Ecumenical Advance: A History of the Ecumenical Movement, Vol. 2: 1948-68* (London, 1970), pp. 263-85.

59. SOAS, CBMS, 567, 'JCRL Minutes and Papers' file, Joint Committee on Religious Liberty, report, Dec. 1947, and 'Occasional Bulletin', Jan. 1948.

60. SOAS, CBMS, 294, 'Correspondence, 1943-50' file, Goodall to Rev. S. G. Pitts, 4 Dec. 1946.

It would be a tragedy for the Church in Southern Africa if the voices of secular bodies were raised in defence of human rights in Africa while world Christian opinion maintained an embarrassed silence. . . . African opinion is watching to see what line the Christian Church will take on such issues. If the Church remains silent they will conclude that it is too identified with the *status quo* to give a lead any more and will turn to secular agencies.[61]

Africans, together with their supporters in Britain, were already turning to such agencies. Knowledge of this did not, for Orchard, negate the continuing need for missions to state their case in relation to colonial affairs, notwithstanding their lack of success with Seretse Khama.

In May 1952 Orchard accompanied Archbishop Fisher to the CRO, to petition Lord Salisbury about Seretse's banishment. Following this fruitless encounter Orchard decided that a change of emphasis was required in relation to African affairs. He contacted Haile, his main confidant: 'I don't think . . . it would be wise to press the Seretse case further; it is too complex and too shaky to form good ground for a major battle'. If it was now certain that government had no intention of reviewing Seretse's case, it was equally clear that government was committed to a Central African Federation, irrespective of African objections. 'I do think', Orchard continued in his letter to Haile, 'we have got to prepare for . . . an all out campaign to convince Government that African opinion in Central Africa must be treated responsibly'.[62]

To the Bangwato of the Bechuanaland Protectorate the LMS had a responsibility that was uniquely special and (as the events of 1948-52 demonstrated) also onerous. In the Rhodesias and Nyasaland the LMS was but one of many missionary societies. The intention of the government in London to establish in central Africa what appeared likely to be a Rhodesian hegemony in support of British imperial interests troubled Ronald Orchard greatly. It troubled many other missionaries also. For that reason Orchard believed it vital that churches and missions present a united front, on behalf of African interests threatened by a British imperial initiative. In the event, a Central African Federation would instead demonstrate how varied and disparate were missionary attitudes to empire and to African nationalism.

---

61. SOAS, CWM AF40/80A, Orchard to Goodall, 26 March 1949.
62. SOAS, CWM, AF33/35E, Orchard to Haile, 12 May 1952.

CHAPTER 3

Missionaries and the Origins
of the Central African Federation, 1949-53

Concerned about Africa, British missionaries strove to relate events there to broader developments in mission and church affairs. One means of doing so was through participation in conferences and other gatherings arranged by the IMC. One such conference took place in July 1947, at Whitby, near Toronto. There, missionaries of many nationalities agreed that they should no longer regard themselves as representatives of 'sending' institutions but rather as invitees of local, indigenous churches, deferring to their leadership. There were many obstacles to the realisation of such a vision, not least the lack, in Africa and elsewhere, of properly trained and adequately paid church leaders.[1] This reality was at least acknowledged. Stephen Neill, drawing on his experiences as a missionary and latterly as an Anglican bishop in India, emphasised also the 'revolutionary' nature of the church itself: 'Christ sent it out', he exclaimed to the conference, 'as an explosive, corrosive, destructive force'. Lengthy periods of stability, according to Neill, might not necessarily be helpful to the church; it might form too close a relationship with temporal power. Change was to be welcomed.[2] The primary message that nevertheless emerged from Whitby was of the necessity for 'partnership' — between Protestant missions and churches throughout the world irrespective of nationality, race or denomination. This message represented a call, in the face of communism, racial tensions and uncertain church-state relations, for greater

---

1. International Missionary Council (IMC), *The Witness of a Revolutionary Church* (New York and London, 1947), pp. 20-3.
2. Stephen C. Neill, 'A Revolutionary Church', in C. W. Ranson, ed., *Renewal and Advance: Christian Witness in a Revolutionary World* (London, 1948), pp. 62-84.

interdependence between mission and church on many levels: of administration; of resources; of commitment to evangelisation; and, above all, of obedience to God's will.[3] British ecumenists such as Norman Goodall and Max Warren (like Neill, a delegate at Whitby) helped spread this message of 'partnership' through missionary societies, churches and national ecumenical agencies.

As the independence of India, Pakistan, Ceylon (now Sri Lanka) and Burma demonstrated during 1947-48, the British Empire was undergoing a process of sometimes uneasy transition. So too were churches outside the West, as shown by the formation (after long delay) of the interdenominational Church of South India in 1947. What effect might imperial change have on the church in sub-Saharan colonial Africa? The situation in Britain's central African colonies in the late 1940s was certainly unsettled, but not revolutionary. During the mid-1940s Africans formed nationalist political parties in Nyasaland and Northern Rhodesia. They took encouragement from developments in south Asia, but it was by no means apparent that devolution of power to indigenous peoples would be repeated in Africa. In the late 1940s Afrikaners and white Rhodesians were better placed than African nationalists to derive advantage from British imperial policy. Pretoria exerted covert influence on the decision of the British government to banish Seretse Khama in March 1950. In discussions on a Central African Federation meanwhile, Rhodesian leaders played on British anxieties about the extension of Afrikaner influence (notably through immigration) into central Africa.

British Protestant missionaries were uncertain if government plans for a Central African Federation would help or hinder ambitions of 'partnership' between mission and church, of the kind affirmed at Whitby. The situation in China boded ill. There, missionaries were denounced as agents of western imperialism not by communist officials alone but also by ordinary Chinese people, both Christian and non-Christian. What occurred in China between 1949 and 1952 was, contemporaries acknowledged, nothing less than a 'debacle' for missions and indigenous church.[4] Notwithstanding Neill's call to heed the lessons of 'revolutionary' change, missionaries had little desire to undergo in other parts of the world an experience similar to that in China. Uncertain as was the situation in Africa, there was at least the prospect of stability — under British imperial aegis. Missionaries valued this prospect.

3. IMC, *Witness of a Revolutionary Church,* pp. 16-28.

4. A China Missionary, 'First Thoughts on the Debacle of Christian Missions in China', *International Review of Missions* 40, no. 160 (1951): 411-20; David Paton, *Christian Missions and the Judgment of God* (London, 1953).

Many missionaries were in consequence guardedly supportive of plans for a Central African Federation. They were attentive to government espousal of another form of 'partnership': that between the races in central Africa, to the ultimate benefit, as it seemed, of the African population. And government went to remarkable lengths to assuage missionary doubts about federation. These efforts were largely successful: British church and mission leaders were as uneasy as ministers and civil servants in Whitehall about Afrikaner expansionism. To many missionaries the Federation, with its promise of racial 'partnership', represented the antithesis of the South African racial state and its policies in support of apartheid. Conversely, some other missionaries believed strongly that federation was not merely contrary but inimical to African interests. They disagreed, just as strongly, with their colleagues. For missionaries, Central African Federation was the most contentious, most difficult of all African colonial issues in the 1950s.

Official Plans for Federation and Missionary Dilemmas

Since the 1920s British settlers in east and central Africa had striven without success to realise ambitions of 'closer union', through means such as the amalgamation of Southern Rhodesia with Northern Rhodesia. Official commissions of enquiry in 1928 and 1938 refrained from recommending amalgamation to the government in London. The conclusions of the 1938 commission proved especially frustrating for Rhodesians: its deliberations were influenced by objections from Africans and from missionaries of the Church of Scotland and of the UMCA. With the onset of war the question of amalgamation was effectively put aside. That did not stop Southern Rhodesia's Prime Minister Sir Godfrey Huggins from raising the issue in 1941. But the British government's only response was to set up, three years later, a Central African Council, with merely consultative powers. Settlers accepted it with poor grace.

The National Party's victory in the South African general election of 1948 had a decisive impact upon British imperial policy. Huggins, now in the fourteenth year of his premiership, had in the past played on British fears of Afrikaner expansionism. He now sensed an opportunity. Visiting London in 1948 with Northern Rhodesia settler leader Roy Welensky, Huggins raised again the possibility of amalgamation. Neither Labour government nor Conservative opposition proved amenable to his suggestions. Following their return to Africa the two men called an unofficial conference of settler representatives, held in Southern Rhodesia, at Victoria Falls, in February 1949. There it was decided that with the route to amalgamation closed off it would be best to campaign instead for a federated colonial state consisting of Southern Rhodesia (which was virtually self-governing) and Northern Rhodesia and Nyasaland (for whose affairs the Colonial Office, in London, was responsible). Such an arrangement would yield considerable economic and administrative advantage to Southern Rhodesia and to its capital, Salisbury, the hub of the proposed federation.

No Africans attended the conference, and the immediate reaction of those in Northern Rhodesia and Nyasaland to news of the proposals was hostile. Rightly fearing that the proposed arrangement would be dominated by Southern Rhodesia, the president of the Nyasaland African Congress, Sam Mwase, denounced the idea of federation. Both Northern Rhodesia and Nyasaland were emphatically 'black African' colonies in terms of population: Europeans made up little more than 1 per cent of their populations (the comparable figure for Southern Rhodesia was 5 per cent and rising).[5] Mwase's objections were echoed in London. Two expatriate Africans, Hastings Banda (from Nyasaland) and Harry Nkumbula (from Northern Rhodesia), issued a pamphlet arguing against federation. They argued instead for an amalgamation of Nyasaland and Northern Rhodesia into a unitary 'black African' colonial state.[6] Both men had links with churches and missions. As a child, Nkumbula had been educated by Methodist missionaries. He was currently studying at the London School of Economics. Banda had received his early education at the Free Church of Scotland mission at Livingstonia. He had subsequently travelled to South Africa and then to the United States, where he qualified as a medical doctor. He completed his medical studies in Edinburgh and became an elder of the Church of Scotland. In 1949 he had a flourishing medical practice in north London. He was also London representative of the Nyasaland African Congress. Banda was fiercely opposed to the idea of federation and would campaign vigorously against it, with the assistance of the Anti-Slavery Society and also the Africa Bureau, formed in 1952. Banda would also receive some support from Scottish churchmen and missionaries.

The settlers' proposals did not immediately commend themselves to the government in London. This had nothing to do with the intervention of Banda and Nkumbula. The government was preoccupied with other matters, domestic, imperial and international. Not until 1951 would plans for federation

5. Due to immigration, mainly from Britain and South Africa, the European population of Southern Rhodesia rose by 64 per cent during the period 1946-51, from 82,000 to 135,000.

6. Hastings K. Banda and Harry Nkumbula, *Federation in Central Africa* (London, 1949). The pamphlet was written by Banda.

receive official backing. British missionary headquarters were no less preoccupied in 1949, with financial, administrative and other problems, especially in China. They paid little attention to news of the Victoria Falls conference.

Racial discrimination was an important characteristic of life in all Britain's African colonies. In 1948, however, with the coming to power of the National Party with its programme of apartheid, the Union of South Africa became the very model of a modern racist state, albeit one for which missionaries held out hopes of redemption, primarily by theological and ecumenical means through the agency of the IMC and the World Council of Churches. In comparison with apartheid, the discriminatory practices of Southern Rhodesia seemed to missionaries relatively insignificant. The genial-sounding, Kent-born former surgeon Huggins was indisputably 'British', and infinitely more capable of inspiring their trust than South African Prime Minister D. F. Malan. British missionaries based in Southern Rhodesia viewed the prospect of federation with equanimity.[7]

Not until June 1951 did a Central African Federation become the subject of widespread debate in Britain. That month, the Labour government issued a White Paper based on the deliberations of a conference of civil servants from Britain and the three central African colonies, held in London in March. Although the government would not commit itself openly to federation, the White Paper provided a blueprint for an immensely complicated set of territorial and federal administrative structures. This envisaged the territories retaining individual responsibility for certain matters, such as taxation and law and order. A federal administration would handle certain other matters, such as defence and external trade policy. Ambiguity surrounded the contentious subject of 'native affairs'. These were to remain largely the responsibility of the individual territories. In addition an African Affairs Board was mooted, to ensure African representation at a federal level.[8]

The White Paper stimulated a great deal of interest among British individuals and organisations interested in Africa. The Conference of British Missionary Societies despatched copies to Christian Councils in central Africa accompanied by a request for information on attitudes to its proposals within local missions and churches. With the exception of some Scots in Nyasaland, Protestant missionaries in central Africa expressed cautious support for federation and took the view that African criticism of the proposals was immod-

---

7. School of Oriental and African Studies, London (hereafter SOAS), Council for World Mission Archive, London Missionary Society Papers (hereafter CWM), AF40/80A, Rev. A. J. Haile to Rev. R. K. Orchard, 19 March 1949.

8. *Central African Territories: Report of Conference on Closer Association, London, March 1951*, Cmd. 8233 (London, 1951).

erate and unjustified.[9] This attitude was influenced on the one hand by fear of Afrikaner cultural and religious infiltration of the Rhodesias and on the other hand by fear of potentially militant African nationalism, enthused from afar by Kwame Nkrumah's February 1951 electoral success in the Gold Coast. In November 1951 the CBMS, after much deliberation, issued one of its occasional public statements on imperial and colonial matters, this time on the subject of federation. The statement acknowledged both the reasonableness of the proposals, on economic and political grounds, and also the doubts of Africans. 'African confidence and consent', the CBMS suggested, 'should be won by patient explanation, by sympathetic understandings of their misgivings and by clear demonstrations of good faith'.[10]

The statement's wording was necessarily bland, and gave little indication as to whether or not a range of opinions existed within missionary societies on the subject of federation. The statement's architect was LMS Africa secretary Ronald Orchard, still at this time grappling with the Seretse Khama controversy. Alarmed by the proposals in the White Paper, he had persuaded colleagues of other denominations of the need to register their concerns publicly. Untypically of mission secretaries, Orchard distrusted Huggins who, he believed, was intent on creating a South Africa-style dominion in central Africa that would be virtually immune to interference from Britain where 'native affairs' were concerned.[11] Orchard had spent some time in Southern Rhodesia in 1948, during a secretarial tour of Africa. Expecting it to be a colony that espoused and practiced 'British' values, he was dismayed by the racial attitudes he encountered. Those attitudes, he admitted later, were 'worse than anywhere else in Africa'. In Southern Rhodesia more than any other place (including Cape Province in South Africa), he had felt '. . . most ashamed of being white'.[12] Orchard believed that federation should not be imposed against African wishes. But he found almost no support for this view within the committees of the CBMS, and its statement on federation duly failed to take it into account.

As missionaries pondered their response to plans for federation, the Labour administration under Clement Attlee fell to defeat in the October 1951 general election. The new Conservative government was more resolutely and

9. SOAS, Conference of British Missionary Societies Papers (hereafter CBMS), 291, 'Christian Council [of Northern Rhodesia] correspondence' file, Rev. G. Hewitt to L. B. Greaves, 18 Aug. 1951.

10. SOAS, CWM, AF34/37A, CBMS, statement, 'Central African Federation', Nov. 1951.

11. SOAS, CWM, AF40/80A, Orchard to Haile, 30 March 1949.

12. SOAS, CWM, BM/5, LMS consultative and finance committee minutes, 24 May; CBMS, 235, CBMS Africa committee minutes, 14 May 1948.

unequivocally committed to a Central African Federation. This worked to Huggins' advantage. In January 1952 Huggins visited London, for further official talks on federation. Away from the talks he promoted the plan at every opportunity. Orchard met with him, at an informal briefing event organised for mission representatives at the Commonwealth Relations Office, in Whitehall. The encounter confirmed for Orchard Rhodesian complacency about African objections to federation. Huggins blithely asserted that protest was being stoked by Banda and other critics of federation in Britain.[13] Certainly, British public interest in the issue increased greatly during 1952, partly as a result of the Conservative government's extension of Seretse Khama's banishment in March. New organisations were formed, with some of which, such as Racial Unity, missionaries openly identified.[14] Conversely, they were less keen to identify with the Africa Bureau, because of Michael Scott's involvement.[15] As Orchard's interest in Seretse waned, so he increased his involvement in matters to do with a Central African Federation. He participated in interdenominational discussions, in forums such as the British Council of Churches' Race Relations Group and in church deputations to government ministers. He met with people such as David Stirling, founder of the Capricorn Africa Society, which promoted the idea of 'multiracial' societies in British east and central Africa.[16] The ferment of ideas and the level of interest in federation convinced Orchard that churches and missionary societies would make a more effective contribution to debate than they had in relation to Seretse Khama.

There were a number of reasons for this optimism. Although Southern Rhodesia would undoubtedly play a major role within a Central African Federation, the imperial authorities in London would retain, through the Colonial Office, ultimate responsibility for government in Northern Rhodesia and Nyasaland. Not only would the Colonial Office probably be more interested in Africans' welfare than the CRO, it would probably also be more receptive to the entreaties on Africans' behalf by religious and humanitarian interests in Britain. Orchard's involvement in a deputation to Colonial Office Minister of State Alan Lennox-Boyd in April 1952 confirmed for him the likelihood of this scenario: Lennox-Boyd appeared welcoming and supportive.[17] Furthermore, unlike the situation in the Bangwato Reserve, where the LMS was the

13. SOAS, CWM, AF34/37B, Orchard, notes on interview with Sir G. Huggins, 30 Jan. 1952.

14. SOAS, CBMS, 262, 'Africa Relations Council' file, C. M. Turnbull to Greaves, 10 Jan. 1952. The Africa Relations Council (1950-52) was an antecedent of Racial Unity.

15. SOAS, CWM, AF34/37B, Orchard to Rev. G. M. Scott, 26 March 1952.

16. SOAS, CWM, AF34/37C, Orchard to A. D. Stirling, 13 June 1952.

17. SOAS, CWM, AF34/37B, Orchard to Haile, 16 April 1952.

sole representative of mission and church, the three central African territories were the location of missions and churches representing many British Protestant denominations, including Congregationalist, Methodist, Scottish Presbyterian and Anglican. Here, Orchard surmised, lay strength in numbers, which would enhance representations to government.

By mid-1952 Orchard was convinced both of the need for such representations and of the unanimity of mission opinion towards the proposals for a Central African Federation. He was now receiving correspondence directly from African church members in Northern Rhodesia that contradicted more sanguine mission reports. Africans were '99% if not 100% opposed' to the proposals.[18] Criticism of federation in Britain had meanwhile provoked its supporters in the UK to establish a London branch of the pro-federation United Central Africa Association (UCAA).[19] Then in early May 1952 further official talks in London took place. The powers of the proposed African Affairs Board, it transpired, were likely to be nugatory, at best.[20] It increasingly appeared that federation would be imposed against African wishes, and with insufficient protection for African interests. Worryingly, the Colonial Office did not seem overtly supportive of those interests. At this time Orchard underwent an extremely discomfiting experience: an interview with Moutlwatsi Mpotokwane, spokesman of the Bangwato delegation to London on behalf of Seretse Khama. He discerned that Mpotokwane's criticism of the LMS might be representative of more general African disenchantment with missions. In June, with explicit reference to the activities of the UCAA, Orchard issued a rallying call to church and mission colleagues. African concerns could not be left to secular agencies: it was time to instigate 'a widespread public campaign' throughout the UK, with the aim of convincing government to postpone federation. In the interim, governments both in London and in Southern Rhodesia should enact legislation in support of racial and economic 'partnership'. Missionaries and clergy in central Africa, meanwhile, should advise Africans not to condemn the proposals out of hand, but to put forward realistic alternatives.[21]

There was nothing radical about these arguments. Orchard was not opposed to federation as such; he was opposed to its imposition against African wishes. Frustrated as he was by the attitude of government in London, he was equally frustrated by African nationalists' inability or unwillingness, as it

18. SOAS, CWM, AF34/37B, E. M. Chalungumana to Orchard, 10 Feb. 1952.

19. Philip Murphy, *Party Politics and Decolonization: The Conservative Party and British Colonial Policy in Tropical Africa* (Oxford, 1995), pp. 75-7.

20. *Southern Rhodesia, Northern Rhodesia and Nyasaland: Draft Federal Scheme: Prepared by a Conference held in London in April and May, 1952*, Cmd. 8573 (London, 1952).

21. SOAS, CWM, AF34/37C, Orchard, confidential memo, 21 June 1952.

seemed, to propose an alternative to federation. Orchard had little understanding of the extent or depth of African opposition in Northern Rhodesia and Nyasaland to the proposals. Nor did he comprehend the extent to which that opposition had now begun to affect church and mission deliberations. Many missionaries *were* privately concerned about the proposals for federation. They had attempted to indicate this through the 1951 CBMS statement and also through a further public expression of concern, made by the BCC in April 1952. But they were a great deal more anxious about the possible impact upon the church in central Africa of two opposing nationalist movements: Afrikaner and black African. This anxiety manifested itself variously: Orchard's fellow-secretaries in other missionary societies rejected his proposal for a public campaign; and officials in the CRO successfully influenced religious opinion against public criticism of the federation proposals.

The CRO had been untroubled and unmoved by LMS representations about Seretse Khama. It took a great deal more interest in Orchard's idea of a public campaign on the subject of a Central African Federation. Its attitude was influenced by the recent growth, in both England and Scotland, of opposition to the government's proposals. At the CRO, assistant undersecretary of state Herbert Baxter kept a close watch on the activities of anyone (including missionaries) with an interest in federation. Chairman of the 1951 London conference on the proposals, Baxter was not at all a dispassionate, objective civil servant: he was obsessed with the necessity of a British imperial counterweight to Afrikaner influence on central Africa. Accordingly, he kept the UCAA informed of CRO policy. Equating almost with treason any criticism of the federal proposals, he regarded Orchard's suggestion of a public campaign as odious.[22] Baxter arranged to meet with mission representatives at Edinburgh House, London, where he trenchantly and convincingly argued the case for federation and informed his audience of their duty to help inculcate in mission staff and in African church congregations a 'responsible' attitude to the proposals.[23]

Baxter's actions owed more to official anxieties than to any power inherent in Orchard's proposal.[24] There had been in any case little need for him to sway missionary opinion; this had already moved against Orchard. The strongest expression of dissent came from Gerald Broomfield, general secretary of the UMCA. For Broomfield the federation question was complicated by another

22. The National Archives of the UK: Public Record Office (hereafter TNA: PRO), DO 35/6794A, G. H. Baxter, minutes, 9 July 1952.

23. TNA: PRO, DO 35/6794A, Baxter, 'Central African Federation: Aide-Memoire', 13 Aug. 1952.

24. TNA: PRO, DO 35/6794A, Baxter, minutes, 23 Feb. 1953.

issue, separate but related. Archbishop Fisher was planning a new Anglican ecclesiastical province — a grouping of dioceses — in the region, as part of his
strategy to devolve ecclesiastical authority from the see of Canterbury. A new
province had already been created in West Africa in 1951. Fisher relied for advice on the central Africa project from the UMCA and also from the bishops of
Northern Rhodesia and of Nyasaland. Frank Thorne, in Nyasaland, had grave
doubts about federation; African congregations in his diocese appeared firmly
against it. But Thorne's doubts were not shared by Broomfield, who had no intention of committing the UMCA to a particular line on federation: politics
were for him a matter of individual Christian conscience. However, he personally favoured a Central African Federation: it promised the political and economic stability upon which development of church and society in central Africa must surely depend. Here, Broomfield believed, the UMCA would have a
crucial role to play, working gradually yet insistently within stable political and
ecclesiastical structures towards greater societal and racial equality. By such
means 'confidence between the races', he would conclude later in 1952, 'can be
established within the Christian fellowship'.[25] African nationalism conversely
appeared to threaten all such prospects. Broomfield adamantly believed that
plans both for federation and for the new province should go ahead. To postpone federation, he argued in contradiction to Orchard, would amount to 'appeasement' of African nationalists.[26]

This negative view of African nationalism proved to be widespread
among missionaries. Hastings Banda continued to fulminate against the federal proposals. He also intervened to prevent Nyasa delegates from attending
the latest official talks on federation, held in London in June 1952. Methodist
missionaries in Northern Rhodesia meanwhile informed their head office of
allegations about Harry Nkumbula, 'a most plausible individual who may try
to cash in on his connection with Methodism'.[27] Nkumbula was also supposed to have demanded of missionaries that they openly take a stand against
federation.[28] Instead, missionaries in Northern Rhodesia had been attempting, at the request of their headquarters and of the CBMS, to convince Africans to suggest amendments to the proposed scheme. Africans rejected these

25. Bodleian Library of Commonwealth and African Studies at Rhodes House, Oxford,
Universities' Mission to Central Africa Papers, SF139, Canon G. W. Broomfield, memo,
'Central African Federation', Dec. 1952.

26. Lambeth Palace Library, London (hereafter LPL), Fisher Papers (hereafter FP), 95,
Broomfield, memo, 'The Church and Central African Federation', 15 July 1952.

27. SOAS, Methodist Missionary Societies Papers, T187, unsigned to Rev. T. A.
Beetham, 22 April 1952.

28. SOAS, CBMS, 285, Federation Group, minutes, 1 Sept. 1952.

overtures. Similar approaches by the Capricorn Africa Society and the Fabian Colonial Bureau fared no better. For many Africans, to suggest amendments to the proposals would in effect have granted the proposals a spurious legitimacy.[29] When the Northern Rhodesia African National Congress did attempt in August to put forward alternatives to federation, the government ignored its suggestions.[30] Unable for the most part to comprehend, much less sympathise with African feelings on federation, missionaries perceived African objections as strident, intransigent and unreasonable. They may have been influenced to some extent by sketchy reports of Mau Mau violence in Kenya during the summer of 1952. They certainly believed that nationalists in central Africa were intent on replicating developments in the Gold Coast, with the intention of creating an 'all black' central African state.[31]

Missionaries still feared the possibility of racial conflict between black African nationalism and its Afrikaner equivalent. There was a further reason for missionary suspicion of what an 'all black' state in central Africa might ultimately entail: unfortunate consequences for the small European populations of Northern Rhodesia and Nyasaland. As far as central Africa was concerned, the state, Broomfield would insist, 'must inevitably be multi-racial', with European interests duly protected.[32] Ultimately, he acknowledged, Africans and Europeans would undoubtedly share political power at some future time, as the 1951 White Paper intimated: the aim of official policy was to 'advance the African to a stage where he is in all respects a full partner exercising all the rights and accepting all the responsibilities of citizenship'. Fisher, for his part, lamented African opposition to federation (which he thought as unwise as it was understandable). He confided to Archbishop David Mathew, Roman Catholic apostolic delegate for British Africa, his belief that the scheme would constitute 'a bulwark against the very doctrine of Apartheid . . .'[33]

As they rejected the overtures of the Fabian Colonial Bureau and of the Capricorn Africa Society, so Africans also rejected efforts by missionaries to encourage in them a 'responsible' attitude to federation. To mission secretaries in London, this rejection demonstrated African irresponsibility and ingratitude. In August 1952 Aaron Mwenya, a government clerk and church

---

29. G. A. Ross, 'European Support for and Opposition to Closer Union of the Rhodesias and Nyasaland, with Special Reference to the Period 1945-53' (University of Edinburgh MLitt thesis, 1988), pp. 251-7.

30. David Goldsworthy, *Colonial Issues in British Politics: From 'Colonial Development' to 'Wind of Change'* (Oxford, 1971), pp. 224-5.

31. SOAS, CBMS, 285, Federation Group, minutes, 1 Sept. 1952.

32. LPL, FP, 82, Broomfield to Most Rev. G. F. Fisher, 12 Oct. 1952.

33. LPL, FP, 95, Fisher to Most Rev. D. J. Mathew, 1 Aug. 1952.

member in Mbereshi, Northern Rhodesia, made an impassioned appeal, via the LMS, for British church leaders to visit central Africa and show solidarity with African Christians in the region. Orchard commended the request to the CBMS and BCC. The reaction was initially equivocal and ultimately negative: a British religious deputation to Africa would be construed as a political act. It could not be allowed.[34] Orchard, chastened, summed up the situation for Rev. Harold Barnes at Mbereshi, who had forwarded Mwenya's request to London: 'To oppose Federation at present on the grounds that there is strong African opposition to it renders us likely to be charged with supporting Nkumbula and his line, which is obviously an impossible one. On the other hand merely to stand aside and to allow Federation to be imposed, if it is going to be imposed, seems likely to lead to a progressive deterioration in race relations. We are at present trying to find a middle course between these two'.[35]

As Orchard had already discovered in relation to the Seretse Khama controversy, a 'middle course' in relation to colonial Africa was difficult to identify and almost impossible to occupy. In British politics the bipartisanship that had supposedly characterised postwar party attitudes to colonial affairs broke down during 1952 as a result of crises in Malaya, Kenya, the Bechuanaland Protectorate and central Africa. New interest groups sprang up in Britain, some intent on representing African interests, others avowedly anti-imperialist. The nature of discourse on empire was changing as a result of developments in east and central Africa, as in relation to race it had already changed because of events in South Africa since 1948. The missionary response was in each case confused and equivocal. In February 1953 Orchard would finally issue on behalf of the LMS a public statement on federation, at once forthright and yet characterised also by anxiety about race. He pleaded that federation be postponed, for as long as five years. Unless African trust and confidence could be restored, he argued, 'the territories would be brought by racial strife to the brink of disaster'.[36]

This was but one of many statements of concern that religious bodies would make in 1953, as a Central African Federation came ever closer to realisation. The CBMS issued a pamphlet proffering guidance on the subject for Christians.[37] It did not advance any argument. Rather it revealed how the

34. SOAS, CWM, AF2A, Orchard to Rev. H. J. Barnes, 15 Aug.; CBMS, 570, BCC International Department, minutes, 22 Oct. 1952.

35. SOAS, CWM, AF34/37D, Orchard to Barnes, 11 Sept. 1952.

36. SOAS, CWM, AF 35/37E, LMS, statement on Central African Federation, 10 Feb. 1953.

37. L. B. Greaves, *Central Africa Federation* (London, 1953).

ideal of 'partnership' between mission and church advocated at Whitby more than five years before might now uneasily sit with a politicised governmental vision of racial 'partnership' in Africa. 'Federation is barren without partnership', the pamphlet asserted; 'partnership is primarily a thing of the spirit . . .' In George Street, Edinburgh, at Church of Scotland headquarters, secretary of the Foreign Missions Committee (FMC) James Dougall read the pamphlet with interest. Central African Federation was currently stimulating vigorous debate and even dispute within the Kirk, and the attitude of Scottish missionaries in Nyasaland was exciting no little interest back in their homeland. Dougall summed up the pamphlet in succinct fashion: 'rather feeble' was his verdict.[38]

The Scottish Mission and Church Response to Federation

In the early 1950s Scotland could seem a long way not only from Africa but from London also. Scottish missionaries co-operated with their English counterparts in ecumenical ventures such as the United Missions in the Copperbelt. And some Scots played an active role in the wider ecumenical movement, maintaining regular contact with like-minded colleagues. To others, however, trips even to the capital city of the United Kingdom (invariably on the sleeper train from Waverley Station in Edinburgh) hardly seemed worth the trouble or the expense: 'one can't spend all ones [*sic*] time in London or in the train', complained Rev. John Watt, FMC secretary for Africa.[39] For reasons of distance as much as of theology or denominationalism, the Scots developed ideas about mission, ecumenism and empire that often differed from those of London-based mission agencies.

All the same, the problems faced by the Scots in central Africa during the late 1940s and early 1950s were little different from those confronting their English counterparts. The need to maintain a mission presence had somehow to be reconciled with a commitment to devolving ecclesiastical authority to the indigenous church. Yet the FMC found itself preoccupied instead by the necessity of retrenchment on every front. A commission of inquiry visited Africa in 1947. Neither the work of the commission nor the subsequent decision to install a Regional Secretary to coordinate mission activity in central Africa

---

38. National Library of Scotland, Accession 7548, General Assembly of the Church of Scotland Foreign Missions Committee Papers (hereafter NLS), A55, Rev. J. W. C. Dougall to Rev. J. A. R. Watt, 23 Jan. 1953.

39. NLS, B272, Watt to Rev. R. G. Macpherson, 3 Jan. 1955.

found much favour among hard-pressed mission staff. The Northern Rhode-sia missions were especially resentful of 'vicious' cuts in expenditure that might entail the ceding of evangelistic advantage to the Watchtower move-ment and of educational advantage to Roman Catholic missions.

Being preoccupied by such matters, Scottish missionaries in central Africa paid little attention at first to the 1949 machinations of Sir Godfrey Huggins and Roy Welensky at the Victoria Falls conference in February of that year. Settler plans were a matter of only passing concern. This was understandable, to a degree. There was no immediate certainty, or even likelihood, that a Cen-tral African Federation would receive approval from the authorities in Lon-don. Every previous settler attempt at 'closer union' had after all come to naught. And Scottish missionaries, especially in Nyasaland, typically kept careful track of official developments relating to African affairs, and relayed their concerns to the FMC in Edinburgh. The Church of Scotland's General Assembly met annually, in late May. Its agenda represented a fair, if by no means always precise barometer of feeling within the Kirk on a range of is-sues, domestic and overseas, religious and secular. The subject of a Central African Federation did not appear on the agenda of the General Assembly, in either 1950 or 1951. In June 1951, however, the London government published its White Paper on federation.

As in England, new organisations formed in response. One of these was the Edinburgh-based World Church Group, which forged contacts between Scots and visiting African students. It also formed working links with the Fabian Co-lonial Bureau and, later, with the Africa Bureau. The likes of John Hatch and Kenneth Little (at Glasgow and Edinburgh Universities respectively) occupied positions at the interstices of these various bodies as did certain visiting mis-sionaries from central Africa, the most active of whom was Rev. Kenneth Mac-kenzie (1920-71) of the Northern Rhodesia branch of the Livingstonia mission. Another Scottish organisation, formed some years earlier for the purpose of Christian engagement with social issues in Scotland, also took a close interest in federation. This was the Iona Community, founded in 1938 by Rev. Dr. George MacLeod. Based on the island of Iona, the Community's main original aim was to imbue in ordinands wishing to work in urban Scotland a strong sense of civic and political responsibility.[40] The World Church Group and the Iona Community fulfilled an important public role. By holding meetings for the likes of Hastings Banda, Michael Scott and others they helped increase Scottish public awareness of colonial issues. They also provided forums for

40. Ronald Ferguson, *Chasing the Wild Goose: The Story of the Iona Community* (Glas-gow, 1998).

continual, year-round debate on African affairs outside the committees of the General Assembly. By the end of 1951 Central African Federation was attracting a good deal of interest in Scotland and would be debated in full for the first time at the 1952 General Assembly.

It was with the upcoming proceedings of the Assembly in mind that the mission council at Blantyre, in Nyasaland, debated federation in February 1952. As the work of Andrew Ross and John McCracken has amply shown,· Scottish mission attitudes both to empire and to African rights might be radical yet also ambiguous.[41] Certainly, the attitude of the Scots to federation was no less ambivalent or confused than that of English Protestant missionaries. The debate in Blantyre was a fractious affair. The mission secretary, Rev. Andrew Doig (1914-97), was determined that the council should assert what he regarded as the mission's historic commitment to African interests. His view prevailed, and the mission council recorded its opinion that any attempt 'to force Federation against solid African opposition would increase racial tension and would delay the hopes for real partnership between the races'. The mission council went further than this, however. It also challenged the General Assembly of the Church of Scotland to come to a similar conclusion, by passing a 'deliverance' or resolution, at its 1952 meeting. Failure to come out in support of African objections to federation would constitute, according to Blantyre, 'a betrayal of trust by the Church of Scotland'.[42] This was a contentious and provocative statement that reflected deep unease within the mission about government plans and Scottish attitudes to federation alike.

The Blantyre resolution set the tone for debate within the Church of Scotland on federation during 1952. It met with a decidedly mixed response at the Kirk's administrative headquarters in Edinburgh. Dougall was sympathetic to the Blantyre point of view but wished it had been more carefully worded. He feared that its tone would antagonise elements within the Kirk at home. So it proved, as the Blantyre resolution underwent the tortuous process of selection and approval for debate by the General Assembly. As far as the Kirk was concerned, Central African Federation was a 'political' matter. It would be submitted for debate by the General Assembly not by the FMC, which was responsible for overseas evangelism, but by another committee, that on Church and Nation. Formed in 1919 to advise the General Assembly on spiritual and moral aspects of social and political affairs, the Church and Nation Commit-

41. A. C. Ross, *Blantyre Mission and the Making of Modern Malawi* (Blantyre, 1996); John McCracken, *Politics and Christianity in Malawi, 1875-1940: The Impact of the Livingstonia Mission in the Northern Province* (Cambridge, 1977).
42. NLS, B330, Blantyre mission council, minutes, 12 Feb. 1952.

tee (CNC) had lately considered such matters as temperance, gambling, birth control, atomic warfare and Scottish devolution. Its remit was eclectic, to say the least. Its outlook was conservative. It was devoid of FMC representation, and lacked a 'radical' overseas missionary presence. The members of the CNC were alarmed by Blantyre's intemperately worded challenge to the General Assembly. Being mistrustful of mission opinion, they turned for advice and guidance to none other than the Colonial Office, in London. Rev. Matthew Urie Baird expressed on behalf of the committee unease about the Blantyre resolution and about the extent to which anti-federation sentiment appeared to be spreading in Scotland. The committee was anxious to do the right thing, Baird explained, and while mindful of African concerns had no wish to give succour to nationalists.[43]

This unsolicited approach attracted a great deal of interest and appreciation in the Colonial Office.[44] It appeared to provide welcome evidence of Scottish support for federation. In reply the Colonial Office encouraged the CNC to view federation in a positive light, and to advise the General Assembly accordingly. The committee devised a moderately worded resolution of its own, to counter that from Blantyre. News of this contact between the Colonial Office and the CNC then precipitated intense lobbying within the Kirk during the run-up to the General Assembly meeting in May. Doig wrote numerous letters to Edinburgh, urging Watt and Dougall to muster support for the Blantyre viewpoint.[45] The two men duly lobbied the CNC, but in vain.[46] The committee and in particular its convenor, Rev. Professor J. H. S. Burleigh, had no wish for the Blantyre view to be regarded as representative of Scottish church opinion. In the General Assembly debate on a Central African Federation the 'moderate' view of the CNC prevailed over that of the Blantyre mission council. The General Assembly adopted the CNC deliverance, which requested of government merely that 'full consideration be given to African opinion and that no scheme should be adopted without the consent and cooperation of the Africans'.[47] The General Assembly did not express support for African opposition to the scheme. The outcome fulfilled Colonial Office expectations. Charles Carstairs, information officer at the Colonial Office, attended the General Assembly in a private capacity. Meeting with him after the

43. TNA: PRO, CO 1015/777, Rev. M. Urie Baird to Colonial Office, 20 April; W. E. Pottinger to A. M. MacKintosh, 9 May 1952.

44. TNA: PRO, CO 1015/777, J. W. Stacpoole, minutes, 9 May 1952.

45. NLS, B334, Rev. A. B. Doig to Watt, 15 March 1952.

46. NLS, A55, Dougall to Urie Baird, 22 April 1952.

47. NLS, Deposition 298, FMC, minute book, 180, General Assembly deliverance, 28 May 1952.

debate, Burleigh assured Carstairs that a small measure of equivocation had been required in the deliverance in order to head off 'more violent amendments and speeches from the floor'.[48]

Both the Colonial Office and the CRO now began to pay greater attention to Scottish church and mission opinion. Conservative Secretary of State for Commonwealth Relations Lord Salisbury paid an informal visit to the Moderator of the General Assembly in July. He was rewarded with assurances that, the occasional recalcitrant missionary aside, the Kirk was firmly in favour of the proposals for federation.[49] In August, Colonial Office Minister of State Henry Hopkinson undertook an official tour of the three central African territories. His report, read with interest in the CRO as well as in the Colonial Office, provided further reassurance. According to Hopkinson, there was little evidence of concerted anti-federation sentiment in the missions: 'even members of the Church of Scotland mission whom I met at Livingstonia and Blantyre are not unanimous in its [*sic*] opposition', he reported.[50]

While not wholly inaccurate, Hopkinson's report owed more to wishful thinking than to precise assessment of the situation in central Africa. Some Scottish missionaries were indeed reconciled to federation. A few supported it. Others were strongly opposed, and those in Blantyre had already made their feelings known, through the mission council resolution. On his return to Britain, Hopkinson publicised in the press and on television his view that African objection to federation was a consequence of Congress intimidation. These comments stirred Doig into further action. He wrote a strongly worded letter to Oliver Lyttelton, Secretary of State for Colonies. Rather than being the product of intimidation, Doig asserted, African opposition to federation had all the makings of a legitimate 'mass movement'. The government of Nyasaland, he suggested, was more likely than Congress to engage in the kind of intimidatory practices referred to by Hopkinson.[51] The colony's governor, Sir Geoffrey Colby, did not in fact consider that Nyasaland would derive any appreciable benefit from federation, and he was sceptical of the proposals. But he was astonished by Doig's imputation. For Lyttelton, Doig's allegations represented the worst aspects of Scottish missionary activism.[52] Dougall had

48. TNA: PRO, CO 1015/777, C. Y. Carstairs to J. E. Marnham, 28 May 1952.

49. TNA: PRO, DO 35/6794B, Lord Salisbury to O. Lyttelton, 1 Aug. 1952.

50. TNA: PRO, DO 35/6759, H. L. d'A. Hopkinson, report on tour of central Africa, 23 Sept. 1952.

51. TNA: PRO, CO 1015/779, Doig to Lyttelton, 29 Sept. 1952.

52. TNA: PRO, CO 1015/779, C. W. F. Footman to Doig, 27 Oct.; Lyttelton to Sir G. Colby, 3 Dec. 1952.

meanwhile also been active. He and Watt inveigled their way onto a sub-committee of the CNC. In correspondence with the Colonial Office, Dougall tried to convince it of the reasonableness and validity of mission opinion.[53] Doig's broadside scuppered his efforts. From Lyttelton downwards, the Colonial Office adopted an ever more contemptuous attitude towards Scottish mission opinion, secure in their knowledge that in the Church and Nation Committee and in the Kirk more widely there were abundant, influential supporters of government policy.

Yet Scottish church opinion on federation was not quite as rigid as supposed in the Colonial Office. Dougall's insistent, patient cultivation of the CNC paid some dividend. Late in 1952 the CNC began to adopt a slightly more conciliatory attitude to the missions, as nervousness grew about the negative impact of federation on Africans. Urie Baird wrote in apologetically worded terms to Lyttelton and to Salisbury that the committee now wished to act as an agent of reconciliation.[54] On 30 December, the CNC issued a new statement on federation. This, remarkably, called for review by Southern Rhodesia of its restrictive laws on Africans. It called also for a strengthening of the powers of the proposed African Affairs Board.[55]

The final official conference on federation opened in London on 1 January 1953. Policymakers in Whitehall had continually ignored or dismissed African opinion. But they now conversely began to pay greater attention to opinion in churches and missions. This was mainly due to developments in Scotland. Some sections of the Kirk now seemed doubtful about federation. Not only that, Scottish Conservative and Unionist MPs were expressing concern to Whitehall at the electoral consequences of adverse reaction among the British public to the imposition of federation against African wishes.[56] The problem, in part at least, was Huggins. His public statements were often a gift to critics of federation. In October 1952, addressing a rally of his supporters in Southern Rhodesia, he ebulliently dismissed as inconsequential African worries about federation. Tailored to its audience, the speech went down well, but in British press reports it came across as insensitive, triumphalist and ill befitting the putative leader of a federated imperial entity of some 5 million African inhabitants. Geoffrey Fisher wrote from Lambeth Palace a letter to *The Times,* chiding Huggins. This momentarily caused panic in the Colonial Of-

53. TNA: PRO, CO 1015/777, Dougall to Carstairs, 26 Nov. 1952.

54. TNA: PRO, CO 1015/777, Urie Baird to Lyttelton; DO 35/6794B, Urie Baird to Salisbury, both 13 Dec. 1952.

55. NLS, B349, Church and Nation Committee, statement on Central African Federation, 30 Dec. 1952.

56. TNA: PRO, CO 1015/777, J. S. Maclay to Hopkinson, 31 Dec. 1952.

fice, where intervention by the archbishop was perceived as being 'immeasurably more serious than that of any number of Fabians or Michael Scotts'.[57] The CRO apprised Huggins of the need to modulate his public utterances in the future. Fisher's hopes for a new ecclesiastical province had made him more sensitive to African opinion. For all that, he had also concluded that federation offered Africans a good deal in both economic and political terms. He was also determined to press ahead with plans for the new ecclesiastical province. Only Frank Thorne's protestations from Nyasaland — that Africans would perceive the province, like federation, as an unwanted imposition from afar — convinced him otherwise.[58] In March 1953 Fisher suspended his plans for ecclesiastical reform. By this time, with the final official conference having brought federation closer still to realisation, both the Colonial Office and the CRO had embarked on a concerted strategy to win British church and mission opinion round to federation.

Having concluded that federation offered, as he put it, 'the one hope for Africans', Fisher was keen to ensure support for the scheme in British Protestant churches.[59] Here he enlisted the help of Kenneth Grubb, an equally strong believer in federation who had been in regular, recent contact with the Colonial Office and the CRO.[60] An Anglican layman, former missionary and president of the Church Missionary Society, Grubb (1900-1980) was an influential and extremely well-connected figure in British and wider ecumenical circles. He was chairman of the Commission of the Churches on International Affairs, an ecumenical body that had been set up in 1946. Grubb arranged a meeting between minister of state Hopkinson and church and missionary society representatives. He advised Hopkinson beforehand: 'Church leaders are acutely divided on this matter . . . there is a great opportunity for you to commend the scheme and to influence waverers, and the people who listen to you will be, in turn, those who have a great deal of influence in their own churches'.[61] At the meeting, in the Colonial Office on 9 February, Hopkinson emphasised the reasonableness and rightness of the government's case. Grubb meanwhile obtained senior Anglican, Free Church and Scottish Presbyterian support for a letter to *The Times*, acknowledging the inevitability of federation. Federation did indeed appear inevitable by this time. In late March 1953 the proposals cleared a significant legislative hurdle in Parlia-

57. TNA: PRO, DO 35/6743, W. L. Gorell Barnes, minutes, 20 Oct. 1952.

58. LPL, FP, 120, Rt Rev. F. O. Green-Wilkinson to Fisher, 11 March 1953.

59. LPL, FP, 120, Fisher to Rev. E. P. Eastman, 19 Jan. 1953.

60. TNA: PRO, DO 35/6794A, Baxter to K. G. Grubb, 17 Dec.; TNA: PRO CO 1015/775, Grubb to A. H. Joyce, 23 Dec. 1952.

61. TNA: PRO, CO 1015/775, Grubb to Hopkinson, 3 Feb. 1953.

ment. Grubb, meanwhile, stage-managed debate on federation in the British Council of Churches.[62] This resulted in a public statement on how racial 'partnership' in central Africa might be attained.[63]

In the meantime, Michael Scott, as well as championing the cause of the Herero at the UN, was campaigning actively on other issues relating to Africa. In January 1953 Scott tried to secure official permission for a delegation of Nyasa chiefs to personally petition the Queen on the subject of federation. Permission was refused. He then attempted to drum up support among church leaders in Britain for the Nyasa cause, again without success.[64] In an all-out attempt to stimulate a critical British Christian response to federation, Scott proposed a national 'Day of Prayer'. Baxter, at the CRO, was apoplectic at the prospect of 'mischievous exploitation of Christian feeling'. Salisbury's successor at the CRO, Lord Swinton, urged Fisher to persuade Scott to desist.[65] Fisher wrote to Scott: '[I]t is not for the Africa Bureau or anybody else to declare that God's will must be on one side or the other in this particular difficult question'.[66] Abandoning the idea, Scott on his own initiative flew to Nyasaland to protest in person against federation, in the process endearing himself to Africans in the colony. He was declared 'PI' (prohibited immigrant) and deported. Scott had 'the desire for martyrdom strong upon him', Fisher explained to Lyttelton.[67]

Scott's maverick exploits exacerbated official uncertainty about Scottish church opinion and caused jitters in the Colonial Office and the CRO. For some time now, the government had been susceptible to criticism on a number of colonial fronts, not least for its anti-insurgent tactics in Malaya and Kenya. Lyttelton admitted to Swinton in late February 1953 being 'increasingly worried about the drift of opinion in this country against Central African Federation . . . the balance of comment is heavily against it . . . our opponents are exceedingly active'. It was time, he suggested, 'to stop the rot . . . this would best be done in Scotland'.[68] Hopkinson and Carstairs were despatched northward to evangelise about federation in Scottish church and political circles. The by now extremely active UCAA also sent a representative to combat Scottish anti-federation propaganda. And at Roy Welensky's suggestion Sir

62. TNA: PRO, CO 1015/775, Grubb to Joyce, 24 April 1953.

63. SOAS, CBMS, 573, 'Race Relations Group correspondence' file, BCC statement, 'Central African Federation', 22 April 1953.

64. LPL, FP, 120, Scott to Fisher, 25 Feb. 1953.

65. TNA: PRO, CO 1015/775, Fisher to Lord Swinton, 12 March 1953.

66. LPL, FP, 120, Fisher to Scott, 12 March 1953.

67. TNA: PRO, CO 1015/243, Fisher to Lyttelton, 11 June 1953.

68. TNA: PRO, DO 35/6726, Lyttelton to Swinton, 23 Feb. 1953.

Gilbert Rennie, the Scottish-born governor of Northern Rhodesia (and Kirk elder), lobbied his compatriots and co-religionists.[69]

Scottish opposition to federation was certainly vocal. New protest groups, such as the Scottish Council for African Questions, were still being formed. But dissent was uncoordinated. This made the task of the government representatives easier. As Hopkinson and Carstairs reported, critics of federation were overemphasising its negative attributes. The critics were not winning support beyond their urban church and university heartland.[70] Having visited St Andrews University, Carstairs sneeringly noted signs of 'hysterical, vocal opposition' from Isobel Forrester, wife of theology professor W. R. Forrester. Carstairs considered her 'a fan of Mr Michael Scott' and 'an able and no doubt unconsciously unscrupulous propagandist'. His opinion of the Women's Foreign Missions Committee was no less patronising: it was, he noted, 'even more rabid than the male branch, and less susceptible to facts'.[71] Nevertheless, Hopkinson, Carstairs and Rennie assuaged the lingering concerns of the Church and Nation Committee. Its members reviewed their recent deliberations and drew up a moderately worded addendum to their December 1952 statement for presentation to the 1953 General Assembly. Dougall, conversely, proved unable to generate support within the Kirk for the 'foreign mission' lobby, despite Doig's continuing, written urgings: none of the other central Africa missions would come out in support of the outspoken line taken by Blantyre.

By the time the General Assembly of the Church of Scotland debated Central African Federation on 25 May 1953, the official proposals had all but received the assent of Parliament in London. The overwhelmingly white electorate in Southern Rhodesia had voted in favour, and the proposals were approved by the territorial governments of Nyasaland and of Northern Rhodesia. The CNC warned that the Kirk now 'must not say anything which would foment strife or encourage unlawful action'. It acknowledged that African consent had not been obtained, but that federation should be given 'a fair trial' in order to prove its worth. The General Assembly approved the deliverance by a large majority. It did so following a rancorous and confused debate. The most vocal opposition came from George MacLeod, who condemned federation as 'an offence against moral principles and African rights'.[72]

69. TNA: PRO, CO 1027/36, B. Hutton-Williams, report of visit to Scotland; Rev. Prof. J. H. S. Burleigh to Hutton-Williams, both 19 Feb. 1953.

70. TNA: PRO, CO 1027/36, Hopkinson to Lyttelton, 4 March; Carstairs, report on visit to Scotland, 9 March 1953.

71. TNA: PRO, CO 1027/36, Carstairs, report on visit to Scotland, 9 March; CO 1015/37, Carstairs, minutes, 7 March 1953.

72. NLS, B349, Church and Nation Committee, report to General Assembly, May 1953.

As MacLeod's contribution to the debate demonstrated, some Scottish clergymen vociferously opposed federation in 1953. But they were a minority within the Kirk. Broadly representative of majority African opinion in Nyasaland as they were, the views of the Blantyre mission were unacceptable to the great majority of General Assembly delegates. MacLeod was disgusted by the outcome, which he believed would cause a damaging loss of African confidence in the church. A despondent Watt informed the Blantyre mission: 'I'm afraid that the Church of Scotland has rather let you down'.[73]

'Dangerous but Not Hopeless': The Missionary Outlook on Central Africa, 1953

During 1953 the LMS, the Methodist Church and the Society of Friends made known to government and public in Britain their fears about the imposition of federation against African wishes. These expressions of concern had no effect upon government policy, and the attitude of the Blantyre mission proved but momentarily troubling to the Colonial Office. In the late 1940s and early 1950s Scotland was experiencing one of its periodic upsurges of interest in self-rule, or devolution. For Scottish nationalists, colonial policy was as good a stick as any with which to beat the government in London. Certainly, its support of Huggins and Welensky and its dismissal of African objections made the government susceptible to criticism, especially in Scotland. But ministers and senior civil servants worked successfully to negate such criticism, from wherever it emanated. Ultimately, the Conservative administration decisively won the argument. The scheme passed its final legislative hurdle in Parliament in July 1953.

No less striking than the extent of government success was the utter failure of the Congress parties in Northern Rhodesia and Nyasaland to effectively mobilise anti-federation sentiment. This may have been in part due to miscalculation by Banda, in London. He believed that the imperial authorities would prove amenable to persuasion by Congress, by sympathetic tribal chiefs and by Congress supporters in Britain such as the Fabian Colonial Bureau. This strategy never found much support among Nyasaland Africans, many of whom wished to reject federation outright. Banda learned a hard lesson in 1953: British democracy was not for export to Africans.[74] Neither were

73. NLS, A76, Watt to Rev. N. C. Bernard, 29 May 1953.
74. John McCracken, 'Democracy and Nationalism in Historical Perspective: The Case of Malawi', *African Affairs* 97, no. 387 (1998): 233-7.

human rights, as understood in the aftermath of the Universal Declaration of 1948. In March 1951 Britain ratified the European Convention on Human Rights, thereby extending, but only in nominal terms, protection of such rights to the Colonial Empire.[75]

However aggrieved they felt about the overriding of objections to federation, many British missionaries had been very worried about the prospect of unrest in central Africa. In the early 1950s, with the independence of India, the continuing growth of communism, recent war in Korea, ongoing states of emergency in Malaya and Kenya and unrest in Egypt, the British Empire appeared to many of its citizens in Britain a beleaguered institution. A Central African Federation brought the prospect not merely of imperial consolidation but also of stability and even of prosperity in the region, for Africans and Europeans alike. 1953 was also a coronation year in the United Kingdom, although celebrations were muted in Nyasaland and the Bangwato Reserve. On 2 September, the Central African Federation was inaugurated in Salisbury, with a display of imperial splendour and pageantry.

Some missionaries took satisfaction from this outcome. Percy Ibbotson was an ordained Methodist missionary in Southern Rhodesia. Long active in 'native' affairs, in 1953 he became vice-chairman of the African Affairs Board and a representative of African interests in the new Federal Assembly (or parliament). He was also a member of the Capricorn Africa Society. Much more surprising, in light of his outspoken criticism of the federal proposals, was Andrew Doig's decision to stand as federal representative of Nyasaland Africans. Having previously represented African interests on the Nyasaland Legislative Council, Doig believed that he could best effect change by working within rather than outside new official institutions. His departure from the Blantyre mission on secondment to the Federal Assembly in early 1954 rankled with colleagues, some of whom questioned his motives and his ideals.[76] Other British missionaries accepted the reality of federation either with foreboding or grudgingly. Among the Scots there was bitterness, almost to the point of self-loathing. Wrote Kenneth Mackenzie: 'The name "partnership" stinks in the nostrils of the Africans'.[77] The cause of yet greater Scottish missionary chagrin, however, was the apparently craven attitude of the Church and Nation Committee and of the General Assembly. Nowhere was this sense of bitterness greater than in the Iona Community.

75. A. W. B. Simpson, *Human Rights and the End of Empire: Britain and the Genesis of the European Convention* (New York, 2001), pp. 838-46.

76. NLS, B351, Bernard to Dougall, 13 July 1953.

77. NLS, B349, Rev. K. Mackenzie, notes, 14 May 1953.

In 1951 the Iona Community formally became part of the Church of Scotland. Yet its ethos resisted easy assimilation into the Kirk at large. Still at this time an all-male organisation (although now with laymen as well as ordinands), Community members were uniformly clad in blue suits and shirts, an idealised version of Scottish island working wear. Service to the Community was rendered through manual labour and spiritual reflection, both undertaken during periods spent on the island of Iona. This disciplined environment helped inculcate in the members a strong sense of purpose. It also caused unease within the wider Scottish church: rumours circulated about homosexuality, monasticism and (given MacLeod's increasingly open espousal of left-wing politics) communism.[78] Several members of the Community would go to Nyasaland in the mid- to late-1950s to serve as missionaries, both lay and ordained. Service with the Community, Scottish nationalism, left-wing politics and controversy about the Central African Federation would combine to politicise these men. Unlike Doig (much less Ibbotson), they had no wish to act as representatives of African interests, whether political or ecclesiastical, in 'foreign', European-dominated institutions. They believed strongly that both church and state in central Africa should be led by Africans, with Europeans in a subsidiary, supporting role. Their views would in time bring them into conflict with colleagues and colonial authorities alike.

That the Central African Federation was a misconceived and fatally flawed imperial project was not universally apparent at the time of its inauguration. Missionaries believed that its success would nevertheless be reliant upon a number of factors, economic and political. One important factor would be the willingness of the authorities to encourage African trust — and participation — in federal politics. Missionaries hoped that under Huggins, the federation's first Prime Minister, its government would prove 'racially liberal, generous and imaginative'. Only then could 'moderate' African opinion develop fruitfully. There was another important factor: the willingness of the government in London to encourage the adoption of 'racially liberal policies' by Huggins and his ministers. Representatives of British churches and missionary societies would hold what they described as 'a watching brief' in this regard. In late 1953 Ronald Orchard made a secretarial tour of central and southern Africa, to assess the work of LMS missions and churches. He visited Tiger Kloof in Cape Province, the Bangwato Reserve, Southern Rhodesia and Northern Rhodesia. On his return to London he reported to colleagues. His

---

78. Ronald Ferguson, *George MacLeod: Founder of the Iona Community* (London, 1990), pp. 234-9.

tone was sombre. There were indeed signs of progress in central Africa, but so too was there evidence of continuing discrimination against Africans, in employment and in politics: 'The general situation in the Rhodesias', Orchard concluded, 'is dangerous, but not hopeless'.[79]

79. SOAS, CBMS, 570, Race Relations Group, minutes, 15 Dec. 1953.

CHAPTER 4

Missionary Problems in Northern Rhodesia and Nyasaland, 1954-60

'A great though risky experiment': that was how Archbishop of Canterbury Geoffrey Fisher described the Central African Federation. Most British missionaries believed that, as the General Assembly of the Church of Scotland had suggested, the scheme should be given 'a fair trial'. IMC secretary Norman Goodall similarly saw the Central African Federation as an 'experiment'. He also saw it as an opportunity for churches and missions. Goodall's thinking was influenced by developments in South Africa, upon which he kept a close watch in the continuing hope of exerting influence through the ecumenical movement and the churches. The Bantu Education Act, which came into effect in January 1954, would impact heavily upon schools run by 'foreign' missions. In April 1955, reporting to the British Council of Churches, Goodall argued in relation to apartheid that 'our attack on a policy from which we dissent in the Union is weakened and even nullified by our failure to demonstrate a more excellent way elsewhere . . . strengthening of the churches in South Africa . . . consists in our more radical obedience to a Christian policy in areas and situations nearer home'.[1] The areas that Goodall had in mind were Britain's colonial territories in central Africa; there missions would work towards 'partnership' with the indigenous church, while the state would implement policies in support of 'partnership' between the races. With other missionaries, Goodall believed in those 'safeguards' for African interests that the planners of federation had built into its constitution

---

1. School of Oriental and African Studies, London (hereafter SOAS), Conference of British Missionary Societies Papers (hereafter CBMS), 565, Rev. N. Goodall, address, 'The Council and South Africa', BCC, Council minutes, 19-20 April 1955.

and institutional structures. He believed also in obedience to the rule of law, as well as to a 'Christian policy' in central Africa. Federation was after all a legal as well as a political entity. Few missionaries disputed its right to exist. In July 1953 Bishop Frank Thorne wrote to Michael Scott, after the failure of Scott's attempt to rouse African opposition in Nyasaland: 'As I think you know, I am opposed to that scheme in its present form and to the way it has been carried through in the teeth of African opposition, but I cannot hold that it is contrary to the law of God . . . and that is the only justification for civil disobedience . . . once it is enforced it is for us to accept it . . .'[2]

It took some time for missionaries to become aware of the contradictory nature of this attitude to federation. In African eyes missionary unwillingness to criticise federation might amount to tacit support for the scheme. Conversely, missionary enthusiasm against federation and in favour of African nationalism might result in official disapproval and even sanction against missions and churches. In ways that missionaries could not envisage in 1953, all these possibilities would become manifest to a greater or lesser degree in both Northern Rhodesia and Nyasaland by the end of the decade.

The stability that the Central African Federation appeared to promise was realised only for a short time. Africans chafed at Rhodesian refusal to countenance other than limited, grudging political concessions. The repressive response of governments both federal and territorial to African protest would in time compromise fatally the legitimacy of the Federation and of colonial authority in central Africa. African dissatisfaction also found other forms such as industrial unrest. Dissatisfaction with missions in the form of African Christian independency might accompany dissatisfaction with empire, as most notably became apparent in Northern Rhodesia in the form of the Lumpa Church of Alice Lenshina.

Northern Rhodesia:
Missions, African Independency and Nationalist Politics

In December 1951 Rev. Fergus Macpherson took up a new posting at the Church of Scotland's mission at Lubwa, in the Chinsali district of Northern Rhodesia's northeast region.[3] He was no stranger to the colony, having first

---

2. Bodleian Library of Commonwealth and African Studies at Rhodes House, Oxford (hereafter RHL), Scott papers, 79, Rt Rev. F. D. Thorne to Rev. G. M. Scott, 1 July 1953.

3. This paragraph draws mainly on Fergus Macpherson, *North of the Zambezi: A Modern Missionary Memoir* (Edinburgh, 1998), pp. 17-28.

arrived there, 25 years old and freshly ordained, in November 1946 to work as part of the United Missions in the Copperbelt (UMCB) at Mufulira. Macpherson's father, Hector, was a minister of the Kirk in Edinburgh, and Hastings Banda became an ordained elder in his congregation while living in the city. Banda and Macpherson became friends. It was not from Banda, however, that Macpherson first learned about Africa. Inevitably, stories about David Livingstone and other missionaries had been a feature of his boyhood. Also, one of Hector's closest friends, Matthew Faulds, had worked as a missionary in Tanganyika and Nyasaland, and he encouraged Macpherson to consider missionary service in Africa. It was Banda, though, who acquainted the adult Macpherson with news of current affairs in central Africa, and also with the basics of Chinyanja, the vernacular of Nyasaland. During his two-and-a-half-year stint at Mufulira, Macpherson (1921-2002) learned a good deal about the ambiguities and inequities of life in a British African colony: like other Europeans, he was required to live in a racially designated area. In April 1947, however, he temporarily fetched up in Lubwa, the UMCB having despatched him there in order to improve his language skills. While there he made the acquaintance of 23-year-old Kenneth Kaunda, who had strong personal links with the Lubwa mission. Kaunda's father, David, had been instrumental in its setting up as an offshoot of the Livingstonia mission in Nyasaland, and the young Kenneth had been educated and would later work there. Kaunda would also subsequently work for a time as a teacher for the UMCB in Mufulira. By the time of Macpherson's eventual arrival as 'missionary in charge' in Lubwa at the end of 1951, Kaunda had effectively given up teaching and was devoting much of his time and energy to political matters: in March of the previous year he had been elected secretary of the newly formed Chinsali branch of the Northern Rhodesia African Congress.

Macpherson initially found life at Lubwa difficult. It was a very different posting from urban, industrialised Mufulira. Also, he had been ill during much of 1951. Not long married (to Myra, daughter of Rev. A. J. Cross, the first leader of the UMCB), he was also worried about money. He felt isolated, and for a time became preoccupied by the ease with which the White Fathers and the Watchtower movement seemed to be extending their influence.[4] He also renewed his acquaintance with Kaunda, but in less happy circumstances. In March 1951 Macpherson preached a sermon based on the Gospel of St John, on the subject of racial and political reconciliation. Believing him criti-

4. National Library of Scotland, Accession 7548, General Assembly of the Church of Scotland Foreign Missions Committee Papers (hereafter NLS), B313, Rev. F. Macpherson to Rev. J. A. R. Watt, 28 Dec. 1951.

cal of anti-federation sentiment, Congress supporters in the congregation took offence. Soon afterwards, Kaunda wrote on their behalf a strongly worded letter to Macpherson criticising him both as a priest and as 'a Scotchman'.[5] A tense meeting ensued, and only with difficulty did Macpherson convince Kaunda of his good intentions. The two men would in time become friends. But it was apparent to Macpherson that the controversy surrounding federation was adversely affecting relations between mission and local people. Like some of his compatriots in the Nyasaland missions, Macpherson hoped that the Church of Scotland would make an unequivocal show of support for African objections to federation during 1952-53, but this did not materialise. Meanwhile, Congress, under Harry Nkumbula's leadership, proved unable to mobilise African opposition to the proposals. Like Michael Scott in England, Nkumbula attempted in 1953 to promote a day of 'national prayer' against federation. This failed partly because of disagreement between Nkumbula and Lawrence Katilungu, president of the African Mineworkers' Union (AMU). It was not in the Copperbelt, however, but rather in rural Lubwa, several hundred kilometres distant, that signs emerged during 1953 of an unforeseen African reaction against federation and against the Church of Scotland missions that had little to do with nationalism.

On 18 September Macpherson received a visitor: Alice Lenshina Mulenga.[6] She was about 33 years of age. She claimed to have risen from the dead, not once but several times. Macpherson was intrigued and, impressed by Alice's sincerity, suggested she give thanks to God and commit to His service. This she agreed to do. In November she was baptised by Rev. Paul Mushindo, the African minister at Lubwa. During 1954 Lenshina began to preach the gospel, in Lubwa and beyond. Her influence and fame began to spread ever more widely and a movement began to develop around her. In 1955 Lenshina and her husband, Petros Chintankwa Mulenga, were suspended from the church. Efforts by African evangelists from Lubwa to win back her supporters failed; by this time Lenshina had her own ministers.

---

5. NLS, B313, K. D. Kaunda, for executive committee, Northern Rhodesia African Congress (Chinsali) to Macpherson, 25 March 1952.

6. This and the following paragraph draw on Andrew D. Roberts, The Lumpa Church of Alice Lenshina (Lusaka, 1972), originally published in Robert I. Rotberg and Ali A. Mazrui, eds., *Protest and Power in Black Africa* (New York, 1970), pp. 513-68. There are many other studies of the Lenshina phenomenon: Wim M. J. van Binsbergen, *Religious Change in Zambia: Exploratory Studies* (London and Boston, 1981), pp. 266-316; Hugo Hinfelaar, 'Women's Revolt: The Lumpa Church of Lenshina Mulenga in the 1950s', *Journal of Religion in Africa* 21, no. 2 (1991): 99-129; At Ipenburg, *'All Good Men': The Development of Lubwa Mission, Chinsali, Zambia, 1905-67* (Frankfurt am Main, 1992), pp. 231-46.

Over the course of several decades historians have studied the Lenshina movement. Its origins are still debated. In one notable study Andrew Roberts emphasised the interplay of two forces: movements towards African Christian independence, and movements towards the eradication of witchcraft and sorcery. Those origins also owed something to social and political change, and the erosion in the face of that change of 'traditional' African forms of social control. Also, Lenshina was perceived by many Africans as divinely inspired, and her visionary experiences, allied to strong personal charisma, granted her tremendous authority. Whatever the nature of the movement's origins, its popularity was unquestionable: during 1956 Lenshina's influence widened, to include the Copperbelt region.

Macpherson, writing in 1958 on the origins of the movement, noted in retrospect the inadequacies of the church at Lubwa: 'The growth of heresy . . . resulted not only from the appearance of malcontents who took over the movement for their own ends, but also from the unhappy fact that what might have been a revival movement found the Church so tied to its set practice and so wanting in zeal and vision that it had not the strength of will to enable it to contain "Alice".'[7] Other Scottish missionaries concurred with this assessment. Reporting on the failure of the church's attempts to win back supporters of the movement, Rev. George Fraser mused that Lenshina had in the space of a few years achieved greater results than had the mission in half a century of evangelistic endeavour.[8] Rev. Vernon Stone, who took up a new posting in Lubwa in late 1956, considered that in the breadth of its appeal to African peoples Lenshina undoubtedly constituted 'a divine judgement on the Church'.[9] In general, missionaries accepted that they had been found badly wanting in theological terms. Furthermore, they recognised that in failing to adequately acknowledge and publicise African bitterness about federation they might also have contributed indirectly to the growth of the movement.[10]

Did the Lenshina movement have links of any importance with Congress? It is difficult to be completely sure, but it appears unlikely notwithstanding the breadth of the movement's appeal to Congress members and non-members alike: Alice was not a politician. Europeans (including Macpherson) had some suspicions about the movement on this point, but failed to identify a specifically 'political' rationale. A few Scots worried that Lenshina might in-

7. Fergus Macpherson, 'Notes on the Beginning of the Movement' (April 1958), IMC Research Department: Department of Missionary Studies, *Occasional Papers* 1, no. 1 (London, Aug. 1958): 4.

8. NLS, B314, Rev. J. G. Fraser to Watt, n.d., but *c.* April 1956.

9. NLS, B310, Rev. W. V. Stone to Watt, 5 Jan. 1958.

10. NLS, B314, Watt to Rev. W. Bonomy, 2 July 1956.

spire a violent African reaction against empire and against the church, such as Mau Mau had in Kenya.[11] This did not occur in Northern Rhodesia, and the sanguinity of most missionaries was attributable in part to their realisation by 1956 that fears of the emergence of another 'kind of Kenyatta national politics-religious movement' had proved unfounded.[12]

Nevertheless, by 1956 the movement had spread to the Copperbelt, with Alice making her first personal visit to the region. The Copperbelt was in turmoil. In January of the previous year the AMU had successfully brought out on strike the great majority of African mineworkers. While this action, which lasted almost two months, forced the mining companies to make certain concessions in terms of pay and status, it did not quell African dissent.[13] Congress tried meanwhile to increase its influence within the AMU.[14] The situation could not be of other than intense interest and concern to missionaries in the locality, one of whom was Dorothea Lehmann, based in Mufulira with the LMS.

Although she worked for a British missionary society, Lehmann was not of British birth. She was born into a Lutheran family in Kassel, in the German province of Hesse, on Reformation Day (31 October), 1910. She developed a strong Christian faith, in part out of adversity: her father died when she was 4 years old, her fiancé when she was 24. She never married. She trained to be a teacher. In 1937, however, possibly due to state strictures on religious education, she decided to become a missionary in Africa, subsequently joining the Berlin Missionary Society as a probationer. Her timing was unpropitious: the Second World War brought the Society's activities to a halt. Through the mission she had become acquainted with Diedrich Westermann, the internationally renowned expert on the languages of West Africa. Lehmann decided to study for a doctorate at the University of Berlin under Westermann's supervision. Her (unpublished) dissertation, on tribal languages in eastern Tanganyika, was based upon missionaries' ethnographic and linguistic records. Lehmann also worked at the university in an administrative or secretarial capacity. After the war she taught for a time in Berlin refugee camps. With Westermann's assistance and through the efforts of the IMC London office (whose officials were facilitating renewed contact with German missionary societies), Lehmann was loaned to the LMS, which was undergoing a recruitment crisis. In June 1949 she arrived in England and after a period in

---

11. NLS, B310, Rev. K. Mackenzie to Watt, 2 Jan. 1956.

12. NLS, B314, Fraser to Rev. J. W. C. Dougall, 19 Sept. 1956.

13. Elena L. Berger, *Labour, Race and Colonial Rule: The Copperbelt from 1924 to Independence* (Oxford, 1974), pp. 131-64.

14. Ian Henderson, 'Wage-Earners and Political Protest in Colonial Africa: The Case of the Copperbelt', *African Affairs* 72, no. 288 (1973): 288-99.

London, and in Birmingham at Carey Hall Missionary Training College for Women, departed for the Copperbelt via South Africa the following year.[15]

In Mufulira the Rhodesian Selection Trust's mining operations exercised an immense influence on economy and society. Lehmann observed at close quarters the difficulties that beset African mineworkers and their families.[16] The colonial authorities funded certain social welfare initiatives aimed at African women; these included training in 'domestic' tasks such as cookery, knitting and sewing. There was a shortage of trained workers, and Lehmann, by now an increasingly fluent speaker of the vernacular Chibemba, participated in many of these initiatives and won the trust of the women.[17] From them she learned a great deal about local attitudes towards a wide range of issues including marriage, divorce, bridewealth — and politics. In 1952, putting to use her interest in and knowledge of African life, she undertook, with the assistance of local teachers, a survey of religious affiliation in the Copperbelt towns of Chingola, Kitwe, Luanshya and Mufulira. Its results indicated a strong following for the African Methodist Episcopal Church and, more noticeably, for the Watchtower movement. Conversely, support for the Church of Central Africa Rhodesia (CCAR) — with which the LMS was closely associated — was comparatively weak.[18]

It seemed to Lehmann that African women were undervalued and underutilised, by mission and by church. She pressed church elders to expand the number of women lay preachers. Strongly conscious of the important social role of women, she was nevertheless ambivalent about their political attitudes. As industrial relations worsened during 1955 and 1956 she noted with alarm the alacrity with which some women expressed support for the 'extreme leaders' of the trade union movement.[19] In July 1956 began a series of 'rolling' strikes. The government responded by declaring a state of emergency

15. John Stuart, 'Dorothea Lehmann and John V. Taylor: Researching Church and Society in Late Colonial Africa', in Patrick Harries and David Maxwell, eds., *The Secular in the Spiritual: Missionaries and Knowledge about Africa,* forthcoming.

16. It is inconceivable that Lehmann and Macpherson did not know each other; but I have found no record of their having met.

17. SOAS, Council for World Mission Archive, London Missionary Society Papers (hereafter CWM), AF/45, D. A. Lehmann, report for LMS on work in Mufulira, Sept. 1954-Sept. 1956.

18. SOAS, CWM, AF/45, Lehmann, report on separatist sects, July 1952. On church formation in Northern Rhodesia, see Peter Bolink, *Towards Church Union in Zambia: A Study of Missionary Co-operation and Church-Union Efforts in Central Africa* (Franeker, 1967), pp. 246-365.

19. SOAS, CWM, AF/45, Lehmann, report for LMS, Nov. 1956.

two months later.[20] This, then, was the environment in which the Lenshina movement began to make its presence felt in the Copperbelt.

Lehmann noted, as had Macpherson at Lubwa, how very strong was the appeal of the Lenshina movement, now becoming known as the 'Lumpa' Church. She would later write that its 'eschatological message and the promise of redemption . . . proved far more attractive than the efforts of the mission churches to keep their flocks in orthodox ways'.[21] Yet the influence of the movement on the CCAR was complex, interacting as it did with the influence of politics and of trade unionism. The actions of the state were also adversely affecting the church. Open-air services were curtailed. Church members associated with Congress and with the AMU were detained. Union officials meanwhile criticised the CCAR, accusing it of being solely the church of salaried (and relatively better-paid) Africans, who were 'blindly following the Europeans'. The AMU, Lehmann reported to LMS head office, 'favours the Lenshina movement as "a truly African church"'.[22]

The Lumpa Church was indeed an African church, for Africans. This extraordinarily powerful manifestation of Christian independency attracted the attention of the colonial authorities, suspicious of its political links. It also attracted a great deal of attention farther afield, in mission and ecumenical circles. What were its origins? What would be its consequences? What lessons did it have for mission and church in Africa more generally? In Scotland Lenshina was reported on and discussed, even in the Edinburgh daily press.[23] For the Kirk's Foreign Missions Committee in Edinburgh the movement appeared as nothing less than a 'striking affirmation of the Divine Presence, a characteristic deficient in the Church'.[24] At the request of the IMC Macpherson and his colleague Stone wrote reports on the phenomenon, to enable information to be shared and disseminated to any missionary of any nationality interested in the church in Africa. Stone sounded what by now amounted almost to a missionary refrain: Alice's ability to bring into being a "People's Movement" showed only too clearly the 'feebleness' of the church in Northern Rhodesia.[25] Remarkable as it was, however, the Lumpa Church was

20. Berger, *Labour, Race, and Colonial Rule,* pp. 137-58.

21. Dorothea Lehmann, 'Alice Lenshina Mulenga and the Lumpa Church', in John V. Taylor and Dorothea Lehmann, *Christians of the Copperbelt: The Growth of the Church in Northern Rhodesia* (London, 1961), p. 252.

22. SOAS, CWM, AF/14, Lehmann to Rev. A. F. Griffiths, 20 Sept. 1956.

23. *The Scotsman,* 22 June 1956.

24. National Archives of Scotland, (hereafter NAS), CH1/8/95, 'Report of the FMC for 1958', in 'Report to the General Assembly, 1959', p. 431.

25. W. V. Stone, 'The Church as the People of God', Dec. 1957; 'The "Alice Movement"

unique only in its scale and in the amount of attention it received. Independency had long been a feature of African Christianity. To missionaries Lumpa nevertheless provided a captivating glimpse of the challenges that African agency on a mass scale might pose, to church and to colonial state. In February 1955, in London, IMC research secretary Rev. Erik Nielsen convened a meeting to discuss how 'younger' churches might best be studied and understood.[26] As a result of this meeting the Anglican missionary Rev. John V. Taylor was commissioned to survey and report on the church in the Ugandan province of Buganda. He had previously spent seven years in Uganda teaching and training clergy. His research findings would be published in book form, as *The Growth of the Church in Buganda* (1958). By then Taylor had already commenced a further IMC-supported research project, on the church in Northern Rhodesia. He did not know the territory and required a collaborator. This would be none other than Dorothea Lehmann. By the time the results of their research were published, in 1961, the political situation not only in Northern Rhodesia but also throughout the Central African Federation had undergone enormous change. We shall return to Taylor and Lehmann and to Northern Rhodesia later in this chapter.

Nyasaland: Scottish Missions, African Church and African Nationalism

The Lumpa Church did not exert an impact in Nyasaland comparable to that in parts of Northern Rhodesia. In Nyasaland the Church of Central Africa Presbyterian (CCAP) seemed able to retain its members' allegiance.[27] The CCAP had been formed through union of the Livingstonia and Blantyre presbyteries of the Church of Scotland in 1924. Until 1945 the CCAP maintained responsibilities in Northern Rhodesia as well as in Nyasaland, but in 1945 three congregations of the Livingstonia presbytery (including that of Lubwa) united with those of the LMS and of the United Church in the Copperbelt to form the Church of Central Africa Rhodesia. In the early 1950s missionaries and African clergy began the gradual process of devolving ecclesiastical authority from Scottish missions to the indigenous church. Certain functions of the mission council at Blantyre were transferred to the church in

---

in 1958', n.d., both in IMC Research Department: Department of Missionary Studies, *Occasional Papers* 1, no. 1 (London, Aug. 1958).

26. SOAS, CBMS, 536, 'Studies in the Life and Growth of Younger Churches' file, Rev. E. W. Nielsen, notes on meeting, 22 Feb. 1955.

27. NLS, A167, Watt to Stone, 23 Dec. 1957; NLS, B310, Stone to Watt, 5 Jan. 1958.

1953. In July 1956 the mission council was wound up. Straightforward as it sounds, the process was subject to many strains. Some were of a distinct religious and theological nature; others related to the level of commitment by mission and church to educational and medical work.[28] Almost all were in some way a consequence of Nyasaland's official enclosure in September 1953 within the Central African Federation. It was in Nyasaland that African opposition to federation was most intense.

Andrew Doig knew this well. He was determined to make known the extent of that opposition, by working within the Federal Assembly in Salisbury. His decision in December 1953 to become a Federal MP met with a mixed response from colleagues. He was seconded from the Blantyre mission, for an initial period of two years, subsequently extended. His replacement was Rev. Tom Colvin, who arrived in Nyasaland in early 1954. Colvin (1925-2000) was aged 29, ten years younger than Doig and with a different attitude to politics. Colvin, unlike Doig, was a member of the Iona Community. He had also been a member of the World Federation of Democratic Youth, an international organisation sympathetic to Moscow. Colvin was no communist, but he was very politically minded. He believed that mission and church should align against political and racial discrimination. Only in this way, he would argue, could the church in Nyasaland claim itself to be truly 'African'.[29]

Colvin's arrival at Blantyre was significant for a number of reasons. His presence helped consolidate anti-federation sentiment within the mission. And when the colonial authorities in Zomba and their federal counterparts in Salisbury learned of his supposedly communistic (as well as anti-federation) leanings he, and the mission as a whole, became the object of increased government suspicion. This suspicion was bound up with the resurgence of the Nyasaland African Congress. In March 1956 Congress members Kanyama Chiume and Masauko Chipembere were elected to the colony's Legislative Council. They advocated secession from the federation. Tensions grew between these younger men and older, more conservative African nationalists such as Manoah Chirwa and Clement Kumbikano, both of whom, with Doig, were now representatives of African interests in the Federal Assembly. At the prompting of Chipembere and Chiume, Hastings Banda agreed to return to Nyasaland as leader of Congress. He eventually arrived back in the colony, to tremendous African acclaim, in July 1958. Scottish missionaries also wel-

---

28. David H. S. Lyon, *In Pursuit of a Vision: The Story of the Church of Scotland's Developing Relationship with the Churches Emerging from the Missionary Movement in the Twenty-five Years from 1947 to 1972* (Edinburgh, 1998), pp. 155-8.

29. NLS, B395, Watt to Rev. N. C. Bernard, 24 Feb. 1954.

comed Banda's return; but they differed in their expectations of him. Colvin and Macpherson (who by now had taken up another new posting, this time at Livingstonia, in Nyasaland's northern province) supported the ideal of secession. Doig conversely perceived Banda as a reformer with whom Africans and Europeans alike could work towards the goal of majority rule for Nyasaland — within the Federation if necessary. Tensions within Congress thus echoed within the missions, at both Blantyre and Livingstonia. In turn, radical nationalists and sympathetic Scots all attracted the attention of Sir Robert Armitage, governor of Nyasaland from April 1956.

Prior to being posted to Nyasaland, Armitage had experienced a troubled governorship in Cyprus, a colony beset by ethnic and religious tensions and anti-colonial violence. His arrival in central Africa coincided with a new phase in the politics of the Federation. Rhodesians were now openly making known their ambition of dominion status for the Federation. Such status, were it to be approved, would render the Federation technically 'independent' of the United Kingdom. In April 1957 the governments of the United Kingdom and of the Federation agreed on a 'joint declaration'. This did not commit Britain to the granting of dominion status but, to the satisfaction of Sir Roy Welensky, federal Prime Minister since 1956, it ostensibly reaffirmed British commitment to the Federation.[30]

The declaration alarmed Doig, now becoming aware of how limited was his influence and authority as a federal MP and as vice-chairman of the politically neutered African Affairs Board. He campaigned ever more vigorously on behalf of Nyasaland, not only in the Federation but also in Britain. He lobbied the Colonial Office and canvassed support for his reformist aims from unofficial organisations both secular and religious. In January 1958 Doig met with Archbishop Fisher at Lambeth Palace, London, in the hope that he (Fisher) might intercede on behalf of Nyasaland African interests with Lord Home, Conservative Secretary of State for Commonwealth Relations. Doig did not receive an especially warm welcome from Fisher. Two months earlier *The Times* had published a letter from Doig on the situation in central Africa. Labour Opposition spokesman on colonies James Callaghan had seized on this, citing the letter (and also a recent statement by the British Council of Churches) as evidence of church antipathy to federation.[31] Fisher was extremely displeased. 'The danger is that enthusiasts in this country for African rights will start protesting . . . and

---

30. Welensky had been knighted in 1953. Three years later he succeeded Lord Malvern (as Sir Geoffrey Huggins had by then become) as Prime Minister of the Central African Federation.

31. UK House of Commons Debates, 578, 808-10, 25 Nov. 1957.

encourage the Africans to resist out there', he noted.[32] He sent Doig away empty-handed. In June 1958 Doig resigned as a member of the Federal Assembly. He resumed work at Blantyre mission, just as Banda's return to the land of his birth began to wreak a transformative effect upon Nyasaland politics.

By 1958 the process of 'integration' of Scottish mission into the indigenous Presbyterian Church was underway in Nyasaland. Following the dissolution of the Blantyre mission council in 1956 a joint council composed equally of Africans and Europeans was formed in order to facilitate the onward transfer of authority to synod. This process was repeated in Livingstonia the following year. European congregations of the overseas presbyteries of the Church of Scotland in Blantyre and Zomba were not enamoured of the prospect of racial change in the leadership of the church in Nyasaland; their members were especially nervous about church and mission association with Congress. Into this unsettled political and religious environment arrived in January 1958 a visitor from Scotland: George MacLeod.

MacLeod (1895-1991) was at once charismatic and controversial. A man whose family had a long history of service to the church in Scotland, he was also thoroughly Anglicised (the process having included education at Winchester and at Oriel College, Oxford). His interests ranged widely, from social conditions in Glasgow to nuclear disarmament. He had been elected Moderator of the General Assembly in May 1957. This had been by no means inevitable. While MacLeod's left-leaning politics and pacifism found some favour within the Kirk, he was also a source of irritation to more conservative Scots. His moderatorship would be marked by controversy, most notably on the interrelated matters of church episcopacy and relations with the Church of England. Since his intervention in the 1953 General Assembly debate on Central African Federation, MacLeod had retained a strong interest in African affairs. He therefore decided to undertake an official visit to Nyasaland and the Rhodesias (as well as to South Africa), the first such visit by a serving moderator. His intentions were twofold: to examine at first hand the religious, racial and political situation in the region; and to demonstrate his support for the indigenous church.

Before his departure from Scotland, MacLeod seems to have sensed the possibility of change in central Africa. The church, he thought, might be able to play an integral role. He intended to use his powers of persuasion to convince colonial and federal authorities that they should both encourage and welcome political reform. He intended to argue that the Church of Scotland

32. Church of England Record Centre, London (hereafter CERC), British Council of Churches papers (hereafter BCC), 5/2/2vi, Most Rev. G. F. Fisher to Rev. K. Slack, 29 Jan. 1958.

was itself committed to indigenisation and devolution. In the event he made no headway whatever with the Europeans he encountered. This may have had as much to do with MacLeod's abrupt, declamatory style as with his politics. Conversely, meetings with Congress representatives went very well. Nyasaland African Congress President-General T. D. T. Banda (no relation of Hastings Banda) welcomed MacLeod warmly and pleaded for the Church of Scotland to denounce federation.[33] Refreshed and even more enthused, MacLeod determined on his return to Scotland that the Kirk should indeed espouse unequivocal support for African protest against federation and also advocate majority rule for Nyasaland and for Northern Rhodesia.

Within the CCAP, MacLeod's visit focussed the minds of missionaries and African clergy alike. The church synods at both Livingstonia and Blantyre decided to advocate Nyasaland's secession from the federation. (The third, remaining CCAP synod, based at Mkhoma, was affiliated not to the Church of Scotland, but to the Cape synod of the Dutch Reformed Church.) In a public statement Livingstonia asserted that 'in the minds of Nyasaland Africans Federation is equated with political subservience, and from it they seek early release'.[34] The Blantyre synod went further than this, in a statement drafted by Tom Colvin and CCAP (and Congress) member Willie Chokani. They noted how a recent upsurge in police surveillance of church properties and church activities was contributing to unrest: for this the local and federal authorities were to blame. But they saved their harshest criticism for the government of the United Kingdom: it had 'betrayed' the people of Nyasaland. Consequently, the Blantyre synod now called on Christians in Nyasaland, on the people of Scotland and on the authorities in Nyasaland 'to take heed of this unrest before worse befalls'.[35]

Support for MacLeod was growing. But so too was opposition to his aims, in Britain as well as in the Rhodesias. To his compatriot Sir Gilbert Rennie, MacLeod was a menace. Governor of Northern Rhodesia in 1953, Rennie became federal high commissioner in London the following year. He promoted the federation's cause tirelessly. MacLeod's return from central Africa prophesying the demise of the Federation galvanised Rennie into action.[36] He enlisted the aid of the Rhodesia and Nyasaland Committee (RNC), a pro-federation lobby group established in London in 1957 at Welensky's instigation. Its chairman was Jack Thomson, formerly general manager of the Roan Antelope

33. NLS, Accession 9084, MacLeod of Fuinary and Iona papers, 68, Rt Rev. G. F. MacLeod, report of visit to central Africa, Jan.-Feb. 1958.

34. NLS, B304, CCAP Livingstonia synod standing committee minutes, 28 March 1958.

35. NLS, Accession 9638, B114, CCAP Blantyre synod statement, May 1958.

36. RHL, MSS Welensky, 660/4/40, Sir G. Rennie to Sir R. Welensky, 2 April 1958.

Mining Company. Its secretary was another proponent of federation, Herbert Baxter, who had retired as assistant under-secretary of state at the Commonwealth Relations Office.[37] Thomson was deputed to lobby church representatives in London. Meanwhile Baxter and Rennie subjected MacLeod to a barrage of correspondence, with the aim of persuading him to reconsider his views.[38]

MacLeod was cannier than his opponents. He had sensed unease in Scotland about Rhodesian intentions and their likely effect upon Africans. Rather than press the General Assembly for a definitive statement on federation, MacLeod, with sympathetic colleagues, conceived the idea of a Scottish church commission of enquiry into federation, ostensibly independent-minded and free of party political links. It would invite representations from individuals and organisations interested in central African affairs. Importantly, this would also take Kirk responsibility for discussion on central Africa away from the conservative Church and Nation Committee. Given the title 'Special Committee Anent [about] Central Africa' the commission was duly set up, with a remit to report on the situation in central Africa within a three-year period. It began its work in September 1958. With MacLeod as its first convenor and the returned missionary Kenneth Mackenzie as its secretary, the Special Committee had (as MacLeod admitted) a 'left of centre' bias. That did not prevent opponents as well as supporters of federation from making representations. On behalf of the RNC Baxter argued to it that 'the Federation must succeed, to prevent the Rhodesias being sucked into South Africa'.[39] Tom Colvin and Andrew Doig both appeared before the committee, as did many others, including Orton Chirwa, a founding member of the Nyasaland African Congress.

During his visit to Africa George MacLeod made quite an impression upon Sir Robert Armitage. An overwhelming mixture, it seemed to the governor, of religion, socialism and (in his antiquated moderator's garb) theatricality, MacLeod was a disagreeable, exotic presence. The two men proved unable to agree on anything. MacLeod could not convince Armitage to take seriously African hostility to federation. Armitage, in return, lamented the Scottish missions' lack of 'loyalty' to the state, and their focus on politics

37. Lambeth Palace Library, London (hereafter LPL), Fisher Papers (hereafter FP), 200, Baxter, memo, 'Electoral Developments in the Rhodesia and Nyasaland Federation', 9 Jan.; Baxter to Rev. D. A. Keighley, 20 Jan. 1958.

38. NLS, 9084, 68, Baxter to MacLeod; Rennie to MacLeod, both 24 March; Baxter to MacLeod, 14 May 1958.

39. NLS, B352, General Assembly Committee Anent Central Africa, minutes, 7 Nov. 1958.

rather than on evangelism.[40] In the aftermath of Hastings Banda's return to Nyasaland on 6 July 1958, the governor's interest in the activities of the Scottish missions intensified. He relied heavily on police intelligence reports, and these painted a disturbing picture. Banda appeared to be preaching sedition from CCAP church pulpits in the northern province. Missionaries from the Livingstonia mission were meanwhile reported as inculcating African school-children in the ways of Congress.[41] In August the Scots plummeted still further in Armitage's estimation. Lord Dalhousie, the Federation's Governor-General, paid an official visit to Livingstonia. He was reportedly booed by Africans, following missionary encouragement. Armitage, a stickler for protocol, was mortified. Missionaries contested the official interpretation of events, to no avail. Relations between missions and state, already poor, degenerated into mutual suspicion and recrimination.

For Armitage, mission and church activities demanded close scrutiny. Much of this scrutiny was directed at Colvin, who by this time had been joined at Blantyre by fellow-Iona Community members Albert McAdam and Rev. Andrew Ross. Consequently, what in other circumstances might have seemed innocuous plans by the CCAP synods at Livingstonia and Blantyre to devolve ecclesiastical authority to African leadership appeared to Armitage evidence of impending Congress appropriation of the church. He found it difficult to conceive of Africans being granted control of church affairs; they were no more ready for such responsibility than were African nationalists for leadership in government. Armitage made little attempt to communicate with missionaries, to ascertain their views. Nor did many missionaries attempt to approach him. On reasonably good terms with local district officers, they had by now little meaningful contact with the state at more senior levels. There developed an atmosphere of mutual suspicion and hostility. As he learned of the situation from reports and from accounts by returned missionaries, James Dougall, in Edinburgh, despaired. In November 1958 he confided to Max Warren:

> . . . all our evidence shows that the African people are being driven to extremes of opposition and non-co-operation. . . . What makes us feel the deterioration badly is that ministers of the Church whom we know well to be cautious and conservative in outlook now associate themselves with the views of the African Congress. What worries us also is

40. RHL, MSS Afr. s. 2204, Armitage papers, Sir R. Armitage, draft memoirs, 2, 27-29; 3, 63-64.

41. RHL, 1959 Nyasaland Commission of Enquiry (Devlin Commission) papers (hereafter DCP), 6, Nyasaland Police Special Branch, top secret dossier, 'The Congress Plan of Violence', April 1959.

that any statement of the facts or criticism of Government is taken to be something approaching high treason . . .[42]

The situation continued to worsen. On 20 February 1959 a brief, violent incident occurred at Livingstonia. This was interpreted by the government as yet further evidence of Congress militancy, linked to church and mission. Days later Armitage was presented with intelligence reports of Congress plans to massacre the European and Asian (and some African) inhabitants of Nyasaland. He consulted with the federal authorities in Salisbury and with the Colonial Office in London. It was decided that coordinated, preventative action should be taken. The Prime Minister of Southern Rhodesia declared a state of emergency on 26 February. Armitage followed suit in Nyasaland on 3 March. Welensky provided federal military assistance. Banda and other senior Congress members were immediately arrested and detained. Other arrests followed. More than forty Africans were killed in the process, by no means all resisting arrest or protesting against government action.

Missionaries were astounded at Armitage's actions. The reaction of Rev. Hamish Hepburn in Blantyre was typical. 'This step seems to me sheer madness . . . I should not be surprised if today's events have finished Federation altogether as a practical policy . . . there must be not a few people in Nyasaland who have the parallel of Cyprus in their minds at this present time — show of force, strife, and in the end constitutional reform'.[43] The layman McAdam took a lead, writing letters to the *Manchester Guardian*, to Alan Lennox-Boyd, as Secretary of State for Colonies, and to the leaders of the Labour Party and the Liberal Party in Britain, vigorously disputing the official account of what had occurred. His combative, accusative writing style unnerved Dougall, who nevertheless concluded that the authorities in Zomba, in Salisbury and in London were all indeed circulating inaccurate reports in an attempt to pin the blame for events on Congress and its supporters — including the missionaries.[44] It now seemed to Dougall imperative that the Church of Scotland speak more firmly and unequivocally than heretofore. But the situation in the Nyasaland missions was, to say the least, confused. Rev. Neil Bernard, a missionary critical of the 'Iona' group, reported from Blantyre on hostility between the 'youngsters', McAdam and Ross (Colvin was on furlough in Scotland), and the 'elders', who included Doig among

---

42. NLS, A140, Canon M. A. C. Warren to Dougall, 19 Nov. 1958.
43. NLS, B346, Rev. J. L. Hepburn to Watt, 3 March 1959.
44. NLS, B346, Dougall to editors of *The Glasgow Herald* and *The Scotsman*, 4 March 1959.

their number.[45] Doig was unwilling to subject the authorities to public criticism. He had met with Lord Perth, visiting Colonial Office Minister of State, to press for a parliamentary enquiry into recent events. His younger colleagues wanted instead an immediate end to emergency conditions. Dougall, exasperated by the bickering among his colleagues, decided that the Special Committee Anent Central Africa, which was shortly due to issue its first report, should immediately assert its moral authority and make a statement on behalf of the General Assembly. On 24 March, just hours before Lennox-Boyd announced a commission of enquiry into events in Nyasaland, Dougall presented a statement to an Edinburgh press conference. Actually written by MacLeod and Mackenzie, this blamed the territorial and federal governments for the current situation in Nyasaland.[46]

Knowing that any report produced by the Special Committee would be portrayed as biased by critics of the missions, Dougall now went to great lengths to assert the committee's reasonableness. He travelled to London to discuss its work with Scottish MPs, both Unionist and Labour. He contacted colleagues in central Africa, stressing the necessity of a united front in the face of official suspicion: 'the particular duty and privilege of the CCAP and the C of S', Dougall wrote, 'is to offer its assistance in restoring peace . . . the Church cannot help as long as it is divided to the point of quarrelling in public or in private'.[47] He eschewed assistance offered by British critics of federation such as Michael Scott.[48] Dougall also declined to be associated with Kirk members hostile to MacLeod, such as the layman Bernard Fergusson. A professional soldier and occasional author whose wartime exploits with the Chindits had brought him some renown, Fergusson organised a conference in Glasgow to publicise an alternative view on federation to that of the Special Committee.[49] Fergusson also kept the Colonial Office and the federal high commission in London informed, and through them, the pro-federation Rhodesia and Nyasaland Committee.[50] In London and in Edinburgh Scottish support-

---

45. NLS, B343, Bernard to Watt, 16 March 1959.

46. The National Archives of the UK: Public Record Office (hereafter TNA: PRO), CO 1015/1864, General Assembly of the Church of Scotland, Special Committee Anent Central Africa, *Report* (March 1959).

47. NLS, B346, Dougall, circular letter; NLS, A140, Dougall to Bernard, both 13 April 1959.

48. NLS, B346, Scott to Dougall, 7 April 1959.

49. NLS, B346, Brig. B. E. Fergusson, report of conference on central Africa, 17 April 1959.

50. TNA: PRO, CO 1015/1866, W. L. Gorell Barnes to Fergusson, 19 May; H. St L. Grenfell to Gorell Barnes, 22 May 1959.

ers of federation marshalled their resources in advance of the 1959 General Assembly.[51] Rennie published a pamphlet, a 'counterblast' to the Special Committee's report.[52] He and Fergusson approached the incoming (for 1959-60) Moderator of the General Assembly, Rev. Dr. Robert Shepherd. One of Scotland's best-known missionaries because of his work at the Lovedale Institution in South Africa, Shepherd (1888-1971) was an arch-conservative, whose antipathy to African nationalism coincided with an abhorrence of communism.[53] On the eve of the General Assembly debate on federation Shepherd and Rennie met with MacLeod and requested that he tone down his planned contribution to the debate.[54] This probably had the effect of further hardening MacLeod's resolve.

On 25 May 1959 the General Assembly debated Central African Federation. MacLeod and Mackenzie had revised the Special Committee's findings, to issue a direct challenge to government in London: follow the lead of the Church of Scotland and devolve political authority in Nyasaland and in Northern Rhodesia to the African majority. 'The time has passed for working with nicely balanced arrangements relating the Colonial Government, the European inhabitants, and the African population', the report observed before going on to declare that 'the time has come for a daring and creative transfer of power to the African people'.[55] The ensuing debate was noisy and intemperate. The outcome was decisively in favour of the report, and owed much to the 'daunting brilliance' of MacLeod's oratory.[56] After years of equivocation a British church had come out in support of African self-determination and against colonial rule. It remained to be seen how effective this call for reform would prove.

The Devlin Report and After

As Lennox-Boyd saw it, the Nyasaland commission of enquiry would investigate and report solely on the disturbances within the colony. There could be no enquiry into African opinion on federation. Thus, the commission's

51. RHL, MSS Welensky, 247/4/19-21, Grenfell to D. Cole, 8 May 1959; Rhodesia and Nyasaland Committee, *The Kirk's New Face in Nyasaland* (London, May 1959).

52. TNA: PRO, CO 1015/1864, J. C. Morgan, minutes, 6 May 1959; High Commission of the Federation of Rhodesia and Nyasaland, *Why Not Be Fair?* (London, 1959).

53. NLS, A167, Watt to L. B. Greaves, 15 Feb. 1957.

54. *The Scotsman*, 25 May 1959.

55. NAS, CH1/6/95, 'Reports to the General Assembly, 1959', pp. 663-91.

56. *The Times*, 26 May 1959.

findings hopefully would not prejudice the formal review of the federal constitution, due in 1960. The four-man commission's chairman would be High Court Judge Sir Patrick Devlin. Lord Perth considered him 'very sensible'; and his judicial qualifications were impeccable. But, as Prime Minister Harold Macmillan later noted ruefully and with the benefit of hindsight, Devlin had certain potentially troublesome deficiencies. He was of Irish Roman Catholic descent (his two sisters were nuns, and one of his brothers was a priest, the other an actor), and his wife was Jewish.[57] This aside, Devlin, as it transpired, was not in the least biddable. He was tough-minded and sceptical.

The commissioners travelled to central Africa. They took care to appear independent of and not unduly reliant upon the Nyasaland authorities.[58] They received more than six hundred written submissions, the great majority from Nyasalanders criticising federation. Missionaries also made submissions, as individuals and as representatives of the synod (and in Dougall's case, on behalf of the Foreign Missions Committee). Missionaries and African clergy testified in person to the commission, which visited Nyasaland between 11 April and 15 May. By no means were all missionaries in favour of Congress. Some registered their disapproval at the links between Congress and the CCAP.[59] Many others, however, spoke in favour of Congress as a legitimate political organisation — the only such organisation available to Africans. In his testimony, Fergus Macpherson insisted that Banda would neither encourage nor condone violence. Macpherson also emphasised the church's need to rebuild relations with government.[60] This was in contrast to McAdam, who was unsparing in his criticism of the authorities.[61] Doig reflected on the frustrations of life as a Federal Assembly member. To the commission he expressed the hope that Nyasaland be granted majority rule as quickly as possible.[62] He also acknowledged that relations between government and the Blantyre mission had been poor for some time.[63] Rev. Stephen

57. Brian Simpson, 'The Devlin Commission (1959): Colonialism, Emergencies and the Rule of Law', *Oxford Journal of Legal Studies* 22, no. 1 (2002): 46.

58. Andrew C. Ross, *Colonialism to Cabinet Crisis: A Political History of Malawi* (Zomba, 2009), pp. 185-91.

59. RHL, DCP, 15, 2, 397-404, testimony of A. Conn, 22 April 1959; 13, 4, 959-61, testimony of Rev. P. W. P. Petty, 2 May 1959.

60. RHL, DCP, 13, 5, 1140-2, testimony of Rev. F. Macpherson, 5 May 1959.

61. RHL, DCP, 15, 2, 222-32, testimony of A. McAdam, 20 April 1959.

62. RHL, DCP, 15, 2, 233-41, testimony of Rev. A. B. Doig, 20 April 1959.

63. RHL, DCP, 15, 2, 171-5, testimony of Rev. J. L. Hepburn; Rev. J. D. Sangaya; Rev. F. S. Chintali; D. D. Mkwaila; 240-1, testimony of Doig, 20 April 1959.

Msiska, who was Moderator of the Livingstonia Synod, preferred to emphasise to the commission the church's ongoing responsibility to the people of Nyasaland.[64]

The commission had to consider the contribution of missionaries and of CCAP clergy along with a great mass of other data. In all, the commission heard testimony from some 450 individual witnesses and from about 1,300 people in groups.[65] Might Scottish missionaries and African clergy and church members have been able to turn the Devlin Commission into a kind of referendum on federation?[66] This does not seem likely. One commission member, Sir John Ure Primrose, was a Scot and not unfriendly towards the missionaries.[67] Yet he seems to have found disappointing their reluctance to initiate discussions with the government in Zomba. The weakness of Armitage's testimony may have weighed more heavily with Devlin.[68] For after examining police records Devlin was unable to find satisfactory evidence of a murder plot. Banda, needless to say, denied any knowledge of a plot: to Devlin's suggestion that even missionaries might have been among his intended victims, Banda retorted 'What a defamation! . . . That is an insult!'[69] The commission concluded its enquiries in London on 23 June, having taken evidence there from other witnesses including Michael Scott. Devlin and his colleagues then began compiling their report.

In the ensuing four-week period prior to publication of the report a good deal happened in Scottish church and mission affairs. The federal authorities finally lost patience with Tom Colvin and declared him (still on furlough) a prohibited immigrant, who would not be allowed re-entry to the Federation. Almost simultaneously, the London journal *The Economist* published an article based on secret sources, revealing the hatred apparently felt within the government of Nyasaland for the 'irresponsible missionaries of the Church of Scotland'.[70] To Dougall's dismay, Scottish Labour MPs took up Colvin's cause in Parliament.[71] Dougall wrote to the synod at Blantyre, counselling restraint

---

64. RHL, DCP, 13, 5, 1143-5, testimony of Rev. S. K. Msiska, 5 May 1959.

65. Colin Baker, *State of Emergency: Crisis in Central Africa, Nyasaland, 1959-60* (London, 1997), p. 105.

66. Baker, *State of Emergency*, p. 85.

67. NLS, A140, Dougall to Sir J. Primrose, 24 June; B347, Rev. W. A. Smellie to Dougall, 3 July 1959. The other two commission members were Edgar Williams, historian and former army officer, and Sir Percy Wyn-Harris, former Governor of Gambia.

68. RHL, DCP, 15, 1, 1-13, testimony of Sir R. Armitage, 15 April 1959.

69. RHL, DCP, 14, 8, 1752, testimony of Dr H. K. Banda, 16 May 1959.

70. *The Economist: Foreign Report*, 18 June; *The Economist*, 27 June 1959.

71. NLS, B347, Dougall to Rev. T. C. Colvin, 11 May 1959.

and a 'dignified protest' instead, to Armitage.[72] He wrote also to the authorities in Zomba and in Salisbury, diplomatically challenging the official view of the missions as revealed by *The Economist*.[73] Colvin meanwhile agreed to a new posting — in Ghana.

Dougall's irenic initiatives won the support of ecumenical colleagues in London. There had been hopes in British religious circles that Garfield Todd, a New Zealand-born former missionary who became prime minister of Southern Rhodesia in 1953, might advance the cause of racial 'partnership'. But although Africans in all three territories derived some economic benefit from federation, their social and political opportunities did not expand. Todd was ousted in January 1958. By then central African affairs were again attracting widespread interest in the United Kingdom. The British Council of Churches attempted to respond. In 1956 Archbishop Fisher had publicly criticised the government in the House of Lords for the deportation of Archbishop Makarios of Cyprus and also for the invasion of Suez. BCC officials took Fisher's actions as a signal to encourage fresh, non-partisan discussion of imperial and African colonial affairs. They canvassed MPs. They organised in July 1958 at the Palace of Westminster a meeting on Africa, attended by MPs, peers and delegates to the Lambeth Conference.[74] They forged personal links with like-minded individuals in organisations such as the Institute of Race Relations.[75] They consulted with historians and other academics in an ultimately futile attempt to devise remedies for the constitutional ills of the Central African Federation.[76] During 1959, with the aim of augmenting Dougall's efforts in relation to Nyasaland, they held meetings in London with senior politicians. These included Labour Party leader Hugh Gaitskell and his colleague James Callaghan and, from the Central African Federation, Sir Roy Welensky and his minister of justice, Julian Greenfield.[77] The churchmen's aims were moderate. They wished to encourage in Gaitskell a commitment by Labour to bipartisanship on African colonial affairs. From Welensky they sought evidence of commitment to greater African self-determination. Neither man showed any willingness to respond as hoped. Gaitskell wanted to use colonial issues

72. NLS, B395, Dougall to Hepburn, 19 June 1959.

73. NLS, B347, Dougall, memo, 'The Next Step in Nyasaland', July 1959.

74. CERC, BCC, 5/2/2vi, Keighley, notes on meeting with P. M. Kirk, MP, 18 Nov; Rev. A. E. A. Sulston to Greaves, 9 July 1958.

75. SOAS, CBMS, 570, Federation Group, minutes, 10 Nov. 1958.

76. SOAS, CBMS, 570, Federation Group, minutes, 18 June 1959.

77. SOAS, CBMS, 570, 'Federation Group' file, Rev. R. K. Orchard, notes on meeting, 7 July 1959.

to attack the Macmillan government. As for Welensky, he described Nyasaland as an 'imperial slum', entirely dependent upon federal aid and with no hope of self-determination. He was confident of vindication by Devlin, and asserted that the federal government's conduct during the emergency would merit 'a clean sheet'.[78]

Missionaries awaited Devlin's report, anticipating that it might become a blueprint for change in central Africa. They were not prepared for its sensational findings, published on 23 July. On the first page appeared the passage that guaranteed the report instant and lasting notoriety. 'Nyasaland is — no doubt temporarily — a police state, where it is not safe for anyone to express approval of the policies of the Congress party, to which before 3rd March 1959 the vast majority of politically minded Africans belonged, and where it is unwise to express any but the most restrained criticism of government policy'.[79] Critics of government seized on the phrase 'police state'. The commissioners had found no evidence of a murder plot. Armitage's response, they concluded, had been misguided but, in the circumstances, probably understandable: he was acting upon the information that had been made available to him and he could hardly have been expected to do nothing. Devlin noted in passing a 'cleavage' between government and the Scottish missions. He also drew attention to the links between Congress and the CCAP.[80] But he made no overt criticism of either church or mission, nor did he comment on official attitudes to the missions. The report did not become a blueprint for change. The Conservative government closed ranks to protect itself — and Armitage.[81] It refused to accept Devlin's findings in full. MacLeod was, once again, disgusted by government inaction. He wrote to Dougall: 'There aint [*sic*] going to be no daring gesture'.[82]

In October MacLeod and Mackenzie issued a further report for the Special Committee Anent Central Africa. It included a plea for the release of detainees and for a new, 'more liberal' constitution for Nyasaland.[83] This plea had the effect only of stimulating anew the forces of reaction within the Kirk. Supporters of federation had by now had enough of MacLeod. They began to organise in earnest against him. Rennie organised a series of pro-federation public meetings in Scotland, hosted by staff from the federal high commis-

78. SOAS, CBMS, 570, Orchard, notes on meeting, 14 July 1959.

79. *Report of the Nyasaland Commission of Inquiry,* Cmnd. 814 (1959), p. 1.

80. *Report of the Nyasaland Commission of Inquiry,* p. 23.

81. *Nyasaland: Despatch of the Governor relating to the Report of the Nyasaland Commission of Inquiry,* Cmnd. 815 (1959).

82. NLS, B352, MacLeod to Dougall, 7 Sept. 1959.

83. NLS, B352, Special Committee Anent Central Africa, report, Oct. 1959.

sion in London.[84] Fergusson, together with Melville Dinwiddie, former head
of BBC Scotland, made plans to pack the Special Committee with new members sympathetic to the white settler point of view.[85] Meanwhile, Shepherd
made representations to the Special Committee and wrote letters and articles
to the Scottish press. Their combined efforts had the effect of weakening
MacLeod's influence. MacLeod's critics paid little attention to Dougall, who
continued to make quiet progress in his efforts to effect a rapprochement between missions and state in Nyasaland. Immediately following the publication of the Devlin Report he had written to Armitage, urging the governor to
meet with church and mission representatives.[86] Suspicious and mistrustful
of missions and church alike, Armitage had no desire to comply with this request.[87] Only after several months and then at the prompting of the Colonial
Office would he finally relent. By that time a general election had taken place
in Britain. Returned to office as head of a new Conservative administration in
October 1959, Harold Macmillan concluded that after a year of crisis in Africa
change in imperial and colonial policy was now imperative. He appointed
Iain Macleod to succeed the retiring Lennox-Boyd as Secretary of State for
Colonies.

Macleod was ambitious, driven and committed to change in colonial Africa. He had been born in Skipton, Yorkshire, in 1913. Both his parents were
Scots, and Macleod also came to regard himself as Scottish. But he had little
personal interest in the tribulations of either the Scottish missions or the
CCAP. Being inexperienced in colonial matters, he sought advice from many
unofficial quarters. Prior to his appointment he had met with David Stirling
of the Capricorn Africa Society. In November 1959 he would meet with Orton
Chirwa, one of the few Congress notables to have been released from detention. Subsequently, during 1960, he would rely for information on a friend of
Banda's, the American Quaker George Loft.[88] Macleod was well aware how
interested churches and missions were in central Africa affairs. One of his
first initiatives upon taking office, therefore, was to seek the views of their
representatives. He invited officials of the British Council of Churches and
the Conference of British Missionary Societies to the Colonial Office. Having
listened to their views on constitutional change and on detainees, Macleod
made his own purpose clear: he needed reliable information on Nyasaland,

84. TNA: PRO, CO 1015/1864, L. F. G. Anthony, 'Tour Report: Scotland, October 11-23,
1959'.
85. TNA: PRO, CO 1015/1864, M. Dinwiddie to C. Y. Carstairs, 3 Dec. 1959.
86. NLS, A141, Dougall to Sir R. Armitage, 31 July 1959.
87. TNA: PRO, CO 1015/1866, Armitage, notes on meeting with Bernard, 19 Aug. 1959.
88. TNA: PRO, CO 1015/2439, G. Loft to I. N. Macleod, 14 and 26 March 1960.

which the churches could help him acquire. His tone was conciliatory. His visitors were taken aback. There was no hint of the hostility towards missions that had typified the recent actions of the Nyasaland authorities. Nor was there any evasiveness, a characteristic of Lennox-Boyd's dealings with them on central Africa. Instead Macleod seemed willing to consider the release of detainees in the interests of political progress.[89] After the meeting, the church delegates rushed to convey to colleagues news of the apparently changed atmosphere in the Colonial Office. If MacLeod wanted information, who better to provide it than Fergus Macpherson, long-standing friend and confidant of Banda? Macpherson had recently returned to Scotland, to take up parish work in Greenock, near Glasgow. On 1 December, Macpherson, accompanied by George MacLeod and Rev. Alan Keighley of the BCC, met with Macleod. As in his testimony to the Devlin Commission, Macpherson emphasised Banda's 'good sense and moderation'. He appealed to Macleod for the release of detainees and for 'a more forward looking policy' for Nyasaland. In response, the new secretary of state was sweetly reasonable, and even flattering. He praised the Church of Scotland's efforts for reconciliation in central Africa, and admitted 'we cannot rule by bayonets'.[90] Two days later Macleod wrote to Macmillan, arguing that the emergency conditions in Nyasaland be ended. He had been influenced not merely by Macpherson but also by recent realisation within the Colonial Office that the state of emergency might contravene the European Convention on Human Rights.[91]

In light of these developments the Colonial Office encouraged Armitage to make formal contact with European and African clergy of the CCAP.[92] On 10 December a meeting finally took place. Dougall had high hopes for a successful outcome. But it was a protracted and at times ill-tempered affair, in which the ostensibly moderate Doig and Neil Bernard took the lead, with Doig now demanding of Armitage that Banda be released immediately.[93] Armitage would not countenance such a decision; but in reality he had little room for manoeuvre: within a week of his meeting with the CCAP representatives he found himself giving way to Iain Macleod's insistence that some detainees be released. Macleod continued to press the matter. Armitage (and

89. CBMS, 573, 'Federation Group papers' file, Keighley, notes on meeting, 12 Nov. 1959.

90. CBMS, 573, Keighley, notes on meeting, 1 Dec.; NLS, B352, Macpherson, report of meeting with Macleod to Special Committee Anent Central Africa, 2 Dec. 1959.

91. Simpson, 'The Devlin Commission', pp. 51-2.

92. TNA: PRO, CO 1015/1866, Lord Perth, minutes, 23 Oct. 1959.

93. TNA: PRO, CO 1015/1866, official notes of meeting between representatives of CCAP and of government of Nyasaland, 10-11 Dec. 1959.

Welensky also) protested, but to no avail. In late March 1960 Macleod journeyed to Nyasaland to expedite Banda's release, on 1 April.

George MacLeod was elated. The timing of the release was perfect. He suggested to church colleagues that Banda be invited to Scotland forthwith, to address the General Assembly.[94] The suggestion was not received altogether favourably. The mood within the Kirk had already begun to change, and not to MacLeod's advantage. For all those Scottish Presbyterians who might have welcomed Banda's release, there were many others who perceived it as a capitulation to extreme African nationalism. One man who thought this was Robert Shepherd. He had accepted an invitation from the government in London to serve on Lord Monckton's advisory commission on the federal constitution. The commission was currently visiting Nyasaland. Shepherd's involvement with its work now brought him into open dispute with missionaries supporting a call by Congress (now renamed the Malawi Congress Party — MCP) for Nyasaland Africans to boycott the commission. When the commissioners arrived at Livingstonia to take evidence, European and African clergy refused to participate. Neither would they meet with Shepherd individually. They snubbed him. Humiliated and angry, Shepherd wrote to Dougall that 'The Church of Central African Presbyterian seems to have "gone political" in the worst sense'.[95] In vain did Dougall protest in response that the church had to maintain 'its own position under Christ' and was 'no more subject to the Malawi Congress than it is afraid to criticise the policy of Federation'.[96] Shepherd fared a little better at Blantyre, where Doig alone agreed to meet with him. On his return to Scotland, Shepherd, with other supporters of federation and critics of MacLeod, succeeded in preventing full acceptance by the General Assembly of a further, critical Special Committee report. They were also able to expand the size of the Committee, and so dilute MacLeod's influence upon it.[97]

Shepherd and others in Scotland feared for the safety of Europeans in Nyasaland, and Banda's release exacerbated these fears. On 1 January 1960 the Church of Scotland's missions in Nyasaland had finally been 'integrated' into the CCAP. Ordained missionaries became clergy of the local church. That same month European settlers in the colony formed an association to campaign against the constitutional changes being planned by Iain Macleod.[98] The

94. *The Scotsman*, 22 April 1960.
95. NLS, B348, Rev. R. H. W. Shepherd to Dougall, 26 April 1960.
96. NLS, A141, Dougall to Shepherd, 28 April, and to Rev. A. C. Ross, 14 May 1960.
97. *The Scotsman*, 27 May 1960.
98. Robin Palmer, 'European Resistance to African Majority Rule: The Settlers' and Residents' Association of Nyasaland, 1960-63', *African Affairs* 72, no. 288 (1973): 256-72.

European congregations at Blantyre and Zomba remained stubbornly resistant to the 'integration' of mission into church. On the face of it, Banda's release from detention seemed to vindicate missionaries both 'moderate' and 'radical'. But no missionary was able to take complete satisfaction from this development. Banda's release precipitated intense jockeying for position and influence within Congress. Rival political parties were harassed and even interest groups sympathetic to but independent of Congress became targets for attack. The CCAP was no exception, and because of its mission origins was singled out: 'All churches are ONE AND THE SAME whatever their names', asserted Congress officials.[99] No one was immune from criticism, whether African or European. African clergy found themselves in an especially invidious position. Doig reported news of the attacks to Edinburgh: even missionaries sympathetic to Congress were now being ' "written off" as Capricornists'. The unquenchably outspoken McAdam, Doig noted, was currently 'No 2 on their list of enemies of Malawi, which just shows how things can change.'[100] As the Scots in Nyasaland were now discovering, it was not enough to be critical of federation, or of empire: Congress demanded unquestioning obedience of its members and supporters.

Anglican Missions and Church in Nyasaland and Northern Rhodesia

Within the UMCA and among the clergy of the Anglican diocese of Nyasaland, developments during 1959 caused incomprehension and horror. The mission had always eschewed involvement in political events. As befitted the apostolic tradition to which it resolutely adhered, all authority was vested in the bishop. Partly for that reason mission and diocesan affairs were characterised by what Andrew Porter has described as 'defensive isolationism'.[101] There were no plans, as in the Scottish missions, for devolution to African ecclesiastical leadership. Such reform as was initiated during the 1950s originated in London and was motivated primarily by the need to preserve a distinct Anglo-Catholic identity within the church in Africa. For UMCA general secretary Gerald Broomfield the Central African Federation, with its promise of 'partnership', had originally promised a stable environment in which the

99. John McCracken, 'Democracy and Nationalism in Historical Perspective: The Case of Malawi', *African Affairs* 97, no. 387 (1998): 242.

100. NLS, 9638, B114, Doig to Bernard, 28 July 1960.

101. Andrew Porter, 'The Universities' Mission to Central Africa: Anglo-Catholicism and the Twentieth Century Colonial Encounter', in Brian Stanley, ed., *Missions, Nationalism, and the End of Empire* (Grand Rapids, MI, and Cambridge, 2003), p. 99.

church might continue to grow, enhancing the spiritual lives of Christian individuals and communities, whatever their nationality or race.[102] The eventual formation of a new Anglican province, in 1955 (delayed because of controversy surrounding Central African Federation), gave cause for optimism. That same year, Joseph Oldham, now 80 years old, published a book, *New Hope in Africa*, to promote the 'multiracial' aims of the Capricorn African Party. Some missionaries approved. Others, like Broomfield, remained suspicious of African nationalism. In November 1958 Broomfield informed one colleague that '[i]t is a tragedy that Africans should blame the Church for Federation . . . the Church had nothing whatever to do with the proposals . . .'[103]

By then Frank Thorne was in the twenty-third year of his episcopate. Learned but in some ways unworldly, he loved Africa and its people, although in a paternal, even idealised way. Nyasalanders, he informed the Devlin Commission, were 'rather a Scottish body of people, stolid quiet folk'. He allowed that for some Africans intolerable conditions might perhaps have provoked thoughts of violence. But he had been mystified and troubled by news of the supposed murder plot.[104] Unfortunately for the bishop he had unquestioningly and unhesitatingly accepted the government's assertion that such a plot existed. Worse, in a diocesan magazine article of April 1959 he naïvely made this belief public.[105] It did him little good to state in the same article his conviction that most Africans, including Congress members, would have found the idea of a plot abhorrent. The article damaged irreparably his reputation in Nyasaland, and led to his denunciation by Congress.

In London meanwhile Gerald Broomfield was being forced to confront his assumptions about 'partnership'. Broomfield was one of a group of clergy who met with the visiting Welensky at the Commonwealth Relations Office in July 1959. He was taken aback by Welensky's bombastic and blustering indifference to African anxieties about white minority rule.[106] Shortly afterwards came news of further disturbing developments in relation to the church in Africa — this time from Northern Rhodesia. The authorities there, like their counterparts in Nyasaland, were now openly suspicious of mission links with African nationalism. Methodist mission reports to London indicated that action similar to that taken against Tom Colvin might now be di-

102. Gerald W. Broomfield, *Towards Freedom* (London, 1957), pp. 92-6.
103. RHL, Universities' Mission to Central Africa Papers (hereafter UMCA), SF 139, Canon G. W. Broomfield to Rev. V. R. D. Hellaby, 10 Nov. 1958.
104. RHL, DCP, 14, 8, 1819-24, testimony of Rt Rev. F. O. Thorne, 20 May 1959.
105. *Nyasaland Diocesan Chronicle* (April 1959).
106. SOAS, CBMS, 573, 'Federation Group papers' file, Broomfield, memo, 'Reflections on Interview with Sir Roy Welensky', 15 July 1959.

rected against the Methodist clergyman Colin Morris, based in Chingola.[107] Broomfield had recently drafted a secretarial message for UMCA staff and supporters, reaffirming his personal belief in 'partnership'. He now decided to seek advice on its final wording and also on the current situation in central Africa from a fellow-Anglican priest who had recently spent an extended period in Northern Rhodesia: John V. Taylor of the CMS.

In 1957, at the request of Max Warren and some lay Christians concerned about African affairs, Taylor had written *Christianity and Politics in Africa,* a Penguin paperback.[108] In this book he considered critically the theological and political implications for the church of condoning racism, both through the maintenance of segregated churches and through church leaders' reluctance to speak out on race and politics.[109] In March of that year Taylor made his first, brief visit to central Africa, to meet at Mufulira with Dorothea Lehmann of the local LMS mission. The World Council of Churches, in collaboration with the IMC, was commissioning research into the effects of 'rapid social change' upon churches and societies in Africa.[110] Taylor and Lehmann were deputed to investigate and report on the churches of Northern Rhodesia. Familiar with Africa only through Uganda, Taylor found Northern Rhodesia a very different sort of place. In the first instance, the effects of industrialisation upon African society appeared to him 'devastating'. The welfare efforts of government and of mining companies had met with little success. Racial problems were endemic. Taylor noted how Africans preferred 'what they regard as the honesty of the Afrikaans [*sic*] to the hypocrisy of the people of British stock'. Not only were the Protestant mission churches complacent, they were also prone to fissiparousness; the Lumpa Church was but the most notable example of this tendency.[111] Following this brief visit in 1957 Taylor returned to Northern Rhodesia in 1958 to commence the research project with Lehmann, and to study the situation in greater depth.

Between February and October 1958 Taylor and Lehmann travelled widely, in urban and rural Northern Rhodesia. They interviewed a great many people about their religious beliefs and about their attitude to social and political

107. NLS, B395, Rev. T. A. Beetham to Watt, 28 July 1959.

108. The laymen included the historian of Africa, Roland Oliver. He made a series of radio broadcasts for the BBC. These formed the basis of a book, with a foreword by Warren: *How Christian Is Africa?* (London, 1956).

109. J. V. Taylor, *Christianity and Politics in Africa* (Harmondsworth, 1957), pp. 15-16.

110. SOAS, CBMS, 558, 'The Common Christian Responsibility Towards Areas of Rapid Social Change' file, Rev. P. A. Abrecht, circular letter, 15 April 1955.

111. SOAS, CBMS, 536, 'Studies' file, Rev. J. V. Taylor, memo, 'First Impressions of Northern Rhodesia', June 1957.

matters. In Chingola Lehmann met with Alice Lenshina Mulenga. 'The prophetess', Lehmann would later write, 'looks a healthy, rather plump and happily relaxed village matron, a chief in her own right, as other women in her cultural stratum of matrilineal Bantu are chiefs through heritage. She is certainly not a medium, or psychopath, used by ruthless and politically ambitious men, as some have described her. Her sense of vocation is the firm foundation upon which her work is built'.[112] Lehmann was immensely impressed, not merely by Lenshina, but also by the services of the Lumpa Church, with their emphasis upon music and song, and by the care and craftsmanship that had been invested in the church's main temple in Kasomo, near Chinsali.

Taylor's view of Anglican missions and church in Northern Rhodesia was neither positive nor sanguine. Like Nyasaland, Northern Rhodesia was a 'UMCA diocese'; the first missions had been set up in 1910. For Taylor the church there faced huge problems. Some of these were doctrinal, such as the UMCA's unhelpful 'Roman' attitude to church unity. Hardly less problematic for Taylor were issues of race and politics. Church congregations were segregated. Like the colonial state the church, as an institution, appeared to be living in 'fear of African freedom'. It was now facing the consequences of its failure to take a stand with Africans on the federation issue in 1953.[113] Five years on, the church's attitude to federation, thought Taylor, was still characterised by equivocation. He developed his ideas in theological and sociological terms, both through correspondence with Broomfield and through writing up his part of the research project with Lehmann. For her it had primarily been a study of African independent churches. For him it became in part a means of confronting the church in Northern Rhodesia with its shortcomings. In April 1959 he began this process of confrontation privately, in response to Broomfield's request for his (Taylor's) views on the draft secretarial message to UMCA personnel and supporters. Taylor took particular issue with Broomfield's underestimation of African feeling about federation and the likely impact of that feeling on the church. He concluded his comments with a deeply personal observation:

> . . . I find myself seeing it in an eschatological light. . . . I cannot but believe that evil has gone too far in Central Africa for judgement to be avoided. . . . Only a miracle can produce in the white population what it takes to live in a real partnership with African fellow-citizens. Only a miracle now can give Africans the ability to forgive and trust once more

112. Lehmann, 'Alice Lenshina', pp. 254-5.
113. Taylor, 'First Impressions of Northern Rhodesia'.

... the Church must fail in her calling if she is not now preparing herself and her people to live through and under that judgement — sharing it inasmuch as she is herself involved in the guilt, and bearing it redemptively inasmuch as she is in Christ, and in a small degree, innocent — or less guilty — than society.[114]

Taylor would develop this theme further and at greater length, in his contributions to *Christians of the Copperbelt,* the book based on the research project and joint-authored with Lehmann.[115]

For Broomfield, impressed and perhaps a little chastened also, the UMCA might learn from Taylor's insight. He invited Taylor to address the UMCA general meeting for 1959.[116] Broomfield had continued to hope in the face of overwhelming evidence to the contrary that the 'ideals underlying the federal scheme' might yet be fulfilled. Gradually during 1959 he came to acknowledge as 'understandable' African recourse to violence in the face of what he now reluctantly accepted as European 'betrayal'.[117] Events during 1959 certainly focussed, and altered, Broomfield's thinking. But in Nyasaland the Anglican Church was much less well prepared for change than its Presbyterian counterpart. Thorne would retire in 1961. There was no prospect of an African successor, and it was far from clear that Africans in the diocese would welcome one.[118] Well might Broomfield assert to colleagues as he pondered the future, that '... the Mission as an organisation does not exist in Africa ...'[119] But the mission's identity had not been subsumed entirely within the church in Africa. And the UMCA still existed as a discrete mission organisation, in London as well as in Africa. During the course of the Nyasaland emergency (which ended in July 1960) Broomfield had to deal with myriad queries to his office about the mission's silence on political matters. Unwilling to subvert the bishop's authority through any official pronouncement, he resorted to personal letters to politicians, to *The Times* and to other publications in an attempt to demonstrate the commitment of the mission to African interests. It was a thoroughly unsatisfactory state of affairs.

114. RHL, UMCA, SF139, Taylor to Broomfield, 20 April 1959.

115. On Taylor's broader contribution to theology, see David Wood, *Poet, Priest and Prophet: The Life and Thought of Bishop John V. Taylor* (London, 2002).

116. J. V. Taylor, 'The Church in the Smelter', address to UMCA general meeting, 14 May 1959, *Central Africa* 77, nos. 920-21 (1959): 120-7.

117. G. W. Broomfield, *1960: Last Chance in the Federation* (London, 1960).

118. RHL, UMCA, SF113iA, Broomfield to Ven. C. Lacey, 29 March 1960.

119. RHL, UMCA, SF113iA, Broomfield, confidential memo, 'The Choice of a New Bishop of Nyasaland,' Advent 1959.

The Situation to 1960

The pace of change in the late 1950s was bewildering. 'I find it very difficult to make up my mind in political matters', admitted Dorothea Lehmann as unrest swept the Copperbelt.[120] The situation reminded her in some ways of Germany in the 1930s: political and trade union agitation and official repression of dissent.[121] Still, she believed that the church might fulfil a much more influential role in contemporary central Africa than it had in Germany two decades earlier. But women, she insisted, must play a larger part, beginning in the Church of Central Africa Rhodesia.[122] The United Missions had been wound up in 1955, its evangelistic work taken over by church organisations, its other responsibilities by a Copperbelt Christian Service Council. That same year the United Church of Canada committed financial resources and people to the CCAR.[123] To Lehmann's delight she was elected a church elder. The example of Lenshina then showed her what women might achieve, albeit in an independent African church. Lehmann was wary of politics, and politicians. So too was Lenshina; yet even in eschewing involvement in politics the Lumpa Church was arguably engaging in a political act, the more so as its growing support and authority undermined that of local chiefs in rural areas. Northern Rhodesian African politics assumed a more radical edge during 1958-59 when Kenneth Kaunda displaced Harry Nkumbula as most influential nationalist leader.[124]

These developments would in time have implications for the church in Northern Rhodesia. By the end of the 1950s, however, more and more missionaries were being forced by events to reconsider their attitude to African nationalism. In response to a request from Broomfield that he be signatory to a letter (on the subject of the Monckton Commission) to *The Times*, Trevor Huddleston wrote: 'African nationalists are capable of making up their own minds', and would 'rightly resent' any attempt by Christians in Britain to speak on their behalf. 'It would be an entirely different thing', Huddleston went on, 'if they could meet us round the table for a frank and full discussion'.[125] There seemed little likelihood of this. It was instead with British government ministers such as Iain Macleod and his successors rather than with

---

120. SOAS, CWM, AF14, Lehmann to Griffiths, 5 Nov. 1956.
121. SOAS, CWM, AF14, Lehmann to Griffiths, 5 Nov. 1956.
122. SOAS, CWM, AF45, Lehmann, report for LMS, Nov. 1956.
123. SOAS, CWM, AF42/66, Rev. D. H. Gallagher to Orchard, 16 June 1955. The CCAR became the United Church of Central Africa Rhodesia in 1958.
124. Roberts, *The Lumpa Church*, pp. 31-4.
125. RHL, UMCA, SF139, Fr E. U. T. Huddleston to Broomfield, 18 Dec. 1959.

representatives of missions and churches that African nationalists like Banda and Kaunda were having full and frank discussions. Having met twice with church and mission representatives in London in late 1959 Macleod subsequently avoided any further direct contact, leaving this to members of his staff.[126] When British Council of Churches officials did meet with a cabinet minister, Duncan Sandys, who was Commonwealth Secretary, in October 1960, they were subjected to a paean by him to the vigorous health of the Central African Federation and the corresponding unlikelihood of full adult suffrage being extended to Africans in the foreseeable future.[127] The report of the Monckton Commission, issued that month, acknowledged the possibility that territories of the Federation might be allowed to secede. Sandys' playing up of the Federation's prospects was an obligatory gesture in defiance. Learning that a federal review conference would take place in London in December, the BCC organised a reception for delegates at Lambeth Palace. The aim was to encourage interracial fellowship away from the negotiating table. The event did not achieve its aim. The review conference broke up unexpectedly early. All the African delegates returned home. The attendance at the reception was entirely European.[128] As had been the case for some time, developments in African colonial affairs exceeded the ability of British churchmen and missionaries to keep pace.

126. SOAS, CBMS, 573, 'Federation Group papers' file, Keighley, notes on meeting, 30 May 1960.

127. SOAS, CBMS, 573, Keighley, notes on deputation, 14 Oct. 1960.

128. SOAS, CBMS, 570, Federation Group, minutes, 10 Jan. 1961.

CHAPTER 5

Anglican Mission, Church, State and Mau Mau: Kenya, 1948-60

In the extent of the disagreement it caused, within missions and between missionaries and colonial governments, developments in central Africa during the 1950s were unique in the history of missions and the end of empire. Hugely controversial as it was in its own right, the situation in Kenya differed in many respects from that in the Central African Federation. At the time that the governor of Nyasaland, Sir Robert Armitage, instituted emergency regulations in March 1959, Kenya had been in a state of emergency for six and a half years. Colonial rule in the colony during this period was notable for its extraordinary harshness: the state hanged more than one thousand Kikuyu men, for capital crimes relating to Mau Mau activity. The period was also notable for certain attempts at political progress, through official encouragement of moderate African participation in 'multiracial' systems of government. State reliance on violence against Africans helped ensure that this encouragement would have limited success. Missionaries doubted government methods, and some were critical of the authorities. Yet missions participated in government-sponsored campaigns to rehabilitate Mau Mau detainees. Missionaries simultaneously worked with secular humanitarian agencies to assist the dependents of detainees. Their involvement in all these varied activities caused missionaries to query their relationship with the state and also with non-mission organisations committed to the relief of suffering rather

---

This chapter is based in part on John Stuart, 'Overseas Mission, Voluntary Service and Aid to Africa: Max Warren, the Church Missionary Society and Kenya, 1945-63', *Journal of Imperial and Commonwealth History* (hereafter *JICH*) 36, no. 3 (2008): 527-43.

than to evangelisation and the building up of the church. In certain important respects the missionary experience in late colonial Kenya would both presage and influence changes in the nature of missionary work at the end of empire in Africa, and also long after.

The missionary presence in east Africa famously predated late nineteenth-century European colonialism: Johann Krapf, representing the Church Missionary Society, had landed at Mombasa with his wife Rosine as early as 1844. By 1914 there were sixteen CMS mission stations, in east and central Kenya as well as on the Indian Ocean coastline. The arrival of Protestant missionaries of other denominations and nationalities precipitated nothing less than an 'intemperate missionary scramble', especially in Kikuyuland in central Kenya. However, friction between missionaries of the CMS and of the Church of Scotland was partly alleviated in 1902 through the first of many 'spheres of influence' agreements.[1] Thereafter, relations among Protestant missions were characterised both by doctrinal controversy, such as that stirred up in Anglican circles by the 1913 Kikuyu Conference on church union, and also by efforts at co-operation such as resulted in a 1918 'alliance' of Protestant missions agreed between the CMS, the Scots, the Methodists and the African Inland Mission, an organisation of American origin. In 1924 these and other missions formed a Kenya Mission Council. This body was superseded in 1943 by a Christian Council of Kenya.

These arrangements had little influence on relations between missionaries and the Kikuyu people. Those relations were often difficult, as the female circumcision and independent schools controversies of the late 1920s and 1930s demonstrated only too clearly.[2] Some missions were more affected than others by these controversies.[3] CMS missionaries were probably less willing than their counterparts in Scottish Presbyterian or other missions to lay down precise rules in relation to Kikuyu cultural practices. As a result their churches and schools arguably suffered less through African defection. Notably, it was in CMS missions, initially in Rwanda and Uganda and later in Kenya and beyond, that the east African Revival or 'Balokole' developed and grew.[4]

Among Protestant missions (which, from Britain, also included Method-

1. Robert W. Strayer, *The Making of Mission Communities in East Africa: Anglicans and Africans in Colonial Kenya, 1875-1935* (London, 1978), pp. 32, 41-7.

2. John Lonsdale, 'Kikuyu Christianities', *Journal of Religion in Africa* (hereafter *JRA*) 29, no. 2 (1999): 206-29.

3. Robert L. Tignor, *The Colonial Transformation of Kenya: The Kamba, Kikuyu, and Maasai from 1900 to 1939* (Princeton, 1976), pp. 203-72.

4. Kevin Ward, *A History of Global Anglicanism* (Cambridge, 2006), pp. 169-79.

ists), Anglicans and Scottish Presbyterians occupied an unusual position in Kenyan society: the colonial state accorded both a kind of 'quasi-established' status.[5] While missionaries represented African interests in the colony's legislative council, they might not be overtly critical of colonial rule. Outspoken missionary critics of colonialism were few. The most notable was probably Rev. Walter Owen of the CMS, Archdeacon of Kavirondo, 1918-45.[6] Missionaries did not in any case always set great store by outspokenness. More often they preferred to utilise personal contacts to effect social change for the benefit of Africans. This well-established tendency would become the subject of disagreement, particularly among Anglicans, during the emergency period. Contrary to what Caroline Elkins has suggested, mission and church representatives were prepared to criticise the Kenya administration.[7] Their criticism took varied form, however. It was not always consistent, and it had limited impact. In their criticism, missionaries were hardly more successful than secular critics of government. The impact of missionary criticism was blunted in part by the ambiguity of the relationship between missions and the colonial government, and also by disagreement between CMS missions and the Anglican diocese of Mombasa (which was coterminous with the colony of Kenya). The attitude of the CMS to matters such as rehabilitation and relief did not readily accord with that of the diocese. Nor did the more general aims and objectives of the Society, as articulated most notably by its general secretary Max Warren, always coincide with the priorities of Leonard James Beecher, the formidable Bishop of Mombasa. Notwithstanding the presence of other British missions in Kenya such as those of the Church of Scotland, this chapter's focus is on the CMS: Anglican missionaries figured prominently in what was and remains still the most controversial aspect of Britain's end of empire in Africa.

Max Warren and Anglican Mission in Kenya and East Africa

The postwar problems facing the CMS, as the largest British missionary society, were little different from those faced by all such bodies, Anglican and oth-

---

5. John Lonsdale, Stanley Booth-Clibborn and Andrew Hake, 'The Emerging Pattern of Church and State Co-operation in Kenya', in Edward Fasholé-Luke, Richard Gray, Adrian Hastings and Godwin Tasie, eds., *Christianity in Independent Africa* (London, 1978), pp. 268-9.

6. Leon P. Spencer, 'Christianity and Colonial Protest: Perceptions of W. E. Owen, Archdeacon of Kavirondo', *JRA* 13, no. 1 (1982): 47-60.

7. Caroline Elkins, *Britain's Gulag: The Brutal End of Empire in Africa* (London, 2005), pp. 298-303.

erwise. Yet the very size of the Society, as well as the extent of its overseas presence in Africa, East and Southeast Asia and the Middle East set it apart: with 980 missionaries on its books in 1948, the overseas staffing of the CMS was approximately double that of the LMS and the Church of Scotland missions combined. And the CMS had developed vast administrative systems to support those missionaries. The value of those systems had largely gone unquestioned in an organisation ostensibly committed to a self-supporting, self-sustaining, self-propagating church overseas. Following his appointment as general secretary in 1942, Max Warren (1904-77) instituted an overhaul of this institutional leviathan.

From the moment of his birth the CMS formed an integral part of Warren's life. His father John, a Church of Ireland clergyman, was a missionary in India, and an older brother of Warren's would serve in Uganda. In 1932 the CMS Africa secretary officiated at Warren's marriage, to Mary Collett. By this time Warren's own missionary service, in Nigeria, had been cut short by serious illness. Ordained also in 1932, Warren remained in close contact with the CMS, notably during his period as vicar of Holy Trinity, Cambridge. By the time of his appointment as general secretary he was very familiar with the CMS and its workings. D. W. Bebbington has identified Warren as a 'centrist', keen to work with a range of fellow-Anglican Evangelicals.[8] As an undergraduate at Jesus College, Cambridge he belonged both to the Christian Union and to the Student Christian Movement, each representing different strands of evangelical thought.[9] This duality went beyond theological matters. Warren had been born not in England (or in India, where he spent his early years), but in Dun Laoghaire, Co. Dublin, and he would mischievously contend that his 'Irishness' endowed him with a level of critical objectivity on matters of church, state and empire denied to fellow-missionaries of English birth.[10]

During the Second World War, and in common with other Christian thinkers in Britain, Warren feared the extent to which official planning for peace appeared likely to bring into being a 'Social Service State'.[11] The institutions of such a state would likely be intrusive, not the least consequence of which might be an overwhelming emphasis on the secular at the expense of

8. D. W. Bebbington, *Evangelicalism in Modern Britain: A History from the 1730s to the 1980s* (London, 1989), pp. 251-3.

9. Adrian Hastings, *A History of English Christianity, 1920-85* (London, 1986), p. 457.

10. M. A. C. Warren, *Caesar, the Beloved Enemy: Three Studies in the Relation of Church and State* (London, 1955), p. 71.

11. University of Birmingham Library Special Collections (hereafter UBL), Church Missionary Society Papers (hereafter CMS), AFg/AP4, Canon M. A. C. Warren, CMS memo, 'Our Society in the Calling of God' (1945).

the spiritual. For missionary societies, meanwhile, intrusive policies of colonial welfare and development would necessitate reorientation of strategy. This was not necessarily a completely bad thing. Too often in the past the CMS had proved unwisely ready to take on additional responsibilities, confident that by God's will the means to fulfilment would somehow become available. With characteristic hard-headedness, Warren's friend and confidant Kenneth Grubb argued, as CMS president in 1944, for a shift away from mission institutions 'many and fair', and a focussing of resources upon the 'few and excellent'.[12] In 1945 under Warren's direction the CMS began a process of 'realignment'.

Warren was committed, as had been his influential nineteenth-century predecessor Henry Venn, to the 'euthanasia' of mission.[13] But 'euthanasia' implied the death, as it were, of overseas mission only where mission could then become the responsibility of the local church. It did not imply that missionary societies such as the CMS should cease to exist. As envisaged by Warren the missionary society in Britain would continue to complement the church overseas. It would serve the need of indigenous churches for recruitment, training and fundraising. Warren strongly espoused voluntary overseas mission service by British men and women. He saw such service as a means primarily of evangelisation overseas but also as a means of individual, spiritual affirmation by British Christians living in the era of the 'Social Service State'. He approved of the arguments in favour of voluntarism that William Beveridge advanced in his book, *Voluntary Action* (1948).[14]

Yet from where in postwar Britain were overseas volunteers to be recruited? Missions encountered difficulty even in locating suitably qualified Christians for teaching and other work in Africa. In 1946 Protestant missions combined to devise a new employment category: the missionary associate. Typically a professional (especially in teaching) and a Christian, the associate would be contracted to work overseas for a specific period, of three to five years. A tireless advocate of mission as lifetime vocation, Warren nevertheless supported this initiative for the encouragement it might give to British laypeople.[15] The missionary associate scheme was a stop-gap. It failed to equip missions with sufficient human resources to respond to the postwar African clamour for education. In the late 1940s that clamour intensified. It

12. UBL, CMS, C/C1, 102, K. G. Grubb to CMS treasurer, 16 Oct. 1944.

13. On Venn, see C. Peter Williams, *The Ideal of the Self-Governing Church* (Leiden, 1990).

14. Lord Beveridge, *Voluntary Action: A Report on Methods of Social Advance* (London, 1948). Beveridge made no explicit reference to religious organisations in this work.

15. UBL, CMS, AFg AM13, Warren to C. W. Williams, 30 Sept. 1946.

was accompanied by African criticism of missions for their failure to fulfil desperately wanted educational needs.

It was in Kenya that the effects of this criticism upon CMS overseas missions were most keenly felt. It was there also that Warren subjected missions to the fullest rigours of 'realignment', in the interests of economy, efficiency and strategic planning. Missionaries in Kenya, denied what they considered their due in terms of finance and personnel, protested to headquarters, but in vain. Their hopes of increased resources had recently been raised by a report from the Colonial Office's Advisory Committee on Education in the Colonies. Entitled *Education for Citizenship in Africa*, this seemed to envisage missions as instrumental in the provision of education to African children. The colonial authorities in Nairobi subsequently appointed a Quaker, Thomas Askwith, to the new post of commissioner for community development. His appointment further fuelled missionary optimism. Their optimism would be short-lived. Askwith's plans and missionary expectations were similarly confounded by government ineptness, interdepartmental wrangling and, ultimately, lack of funds.[16]

Missionary unease about African criticism was indicative of wider perception among Europeans in Kenya that African society was in danger of communist-inspired collapse, perhaps into anarchy. A major dock strike took place in Mombasa in 1947. Government action against African squatters on European-owned land exacerbated racial tensions and stimulated migration especially to Nairobi, where overcrowding and crime became rife. The city was also the undisputed centre of militant African politics. For all these reasons missionaries in the colony became receptive to official ideas about making citizens of Africans, as especially suggested by the Colonial Office. Rev. Martin Capon of the CMS was a veteran of mission in Kenya. His views on African propensity for unrest were by no means untypical. In May 1949 Capon urged that missions work more closely with government to combat 'agitators' among the Kikuyu. By so doing missions could help 'produce the core of Christian citizens which alone can be an answer to any communist threat and the foundation for a continuance of the British way of life in Kenya'.[17] Education, Capon argued, was central to this process.

In January 1949 the government of Kenya formed a committee to inquire into the provision of education to Africans. Its members included European laypeople and clergy of various denominations, and the moderate Kikuyu pol-

---

16. Joanna Lewis, *Empire State-Building: War and Welfare in Colonial Kenya, 1925-52* (Oxford, 2000), pp. 330-40.

17. UBL, CMS, G/EW/5/7i, Rev. M. G. Capon, report, May 1949.

itician, Eliud Mathu. But the most important member of the committee was its chairman, Archdeacon Leonard Beecher. Born in London, Beecher (1906-87) came to Kenya as a mission teacher for the CMS at the age of only 21. He knew a good deal more about the colony and its people than the typical new mission recruit, for he was already affianced to Gladys Leakey, the Kenyan-born daughter of missionaries Harry and Mary Leakey and sister of palaeontologist Louis Leakey. Beecher and Gladys Leakey had met in London. They married in Kenya in 1930, in a ceremony notable for the presence of many Africans among the guests. With his wife's assistance and encouragement Beecher immersed himself in African languages and culture. By this time ordained, he took on a host of responsibilities, including those of nominated representative for African interests on the legislative council. In 1949 Beecher was one of the best-connected and best-informed Europeans in Kenya. As the work of the committee of enquiry into African education proceeded under his leadership, missionaries watched its progress with great interest.

The committee made its report in November 1949. It recommended an increased emphasis upon Christian teaching, as undertaken by the missions. Missions should work more closely with government on all aspects of African education, including teacher recruitment and training and school inspection. Together, these measures, according to the committee, would best remedy the recent 'breakdown in moral standards in African society . . .' Ultimately the aim of education in Kenya 'must be to produce at all levels of African society morally sound, economically valuable citizens'.[18] Historians' interpretation of the committee's findings has thus far focussed on the adverse African reaction. Africans were strongly critical, justifiably interpreting the committee as biased against the independent schools that had developed as a reaction against missions and mission education during the 1920s.[19] The Beecher Report gave further stimulus to Africans' sense of grievance. What of the missionary reaction? The report had a galvanising effect upon CMS missionaries in Kenya, who, with support from Beecher and from the diocese, began to draw up ambitious plans whereby the report's recommendations could be met — and even exceeded. This was not at all to Warren's liking. He deemed the proposals unrealistic and impractical and contrary to his own plans for a more focussed and efficient approach to mission. To Reginald Crabbe, Bishop of Mombasa, Warren wrote: '. . . you will be failing in your responsibility . . .

18. Kenya Colony and Protectorate, *African Education in Kenya* (Nairobi, 1949), pp. 55-78.

19. Derek R. Peterson, *Creative Writing: Translation, Bookkeeping and the Work of Imagination in Colonial Kenya* (Portsmouth, NH, 2004), pp. 193-5.

and frustrating your purposes . . . if you do accept the Government's propos-als . . . for we do not believe that you will be able to implement them . . . it will be found wisest to concentrate our resources and to resist the temptation to expand . . .'[20] Dispute ensued between Nairobi and London. The Kenya mis-sions aligned with the diocese, whose officials intimated their intention to mount a recruitment campaign for teaching staff independent of the CMS. Worried that developments in Kenya might precipitate 'unilateral' action on the part of missions elsewhere in Africa, Warren relented. In April 1951 he conceded that the CMS would work with other Protestant missions, the Insti-tute of Christian Education and the Colonial Office to recruit teachers and inspectors for Kenya. This decision led to a further small but significant de-velopment: the setting up early in 1952 of the Overseas Appointments Bureau. Supported by colonial development and welfare funds, this employment agency would place teaching staff in mission-run and other Christian schools overseas.[21] It would place only twenty teachers in its first year of operation, but it represented an alternative to the missionary society as recruiter of Brit-ish Christians for overseas educational work in Africa.

As the question of African education demonstrated, mission 'policy' could be the subject of contestation and even dispute. There was nothing un-usual about this. It was in part a consequence of CMS suspicion of episcopal authority, a characteristic evident in its origins as a voluntary society. Warren believed that bishops would invariably put diocesan interests ahead of those of the church at large. And CMS in London had no wish for the Society to be-come merely 'a feeder into a Diocesan machine', as its Africa secretary put it in correspondence with colleagues in Kenya.[22] What missionaries in Kenya wanted at this time were increased resources — mainly to expand educational provision for evangelistic purposes but also to counter radical nationalism and communism. Warren's unwillingness to commit resources rankled with those in Kenya. The effect was exacerbated by Warren's apparent eagerness (as it appeared from Kenya) to support mission in Sudan, and his imposition in 1948 of a Nairobi-based regional secretariat, to coordinate mission in Kenya, Uganda, Rwanda, Tanganyika and Sudan. That decision had been taken with-out reference to, much less consultation with, the Kenya mission secretary. In the circumstances it was not surprising that CMS missionaries in Kenya found the recommendations of the Beecher Report so congenial. Neither was

20. UBL, CMS, A5e1, Warren to Rt Rev. R. P. Crabbe, 27 Feb. 1951.

21. The National Archives of the UK: Public Record Office (hereafter TNA: PRO), CO 859/447, C. G. Gibbs to L. B. Greaves, 17 Jan. 1952.

22. UBL, CMS, A5e1, Canon T. F. C. Bewes to Ven. A. Stanway, 5 Sept. 1950.

it surprising that they were less concerned than colleagues in London as to how their support both for Beecher and for government plans for education might affect the relationship between missions and colonial authority.

State of Emergency in Kenya

By 1950 social and political unrest in Kenya was attracting increased attention outside Africa. In September of that year Fenner Brockway, the radical Labour MP, visited the colony. Brockway was co-founder of the Congress of Peoples against Imperialism. He was also a friend of Jomo Kenyatta, a Kikuyu and leader of Kenya's main political party, the Kenya African Union (KAU). In late 1951 two KAU representatives, Koinange wa Mbiyu and Achieng' Oneko, accompanied Brockway to Paris, to petition the United Nations on behalf of the Kikuyu, the largest ethnic group in Kenya. They subsequently travelled to London with the intention of petitioning Parliament on the subject of land reform. For CMS Africa secretary Canon Cecil Bewes, the presence of the two Kikuyu men in London represented an opportunity to learn at first hand more about the current situation in Kenya. Bewes (1902-92) had worked as a missionary in Kenya for almost twenty years before returning permanently to London in 1949. He corresponded regularly with the many Kikuyu he had befriended. Now he learned in conversation with Oneko in February 1952 that Africans despaired of missionaries because of their uncritical willingness to support government initiatives, in education and social affairs. Nor, it appeared, were missionaries actively supportive of African expressions of grievance. Here the contrast between their inaction and Brockway's energy and resourcefulness seemed especially apparent.[23] Brockway's parents had been missionaries in India. His sister Nora ran a Christian girls' college in Madras. Bewes took him seriously, and respected him for his advocacy of African interests. But Bewes was less worried about African support for Brockway than about Africans' perception that missions in Kenya were too close to government. Bewes had in mind the current situation in China, from where missionaries were being expelled because of their links — both real and imagined — with western imperialism. Might a similar eventuality occur in Africa? Bewes was prepared to consider the possibility. To a fellow veteran of mission in Kenya he confided that missionaries there might 'have to be as prepared as possible to hand over full control to Africans at the shortest possible notice'.[24]

23. UBL, CMS, O16/1, Bewes to Greaves, 21 Feb. 1952.
24. UBL, CMS, O16/1, Bewes to Greaves, 21 Feb. 1952.

Notwithstanding his meeting with Oneko and his regular correspondence with other Kikuyu, Bewes had little clear idea of the situation in Kenya in early 1952. What no one in the Kenya missions much less at CMS headquarters realised was the extent to which Kenyatta's authority was being undermined by militant elements within the KAU. African politics was increasingly characterised not only by radicalisation but also by criminality and extreme violence.[25] In August 1950 the government had banned an organisation known then to the police as 'the Mau Mau Society'. But the authorities, including the governor, Sir Philip Mitchell, were unable to comprehend either the nature or the scale of rebellion, spread via secret oathing ceremonies. With the assistance of Kikuyu chiefs and elders the government launched a 'counter-oathing' campaign. African clergy denounced oathing. As a result, Mau Mau adherents attacked Kikuyu Christians as well as other Kikuyu loyalists — government employees and those deemed sympathetic to government. A wave of assaults, arson and murder swept Kikuyuland during 1952. European settlers clamoured for action in response. Incapable of effective leadership and due for retirement, Mitchell left office in June 1952. One of his valedictory actions was to warn missionaries against involvement (in the manner of Michael Scott) in political agitation.[26] His successor, Sir Evelyn Baring, would not arrive in Nairobi until the last day of September. During the interregnum the situation in Kenya worsened. Three weeks after his arrival Baring declared a state of emergency. Kenyatta and many other Africans were detained without trial. Kenyatta would ultimately spend more than eight years in custody.

Now assistant bishop, Leonard Beecher was assuming an increasingly influential role in Kenyan society. Bishop Crabbe (1883-1964) would soon retire and in mid-1952 was away from Kenya, on an extended visit to Tanganyika and Egypt. It seemed to Beecher that the worsening situation in Kikuyuland demanded an unambiguous response from the church. In August he appealed to the CMS and to the church in England for support to spread the gospel more widely among the Kikuyu. By such means, he argued, might the pernicious effects of oathing be combatted and support given to "revived" Kikuyu Christians, some of whom had already paid for their faith with their lives.[27] To Beecher, Mau Mau seemed to be a violent outgrowth of a 'politico-

25. David Anderson, *Histories of the Hanged: Britain's Dirty War in Kenya and the End of the Empire* (London, 2005), pp. 9-53.

26. School of Oriental and African Studies, London (hereafter SOAS), Conference of British Missionary Societies Papers (hereafter CBMS), 274, Christian Council of Kenya (hereafter CCK), minutes, Sir P. Mitchell, address, 8 May 1952.

27. UBL, CMS, A5/6/1, Ken L. J. Beecher, personal newsletter, Aug. 1952.

religious' cult, with its origins in what appeared as syncretistic and separatist tendencies within African religion.[28] He was in little doubt that Christian missions and churches had contributed to the situation, through failures of understanding and inadequate primary evangelism. Through the restoration of Christian faith among the Kikuyu the situation might, however, be stabilised and then remedied. Government action would also be necessary, and Beecher approved of the state-supported counter-oathing initiatives undertaken by 'loyal' chiefs.

Churches and missions deployed Christian theology against Mau Mau. In late 1952 missionaries and African clergy formulated a religious service of 'confession' or 'cleansing' for Christians who had taken the Mau Mau oath. The idea had sprung from within the Kikuyu church, in places such as Kahuhia and Weithaga in the Fort Hall district. Rev. Obadiah Kariuki (c.1902-78), rural dean at Weithaga, strongly advocated the service as a means whereby Revival within the African church could also be further encouraged. Using information from the Fort Hall area, the Australian-born CMS missionary Rev. Keith Cole devised a method of service. Beecher ordered circulation of the details throughout the diocese. At his insistence, there was to be no 'pushing of the issue'; any penitent should confess their sin willingly, to priest, elders and congregation, and commit, again willingly, to observance of their Christian faith. The confession might take the following oral form.

> I confess to God Almighty, the Father, the Son, and the Holy Ghost, that I have sinned through my own fault in having taken a heathen oath which I most earnestly believe to be contrary to God's most holy law; I truly repent, and pray God to have mercy upon me, to cleanse and purify me through the blood of Christ my Saviour, who died on the Cross that I might cease from sinning, and I pray that, in the power of God, the Holy Spirit, I may be enabled to live faithfully in accordance with God's will and commandments.[29]

The service of 'confession' or 'cleansing' would constitute a significant aspect of the church's response to Mau Mau. However, Beecher was now more than ever conscious of a lack of resources. In November 1952 he wrote to Geoffrey Fisher, Archbishop of Canterbury.[30] He followed this message up

---

28. Lambeth Palace Library, London (hereafter LPL), Fisher Papers (hereafter FP), 105, Beecher, personal newsletter, Feb. 1952.

29. UBL, CMS, A5/6/1, unsigned memo, 'The Restitution of Church Members Who Have Taken the Mau Mau Oath', n.d., but Nov. 1952; Beecher, circular letter, 26 Nov. 1952.

30. LPL, FP, 102, Beecher to Most Rev. G. F. Fisher, 11 Nov. 1952.

three months later with a plea that an evangelistic 'task force' be despatched from England to Kenya.[31] Fisher took a close interest in African colonial affairs.[32] Both he and Warren reacted positively to Beecher's entreaty.[33] Accordingly, on 5 December the CMS published a special pamphlet entitled *Mau Mau — What Is It?* This document, aimed at the British public in general as well as CMS supporters, attempted to explain the circumstances that had contributed to the current situation in Kenya. It referred to African difficulties connected with land ownership, unemployment and race discrimination. It described Mau Mau as 'an evil but not surprising echo from a very recent savage past'. The pamphlet's main message was an appeal for volunteers from Britain, such as teachers, to work in Kenya and for £7,000 to assist church and mission work in the colony.[34] The CMS would forward funds to Beecher for use as he and his church colleagues in Kenya saw fit.

The appeal for funds was successful, and quickly met its target. It inspired the Foreign Missions Committee of the Church of Scotland to launch a similar though less rewarding initiative that brought in almost £2,000. Anglicans in London discussed with colleagues in Nairobi how they might demonstrate in other ways their concern for and commitment to the Christian Kikuyu. It was decided that Bewes should make an official visit to Kenya, on behalf of the Archbishop of Canterbury. Bewes' main role would be that of envoy, but at Warren's insistence he would carry out another important task: gathering information not only about church and mission affairs, but also on matters relating to the conduct of the security forces. To CMS officials, the British press were reporting Kenyan events in sensationalist and biased terms. Such information as emanated from the authorities in Nairobi appeared of doubtful accuracy. It was therefore vital, Warren reasoned, that Bewes utilise his good offices and his personal contacts to ascertain the true nature of the situation. This was particularly the case where official maltreatment of Africans was suspected. Even Fisher had been perturbed by reports from Kenya that referred to the phenomenon of 'collective punishment' of detainees. Prior to Bewes' departure he was briefed by the CMS information officer, Bernard Nicholls, who was responsible for press and public relations and who had written the pamphlet *Mau Mau — What Is It?* Nicholls emphasised the Society's obligations to ensure the upholding of 'human rights and liberties' in Africa. He advised

31. LPL, FP, 127, Beecher to Fisher, with confidential enclosure 'The Church's Response to the Challenge of Mau Mau', 10 Feb. 1953.

32. Sarah Stockwell, "'Splendidly Leading the Way'? Archbishop Fisher and Decolonisation in British Colonial Africa", *JICH* 36, no. 3 (2008): 545-64.

33. LPL, FP, 102, Warren to Fisher, 3 Dec. 1952.

34. Church Missionary Society, *Mau Mau — What Is It?* (London, 1952).

Bewes to ensure '. . . that we are not led unawares into the position of appearing (by absence of comment or criticism) to condone emergency regulations which are responsibly judged in due course to be beyond the limit of compromise and conscience'.[35] Nicholls had previously worked for the Associated Press news agency in London. He well knew the value of publicity. He was determined that Bewes should not only ascertain the facts about Kenya, but that the Society should also make those facts known publicly.

Bewes sympathised with the incomprehension and anxiety that missionaries in Kenya felt, and which they expressed in their correspondence to him. But he worried about their readiness to regard Mau Mau as a local or even isolated phenomenon and their willingness to condemn African nationalism and individual nationalists such as Kenyatta out of hand. The retired Anglican bishop Walter Carey, who lived at Kitale in east Kenya, dismayed CMS headquarters with his intemperate condemnation of Mau Mau.[36] Warren by now knew that the danger to missionaries was slight compared with that currently being experienced by Christian and other Kikuyu. In November 1952 a friend of Bewes, Rev. David (Daudi) Petero, had written to him (and also to Warren) from Embu, northeast of Nairobi. Arsonists had attacked his home, although he and his family had escaped. Petero's message was stark and simple: 'We need your prayer and help'.[37] Even before his arrival in Kenya, on 7 January 1953, Bewes was determined that voices such as Petero's should be heard in Britain.

To begin with, however, Bewes had first to make heard in Kenya the words (if not the voice) of Geoffrey Fisher. The archbishop had entrusted him with a personal written message of support for the Christian Kikuyu. At the Nairobi premises of the government's information office Bewes made a sound recording of the message, in English, for broadcast purposes. Gladys Beecher recorded a version in Kikuyu, which, as well as subsequently being broadcast, was also transferred to vinyl disc to be played directly to African audiences. Bewes then set off on his mission, in Nairobi and beyond. He would publish later in 1953 a largely celebratory account of his three-week visit. This book, *Kikuyu Conflict*, was also in part a work of martyr literature, in which Bewes attempted to give voice to Africans' experiences, both good and bad. He also emphasised the importance of their taking 'a creative and responsible part in political activity'.[38] In other published writings Bewes acknowledged what 'a

35. UBL, CMS, A5/6/2, B. D. Nicholls to Bewes, 7 Jan. 1953.
36. Bishop Walter Carey, *Crisis in Kenya: Christian Common Sense on Mau Mau and the Colour-Bar* (London, 1953); LPL, FP, 120, Warren to Fisher, 14 Jan. 1953. The London *Evening Standard* also published Carey's opinions.
37. UBL, CMS, A5/6/1, Rev. D. Petero to Warren, 17 Nov. 1952.
38. T. F. C. Bewes, *Kikuyu Conflict: Mau Mau and the Christian Witness* (London, 1953).

proud and humbling experience' it had been for him 'to witness the joy and the courage, the radiance and the fire of the Church in persecution'.[39] He could hardly report openly (as he did privately instead, in his journal) that African clergy might be regarded as '"white men's stooges"', that Kikuyu in the slums of Nairobi might be 'hard and bitter' or that clergy could accuse the missions of disinterest in devolution of ecclesiastical authority: according to Kariuki '. . . you missionaries think that by laying down a task and letting an African pick it up you have devolved'.[40] For all that, Bewes was genuinely impressed by Kikuyu Christian resilience and resolve.

But Kenya was a colony at war with itself. Loyal chiefs, urged on by government, encouraged the formation of a Kikuyu Home Guard that would eventually number more than 25,000 recruits. To some missionaries this gave evidence, initially at least, of active Christian resistance to Mau Mau. But the Home Guard was 'a rag-bag' army, the members of which were not necessarily loyal to church, to state or even to their chiefs.[41] It did not take Bewes long to learn details of violence by African against African, and by police and (British) army personnel against Mau Mau suspects. Having interviewed a number of men who had suffered police beatings, he raised the matter personally with Governor Baring. All the time Bewes maintained close contact with Warren; he it was who urged Bewes to obtain and present to the governor 'incontrovertible evidence' of police brutality.[42] Warren then decided that Bewes, on his return to London, should make publicly known what was actually occurring under emergency conditions in Kenya. Nicholls organised a press conference at CMS headquarters in Salisbury Square, London EC4 for 9 February, explaining to colleagues that 'It cannot be long before the truth — or worse — a garbled version of the truth — gets out. Then will come a day of reckoning if CMS appears to have "suppressed" such information'.[43] At the press conference Bewes presented to journalists a sober, even restrained account of what he described as unjustifiable lapses of discipline and of behaviour by the security forces. He refused to divulge details of specific instances of abuse, explaining that he had already presented these to Baring, who had promised to take action. He also explained his intention to inform Fisher.[44] Subsequently, Fisher contacted the Colonial Office and se-

39. T. F. C. Bewes, 'The Work of the Christian Church among the Kikuyu', *International Affairs* 29, no. 3 (1953): 324.

40. UBL, CMS, A5/6/2, Bewes, journal of visit to Kenya, 7 Jan.-2 Feb. 1953, I, 5; III, 7; VI, 5.

41. Anderson, *Histories of the Hanged,* pp. 238-43.

42. UBL, CMS, A5/6/1, Warren to Bewes, 23 Jan. 1953.

43. UBL, CMS, A5/6/2, Nicholls, memo, 5 Feb. 1953.

44. *The Times,* 10 Feb. 1953.

cured the attendance at Lambeth Palace of the secretary of state, Oliver Lyttelton, who heard Bewes' report at first hand. In Nairobi meanwhile Baring, who had failed to act in the aftermath of his meeting with Bewes, issued belatedly and for the sake of appearances a directive to the security forces on methods of interrogation.

In June 1953 Warren contacted Bewes: 'we have made our point about police misbehaviour. . . . Parliament is on to it, & Lyttelton will get no peace. . . . We've made our negative criticisms. I think the time calls for a constructive approach as well.'[45] Since his return to Britain four months earlier Bewes had discreetly pursued his own inquiries into certain cases of police brutality. He had personal as well as professional reasons for doing so in the case of Elijah Njeru, beaten to death in January: Njeru was a nephew of his friend David Petero. Due in part to Bewes' persistence the two police reserve officers responsible for the beating were eventually convicted, although punished only by a fine.[46] Anglican leaders in London and Nairobi felt that Baring and his administration should now be allowed to get on with defeating Mau Mau.

In April 1953 an important matter of church leadership was clarified, with Beecher's enthronement as bishop of Mombasa. Nominally at least this gave him equal ecclesiastical (and political) status in the colony with the moderator of the Church of Scotland in East Africa, Rev. David Steel (1910-2002).[47] But Beecher regarded himself as *primus inter pares,* not least because of his experience and expertise in Kenyan affairs. He regarded Steel (four years younger and resident in Kenya since 1949) almost as a neophyte where Africa was concerned. Beecher, in contrast, *knew* Kenya and its people and he was committed to African advancement, in governmental and in church affairs. He was a man of immense energy, determination and single-mindedness. He was pragmatic, and good with money. He was compassionate, but he was also high-minded, and prickly with it. In late October 1952, ten days after the declaration of a state of emergency, Oliver Lyttelton made an official visit to Kenya. Among those he met with were church and mission representatives of various denominations, who expressed to him their concern about police behaviour. Beecher's attitude towards the secretary of state was one of menace mixed with hostility: 'Do not think of us as a crowd of amateur politicians', he warned Lyttelton; 'we are concerned in these things because as ministers to both black and white we feel we have certain civic responsibilities as well as

45. UBL, CMS, A5/6/1, Warren to Bewes, 7 June 1953.
46. UBL, CMS, A5/6/1, Bewes to Beecher, 1 Oct. 1953.
47. On Presbyterian Church developments in Kenya, see Robert MacPherson, *The Presbyterian Church in Kenya: An Account of the Origins and Growth of the Presbyterian Church of East Aftica* (Nairobi, 1970).

spiritual ones'.[48] Lyttelton was brusque and businesslike. Beecher thought him uninterested in and incapable of understanding the complexities of the situation in Kenya.[49] Conversely, Beecher would be untiring and unstinting in his support of Baring, whom he considered a decent Christian man faced with a hugely difficult task. It mattered not to Beecher that the Barings (and more particularly Lady Baring) were Anglo-Catholic in their religious outlook: the governor, he believed, should be able to count on the support of the church in the conduct of his work. This did not mean that the church should refrain from criticism of either governor or administration. But it did mean that the church should offer criticism only in terms that were helpful and not harmful to gubernatorial authority. As the emergency continued, a divergence of opinion would develop on this point between the diocese in Kenya and mission headquarters in London.

Rehabilitation

John Casson has noted how missionaries found in the resilience of the Christian Kikuyu 'new grounds to assert the essential part which Christian faith, and specifically missionary enterprise, must play in the African future'. It was in the aftermath of the massacre by Mau Mau of 120 loyal Kikuyu at Lari in late March 1953 that missionaries began in earnest to reformulate in theological terms not only the importance of the Christian Kikuyu to the church but also the origins of Mau Mau itself.[50] The horror of Lari demonstrated the necessity of moving beyond conceptualisation of Mau Mau as 'African' and thence by implication 'evil', towards an interpretation based on remedying the harmful effects of westernisation upon the Kikuyu. Missionary aims coincided to a notable degree with those of a colonial state intent on remaking Kenyan African society. Nowhere was this co-incidence more apparent than in relation to the controversial idea of rehabilitation.

During the first six months of the Emergency thousands of Africans suspected of Mau Mau involvement were confined to detention camps. Only a few were ever likely to be convicted of indictable offences. Many, if not most, were considered by the authorities to be strongly susceptible to the doctrines

48. TNA: PRO, CO 822/460, official report of meeting, Government House, Nairobi, 31 Oct. 1952.

49. LPL, FP, 102, Beecher to Fisher, 11 Nov. 1952.

50. John Casson, 'Missionaries, Mau Mau and the Christian Frontier', in Pieter N. Holtrop and Hugh McLeod, eds., *Missions and Missionaries* (Woodbridge, 2000), pp. 205-7, 210.

of Mau Mau. For that reason the government of Kenya began during 1953 to consider by what means detainees could be persuaded to renounce their supposed allegiance to the movement. It took some time for systems and methods of rehabilitation to be formulated. It is clear from the outset that the government envisaged the process as to some degree punitive as well as remedial. Detainees would receive education and training, to facilitate their re-entry and re-absorption back into society upon release. But while in detention they would be required to undertake physical labour.[51] And rehabilitation constituted part of a much broader strategy for dealing with Mau Mau. It would complement official schemes of land reform (and land confiscation) and, subsequently also, of forced villagisation, which was intended to physically separate Mau Mau activists from their families and supporters.[52] Official discourse on rehabilitation was sometimes couched in quasi-religious terms with the reintegration of rehabilitated Kikuyu into Kenyan African society likened to their being brought back into '"the body of the kirk"'.[53] In terms of intended outcomes (as distinct from methods), rehabilitation as envisaged by the authorities in 1953 did not seem greatly different in some respects from those ceremonies of 'cleansing' and 'confession' devised by Anglican clergy for use among the Kikuyu. From the outset missionaries expressed great interest in the transformative potential of the process.

It was not the CMS (or the missions of the Church of Scotland) but rather the Kenya branch of Moral Re-Armament (MRA) that first attempted to conduct rehabilitation along explicitly Christian lines. An international, interdenominational body set up in 1938 by the American pastor Frank Buchman, MRA, according to Philip Boobyer, 'can partly be seen as Buchman's attempt to universalize a personal spiritual experience of the cross, and to show its relevance to international as well as spiritual life'.[54] MRA was also active in central Africa and parts of north Africa. The government entrusted its Kenya branch with the rehabilitation programme at Athi River detention camp, southeast of Nairobi. A CMS missionary, Rev. Howard Church, was seconded to the camp and worked there for nine months.[55] MRA made innovative use of music and drama at Athi River; but it had limited success in persuading detainees to renounce their oaths. The govern-

---

51. TNA: PRO, CO 822/703, Sir E. Baring to O. Lyttelton, 24 June 1953.

52. M. P. K. Sorrensen, *Land Reform in the Kikuyu Country* (Nairobi, 1967), pp. 104-10.

53. *The Times*, 16 Dec. 1952.

54. Philip Boobyer, 'Moral Re-armament in Africa in the Era of Decolonization', in Brian Stanley, ed., *Missions, Nationalism, and the End of Empire* (Grand Rapids, MI, and Cambridge, 2003), p. 216.

55. UBL, CMS, A5/6/1, Rev. H. J. Church, personal newsletter, Sept. 1953.

ment closed the camp in 1956.[56] Notwithstanding Howard Church's involvement with the organisation, other CMS missionaries were sceptical of MRA for what they perceived as its emphasis upon indoctrination rather than evangelisation. Yet missionaries were also uncertain how readily their own techniques of 'confession' and 'cleansing' might be adapted to rehabilitative use, as the government now appeared to think possible. As Bewes noted, any person undergoing 'cleansing' had by definition to be Christian, and not 'pagan'.[57] The church, he considered, could not 'cleanse' non-Christians: '. . . it would be a mockery to attempt it. It can only preach the Gospel to them'.[58] It was one thing for a non-Christian Mau Mau adherent to deny his or her oath; it was quite another for them to commit unequivocally to Christ. How was it possible that rehabilitation might somehow constitute some form of evangelistic activity? In 1953 it was by no means clear to missionaries what the government even understood rehabilitation to entail.

From mid-1953 the authorities in Nairobi began to consider in greater detail what rehabilitation might mean in practice. For advice on the causes of Mau Mau and on how it might be overcome they relied upon people such as Louis Leakey and the British psychiatrist J. C. Carothers, both of whom produced influential written works on the matter.[59] Rather more influential in terms of mission and church involvement in rehabilitation would be advice provided from within the colonial administration by commissioner for community development Thomas Askwith. In August he was sent to Malaya to study the 'hearts and minds' methods utilised against communist insurgents by high commissioner Sir Gerald Templer. Such methods, Askwith later discerned, would be of limited use in Kenya, the circumstances there being different from those in southeast Asia. For Askwith rehabilitation was primarily a means by which 'moral values' might be re-established among the Kikuyu, especially through education and through training in economically useful skills. He regarded as essential participation by missions and churches in the process.[60] In this view he was supported by Baring who, almost from the moment of his arrival in Kenya, invariably characterised Mau Mau as 'anti-Christian' and 'anti-mission'.[61] At a meeting in Government House, Nairobi, on 2 October official plans were made for rehabilitation. Askwith (now designated commissioner for community

56. Boobyer, 'Moral Re-armament', pp. 223-7.
57. UBL, CMS, A5/6/1, Bewes to Rev. E. Jay, 1 Jan. 1953.
58. UBL, CMS, A5/6/2, Bewes, journal, III, 3.
59. Anderson, *Histories of the Hanged*, pp. 281-4; Elkins, *Britain's Gulag*, pp. 106-11.
60. TNA: PRO, CO 822/794, T. G. Askwith, memo on rehabilitation, 6 Jan. 1954.
61. TNA PRO, CO 822/444, Baring to Lyttelton, 9 Oct., and 18 Oct. 1953.

development and rehabilitation) would contact religious organisations to enlist their assistance.[62]

As Elkins has noted, rehabilitation was not intended by Askwith to be a mandate for conversion (or reconversion) of the Kikuyu to Christianity. But Askwith did wish to instil in the Kikuyu moral social values best represented, as far as the needs of the state were concerned, by Christianity.[63] Askwith's wishes coincided closely with those of Baring. Beecher also perceived rehabilitation as important. In November 1953 he delivered a charge to the diocesan synod, stating that '. . . it is not too soon to impress upon the Government both of City and of State, that their plans for rehabilitation and advance as well as those of the Church must be formulated explicitly now'. The authorities, he emphasised, must also ensure the restoration of law and order. The church, Beecher asserted, would meanwhile work on its own account and also with government 'to bring an end to all those negative aspects of racialism which hinder the development of true partnership on this land'.[64]

Beecher was in no doubt that faced with the challenge of Mau Mau, the church was undergoing trial. It had to stand firm. It also had to use whatever resources it could muster to assert itself in the interests both of the Christian Kikuyu and of the wider Christian community in Kenya. In his charge Beecher acknowledged how vital had already been support from external Christian sources, notably the £7,000 raised by CMS through its appeal — not for mission as such but for the work of the diocese. More funds would now be required. Askwith too believed that rehabilitation work would necessitate funding from unofficial external sources: the Society of Friends, he informed his contacts within the administration and at the Colonial Office, 'may well be prepared to help'.[65] In January 1954 Baring approved in principle Askwith's proposals for rehabilitation. In February Askwith met with representatives of the Christian Council of Kenya to inform them that the government would support church work for rehabilitation.[66] The Council co-opted him onto a committee that would facilitate its member organisations' involvement in the new enterprise. Askwith would also develop links with the Roman Catholic Church in Kenya. Rehabilitation, according to Baring's dep-

62. TNA PRO, CO 822/703, minutes of meeting at Government House, Nairobi, 2 Oct. 1953.

63. Caroline Elkins, 'The Struggle for Mau Mau Rehabilitation in Late Colonial Kenya', *International Journal of African Historical Studies* 33, no. 1 (2000): 38-9.

64. TNA: PRO, CO 822/441, Beecher, charge to Mombasa diocesan synod, 10 Nov. 1953.

65. TNA: PRO, CO 822/794, Askwith, memo on rehabilitation, 6 Jan. 1954.

66. SOAS, CBMS, 274, CCK, executive committee minutes, 25 Feb. 1954.

uty, Sir Frederick Crawford, would be '. . . a combined operation between the Government and the Church'.[67]

For Beecher rehabilitation was a vital adjunct to the work of the church. Consequently he believed that its educational and social-work aspects should be carried out by Christians. But neither diocese nor mission had personnel available for extra activities beyond those focussed on 'confession' and 'cleansing'. In late March 1954 Beecher travelled to England, ostensibly on furlough. Over the course of a two-month stay he rested little but instead campaigned forcefully for funds and for workers in the detention camps, in the villages and in urban areas. He addressed a CMS rally at Earls Court, London. He met with MPs. He conducted interviews with the press and with the BBC. He left the many audiences to which he spoke in no doubt that he regarded as vital their involvement at this time in remaking Kenya's future. Beecher wanted Christian workers for rehabilitation projects. He also wanted volunteers prepared to work in the service of the church in Kenya. Addressing the Conference of British Missionary Societies, he identified three main priorities for the church: evangelism; the training of African Christian leaders; and work among women. Kenya, he insisted, was at a turning point in its history: 'it would never be the same country again'.[68] Beecher's energy was fuelled primarily by his concern for the Christian Kikuyu and for the future of the church in Kenya. But his energy was also fuelled by indignation, directed at none other than Oliver Lyttelton. Shortly before Beecher's departure for London, Lyttelton visited Kenya again, and imposed on the colony a new constitution intended to stimulate moderate African involvement in politics.[69] Both Beecher and Steel attempted to meet with him, to put the churches' point of view. Lyttelton snubbed them both. Beecher was outraged: Lyttelton, he stormed, was 'stupid and wrong' to disregard the churches in this way.[70] With its niggardly concessions to African political aspirations the new constitution confirmed Beecher's suspicions about the secretary of state's inability to understand the situation in Kenya and the necessity of greater African involvement in its administration. While in London Beecher visited the Colonial Office and harangued Lyttelton about African under-representation in the updated administrative structures. He made little impression, and evoked no useful response. He departed the encounter 'utterly dejected'.[71]

67. TNA: PRO, CO 822/794, Sir F. Crawford to Lyttelton, 14 June 1954.

68. SOAS, CBMS, 235, CBMS Africa committee minutes, 30 April 1954.

69. B. A. Ogot, 'The Decisive Years, 1956-63', in B. A. Ogot and W. R. Ochieng', eds., *Decolonization and Independence in Kenya, 1940-93* (London, 1995), p. 51.

70. LPL, FP, 143, Fisher, notes of conversation with Beecher, 2 April 1954.

71. LPL, FP, 143, Beecher to Lyttelton, 13 April 1954.

Beecher did not trust Lyttelton to instigate meaningful political progress in Kenya. This strengthened his conviction that Baring should be supported and that the church should take a more active role in social matters. During Beecher's London sojourn, however, developments occurred in Kenya that would have important consequences for the Kikuyu and also for church and mission involvement in rehabilitation. Beecher was less than fully aware of the extent to which the government's struggle against Mau Mau was at this time still being conceived in military terms. In March an official War Council was formed in Nairobi, composed of Baring, army commander-in-chief General Sir George Erskine and settler representative Michael Blundell. On 24 April the authorities unleashed Operation Anvil, an enormous military undertaking. More than 20,000 Africans were rounded up and sent to reception camps, joining tens of thousands of other inmates already waiting to be screened or graded according to the supposed extent of their loyalty to Mau Mau. Conditions in the camps, already terrible, worsened greatly. The authorities struggled to cope and detainees became subject not only to overcrowding, hunger and disease but also to violence indiscriminately meted out by security personnel. In such circumstances rehabilitation could not be expedited along the reformist lines envisaged by the likes of Beecher and Askwith: in the hands of untrained, undisciplined and unaccountable security and detention staff the process would become excessively, even brutally, punitive rather than remedial.

Religious and Humanitarian Intervention and the 1955 Kenya Appeal

By 1953 the state of emergency in Kenya had become a party political issue in Britain. The situation was also attracting the attention of a disparate and uncoordinated collection of individuals and organisations whose interests ranged from the political to the humanitarian. In these respects the situation resembled only too closely certain other controversial African matters, notably the banishment of Seretse Khama and the Central African Federation. Yet whereas most missionaries (with the exception of certain Scots) had been uncertain and ambivalent in their response to those other controversies, missionaries of the CMS in Kenya were during 1953-54 unhesitant in their readiness to engage with the problems of the colony, whatever difficulties might ensue. In mid-1953 Max Warren decided that the Society would support Beecher in his efforts to organise a Kenyan Christian response to Mau Mau. The CMS would not risk undermining those efforts by publicly criticising the authorities in Nairobi. Only months later, however, in October 1953, officials at the Society's headquarters were reconsidering the situation, in light of secular interest-group activity. In October Bernard Nicholls wrote to Cecil Bewes: 'I am finding it increasingly irritating to have it thrown at me that the only champions of the Africans in Kenya are Fenner Brockway and his friends'. Nicholls went on to note that

> To-day Conservatives, Liberals, Labour and Communists, and innumerable associations and pressure groups, including the whole phalanx of international agencies, vie with each other for the reputation of being the biggest and best champions of the interests and true welfare of the under-privileged peoples. Many people's livelihoods and much [*sic*] vested interests are concerned in this struggle.[72]

In June the KAU had been proscribed. The following month Brockway helped present to Parliament a KAU petition on land reform. A week later a British communist-backed Kenya Committee was formed in London. Increased attention now focussed on police brutality, on violence in the camps and on Baring's inability to remedy the situation.

In December, prompted by the case of Gerald Griffiths, an army officer court-martialled for murder, the churches in Kenya responded en masse. Beecher, Steel and other Protestant church and mission representatives met with deputy governor Crawford and army commander Erskine (Baring was away in London). In response to their requests Crawford pledged reform of the police. A few days earlier church representatives had called publicly for such reform, and in January 1954 they released a further statement, acknowledging the government's ostensible commitment to improving police behaviour. These statements served to reassure CMS headquarters that Beecher was as interested in holding the authorities to account as he was in promoting rehabilitation.[73] Yet as Beecher admitted to Fisher, he had agreed to the statements only with the greatest reluctance and to satisfy the insistence of Steel and others that the churches make their dissatisfaction publicly known.[74]

Why was Beecher wary of churches expressing dissatisfaction with the security situation? He feared that public statements would be misrepresented for political purposes by the British press and by organisations and individuals (such as Brockway) in Britain hostile to Baring. The churches would need

---

72. UBL, CMS, A5/6/4, Nicholls to Bewes, 20 Oct. 1953.
73. LPL, FP, 143, Warren to Fisher, 8 Jan. 1954.
74. LPL, FP, 127, Beecher to Fisher, 4 Dec. 1953.

to work with the authorities in order to expedite rehabilitation. They could not afford to be publicly critical: rather they should make their representations firmly but discreetly — as Beecher by now habitually did in person to the governor. During the first year or so of the emergency David Steel was determined to maintain a similar approach. In January 1953 he made the first of many private written representations to Baring, urging action against the violent behaviour of the security forces.[75] Baring all but ignored this request, as he did that of Bewes, made during the latter's visit to Kenya the same month. Steel's insistence to his fellow church leaders in late 1953 that the churches press for reform of the police was a measure of his frustration and anger at the authorities' tolerance of official misconduct and violence. It was also indicative of tension within the Christian Council of Kenya, between Beecher and the representatives of other Protestant denominations — especially Steel. The bishop was now perceived as insufficiently critical of the administration. Individual missionaries, both Anglican and Scottish Presbyterian, made strong efforts to remedy individual cases of injustice, such as the wrongful detention and maltreatment of innocent Kikuyu.[76] In the process they met with official indifference and obstruction, and came to be regarded by the authorities as 'trouble-makers'.[77] But they could do little as individuals to effect change in the system of detention. The headquarters of the CMS and of the Church of Scotland missions meanwhile preferred to leave matters to the discretion of colleagues in Kenya. There was no coordinated mission response to abuses of authority.

In early 1954 further developments of interest to missionaries occurred, not in Kenya but in London. On 22 January a meeting took place, to discuss a public appeal for dependents of detainees. Those present included Canon John Collins, founder of Christian Action, the publisher Victor Gollancz, Paul D. Sturge of the Society of Friends and Joseph Murumbi of the now-proscribed KAU. Nicholls also attended, on behalf of the CMS. Collins was the main instigator of this meeting and of another, on 17 February. Nicholls was concerned about Collins' intentions. 'I see the possibility of immense confusion . . .' he reported to colleagues.[78] CMS officials doubted Murumbi's bona fides (he was involved with the communist-inspired Kenya Committee). They suspected

75. National Library of Scotland, Accession 7548, General Assembly of the Church of Scotland Foreign Missions Committee Papers (hereafter NLS), B278, Rev. D. Steel to Baring, 14 Jan. 1953.

76. Anderson, *Histories of the Hanged*, pp. 206-8.

77. NLS, B271, Rev. R. Macpherson, memo, 'The Church of Scotland Mission and the Emergency', April 1954.

78. UBL, CMS, A5/6/5, Nicholls, memo, 18 Feb. 1954.

that Collins' interest in detainees' dependents was in part at least politically motivated. Yet there could be no doubting the sincerity of the Friends' involvement; and other non-political organisations such as the Oxford Committee for Famine Relief (later OXFAM) were already displaying active interest in the welfare of Kenyan Africans. Nicholls suggested that the CMS pre-empt Collins and move to help detainees' dependents with the assistance of other religious organisations and the Oxford Committee for Famine Relief.[79]

To missionaries, Collins was a gadfly. They little realised the effectiveness of much of his (sometimes unpublicised) work. They did not acknowledge how influenced they actually were by his activities. For Collins was more provocateur than gadfly. He actually goaded missionaries into action they might otherwise have balked at — such as a coordinated appeal for Mau Mau detainees' dependents. Such an appeal was unchartered territory for missions. Its objective would not be evangelisation, but relief. How well did this fit with mission priorities in the mid-1950s? The CMS did have some prior experience of such matters. In 1948, on account of its long-standing mission presence in Egypt and Palestine, the CMS had become involved in an international, interdenominational project by Christian organisations to relieve the suffering of refugees displaced by the Arab-Israeli War.[80] In 1954 that project was still in progress. It had met with only limited success, the needs of the refugees being far greater than the ability of aid agencies to help.[81] CMS involvement with the Palestine refugees had proved complicated and troublesome. The Society would not easily be drawn into any other similar venture. Collins meanwhile made plans of his own. He consulted with Michael Scott of the Africa Bureau, and then made a controversial visit to South Africa to draw attention to the iniquitous effects of the Bantu Education Act. In so doing he panicked the Society for the Propagation of the Gospel into a precipitate and pre-emptive fund-raising effort of its own.[82]

Within CMS Kenya and the diocese of Mombasa interest in a church-backed relief project was generally strong. Beecher was especially enthusiastic. CMS headquarters emphasised to those in Kenya that if such a project was to be instigated the Society should be closely involved to ensure proper planning and coordination, preferably from London. On 7 April, at Friends House on London's Euston Road, a meeting took place, to plan a public appeal.

79. UBL, CMS, A5/6/5, Nicholls, memo, 5 Feb. 1954.

80. UBL, CMS, A5/6/5, L. G. Fisher to W. H. Carey, 24 Feb. 1954.

81. International Missionary Council and Department of Inter-Church Aid and Services to Refugees of the World Council of Churches, *A Report of a Conference on Arab Refugee Problems, Beirut, Lebanon, May 4-8, 1951* (Geneva, 1951).

82. LPL, FP, 148, Fisher to Sir J. Hubback, 6 Dec. 1954.

Beecher had arrived in England from Kenya ten days earlier. He took an active part in the discussions. So too did Sturge, Nicholls and Oxford Committee general secretary Leslie Kirkley among others. Also present was the man who, it was decided, should coordinate the proposed relief project within Kenya: CMS lay missionary Stanley ('Sam') Morrison, general secretary-designate of the colony's Christian Council. Morrison (1894-1956) was sixty years old and about to enter a new phase of an already lengthy missionary career. Between 1920 and 1951 he had worked with the CMS Egypt mission. During that time he developed a strong interest in Islam and in Arabic culture and language. This interest led in turn to more active interest and involvement in matters relating to the religious freedoms (or lack of such freedoms) of Christian minorities in Islamic countries such as Egypt. On these matters Morrison published widely in missionary journals. He corresponded regularly and to some effect with Christian thinkers in Britain and in the United States, even positing, in 1940, the idea of an internationally agreed 'declaration of human rights' that would have religious freedom at its core.[83] Despite his efforts Morrison was unable to effect any change in official Egyptian attitudes to Christian missions. But it was not primarily for his interest in matters of religious freedom that he had been asked to go to Kenya. In September 1951 CMS Egypt had seconded him to Gaza, to assist the international relief effort for Palestinian refugees. He adapted quickly to the peculiarities of a situation in which religious and secular agencies worked in uncomfortable proximity to each other and to official authority. Through his interest in religious freedom as well as through his work in Gaza, Morrison had acquired excellent contacts in the international ecumenical world. He was an efficient and effective organiser. He was strong-willed to the point of bloody-mindedness. Above all, he had no qualms about collaborating with government on a church- and mission-supported relief project. He would first assess the situation in Kenya, while others in London finalised arrangements for a public appeal. In June Morrison left London to take up his new post with the Christian Council.

Before Morrison, general secretaries of the Christian Council of Kenya had to combine their duties with other mission or church responsibilities. Morrison would be free of such constraints. But he would be secretary of the Council for only two years, until his unexpected death. Nevertheless, he invigorated it and gave it a sense of purpose that it had previously lacked. In so doing he aligned the Council's aims ever more closely with those of the colonial authorities, not only with regard to the relief of detainees' dependents

---

83. John Nurser, *For All Peoples and All Nations: Christian Churches and Human Rights* (Geneva, 2005), pp. 86-8.

but also with regard to the policy of rehabilitation. Morrison saw the churches' role in Kenya as encompassing evangelism, education, social work and relief. He welcomed participation in social work by Christian organisations such as the Society of Friends and the Salvation Army. Morrison was very enthusiastic about the possibilities that rehabilitation seemed to represent. He summarised the situation in June 1954.

> . . . the rehabilitation of the African tribes is not only linked with Mau Mau, it is also tied up with the question of the future of Kenya. One of the speediest ways of effecting change in African attitude towards the government is an assurance that the Africans will be given their fair share in the development of a multi-racial society. . . . So radical a change of mind and heart will be a major spiritual achievement. It will involve a 'spiritual rehabilitation' of all communities.[84]

This of course was what Askwith also had in mind. In Morrison's vision the church occupied an even more important position in society. Ideas for advancing the church that drew on Christian Revival alone, he contended, were too 'other-worldly' to be effective. A 'revolution in the thinking of the church' would be required, with greater emphasis on the training and promotion of African Christian leaders who would take forward the work undertaken within and beyond the detention camps.[85] What otherwise set Morrison apart from his peers was the scale of his ambition: 'We shall probably have to look to the USA rather than to the UK for the major proportion of the money we shall require', he matter-of-factly informed Bewes.[86]

Almost from the moment of his arrival in Nairobi Morrison concluded that Kenyan society was in urgent need of transformation and that government funding alone was inadequate to the task. He began to make insistent demands of his contacts in London that they proceed at once with plans for a public appeal to raise the necessary funds. He was impatient of hesitation or delay.[87] For that reason he also made full use of his ecumenical contacts, which included the Geneva-based Scottish clergyman Robert Mackie, director of the Inter-Church Aid and Refugee Service of the World Council of Churches. In response to Morrison's urgings Mackie pledged to bring the

84. UBL, CMS A5/6/5, S. A. Morrison, memo, 'What Does Rehabilitation Mean?', 5 June 1954.

85. UBL, CMS A5/6/5, Morrison, memo, 'Relief and Rehabilitation in Kenya', 12 May 1954.

86. UBL, CMS A5/6/5, Morrison to Bewes, 26 June 1954.

87. UBL, CMS A5/6/5, Morrison to Greaves, 21 July 1954.

subject of Kenya to the attention of the WCC assembly, due to take place at Evanston, Illinois, in August. It so happened that through coverage in newsmagazines such as *Time* and *Newsweek* the American public had been receiving a good deal of information about events in Kenya. Of particular influence on American Christian opinion, however, was a May 1954 article in the mass-circulation *Reader's Digest* publicising the resilience of the Christian Kikuyu.[88] By the time, therefore, that the sizeable British contingent arrived at Evanston, American and other national church representatives were ready and willing to listen to their ideas. Beecher was present (he would also publicise Kenya at the Anglican Congress, held at Minneapolis that month); so too was Mackie, Warren, IMC secretary Norman Goodall, James Dougall of the Church of Scotland and Janet Lacey, secretary of the Inter-Church Aid and Refugee Service of the British Council of Churches (Inter-Church Aid, or ICA). But their discussions failed to completely resolve some salient questions. How realistic were Morrison's escalating demands? Would an interdenominational appeal for dependents hurt missions' own fund-raising efforts? Would funds raised for relief also be used for rehabilitation work? What would be the role of the Christian Council, and of ICA?[89]

ICA was a church-based organisation. In terms of priorities as well as structure and administration it differed from the missionary societies: its aims were not primarily evangelistic. But since its founding in the aftermath of the Second World War, ICA had acquired considerable experience and expertise in working with refugees and other displaced peoples, within and outside Europe. In subsequent discussion in London, after the Evanston event, Lacey (1903-88) argued strongly that ICA possessed the experience and expertise required; and she asserted with equal vigour that the missionary societies had nothing to fear from ICA. It could raise large funds, some of which would be made available to missions, to use as they saw fit. ICA would also assist with the recruitment of overseas Christian personnel for work in Kenya: the Christian Council would fulfil a similar role within Kenya, and would coordinate the allocation of personnel to specific tasks and locations. In January 1955 Lacey visited Kenya, touring detention camps and the makeshift villages to which Kikuyu were being relocated in huge numbers. Conditions were everywhere dreadful: 'if Christians don't go and don't witness when they get there', she reported, 'the situation will be lost'.[90] Lacey did not completely win

88. Stanley High, 'The Mau Mau's Unexpected Enemy', *Reader's Digest* 64, no. 385 (1954): 57-9; NLS, B278, E. Ross to Rev. J. W. C. Dougall, 5 May 1954.

89. SOAS, CBMS, 577, 'Kenya Appeal' file, Greaves to J. Lacey, 4 Aug. 1954.

90. SOAS, CBMS, 577, Lacey, report on visit to Kenya, ad hoc Kenya Appeal meeting, minutes, 24 Jan. 1955.

over missionaries such as Warren; but she reconciled them to the participation of ICA in the administration of the relief effort. Her energy and acumen complemented that of Morrison in Nairobi. Together they drove forward plans for the appeal, constantly revising upward the target amount. This was finally agreed at £50,000 — an unprecedentedly large figure.

The security situation was not uppermost in the minds of those planning the appeal. So closely was Morrison by now involved in Kenyan affairs, however, that he could not but be aware of the arbitrary and sometimes violent behaviour of the security forces and those Africans (including the Home Guard) with authority and power over detainees and their dependents in the villages. He acknowledged that by its nature the emergency was repressive, and admitted to colleagues his unease at the use of detention without trial and the imposition of the death sentence for crimes other than of murder. But he insisted that objections made by the church should be 'well-informed, fair and constructive'; there had already been 'far too much ill-advised and negative criticism of the authorities'.[91] Morrison, like Beecher, adopted a protective attitude towards Baring, who, he felt, was being unfairly subjected to hostile comment by critics in Britain. The governor continued to express firm support for church and mission involvement in rehabilitation.[92] He also appeared to be receptive to reform of the police. In April 1954 a new commissioner was appointed: Colonel Arthur Young. He had extensive experience, and was becoming known for his progressive methods. Church and mission leaders in Kenya (who had lobbied for this development) welcomed his appointment, none more so than David Steel who had pressed so firmly for reform of the police. Young attempted to eradicate inefficiency and corruption. But he made little headway, and quarrelled with Baring about the extent of executive authority over police matters. Baring refused to support Young's methods. In December 1954 Young resigned.[93] In so doing he provoked an outburst of anger in religious circles, both in Nairobi and in London.

For two years Steel had tried to maintain faith in Baring's ability to effect change for the better in police conduct. Young's enforced resignation finally convinced him to speak out publicly and critically. He did so in a sermon (also broadcast on radio) at St Andrew's Church, Nairobi, on 9 January 1955. Steel lambasted official security policy, comparing Operation Anvil to a po-

91. UBL, CMS A5/6/5, Morrison, confidential memo, 'Kenya Survey and the Christian Council of Kenya', Sept. 1954.

92. UBL, CMS A5/6/5, Baring, memo, 'The Churches and Rehabilitation', n.d., but Sept. 1954.

93. Georgina Sinclair, *At the End of the Line: Colonial Policing and the Imperial Endgame, 1945-80* (Manchester, 2006), pp. 74-7.

grom and the government's thinking to that of Herod. The agencies of the state, he argued, had made use of the threat posed by Mau Mau to justify wholly unacceptable action on the part of the police and other organisations. Now, Steel insisted, the church 'dare not and will not stand aside when Christian principles are abrogated and when our great traditions of government based on those principles are being violated and shamed'. Yet the church, he pointedly noted also in his sermon, was far from guiltless, having kept silent for too long. His sermon, he concluded, was by way of 'small repentance' for that shortcoming.[94] Steel wrote to Young, assuring him of his personal support. He hoped that Young would publicise the difficulties that had forced his resignation.[95] CMS headquarters had by now received news of Young's predicament. Bewes invited Young, on his return to London in January 1955, to meet with Fisher to discuss the matter confidentially.[96] Young did so, but for reasons of duty and career refused to make public his reasons for resigning. This refusal sparked Warren into action.

Throughout Africa the CMS was being subjected to pressures financial and political. The situation in Kenya was the most complicated and the most fraught. But in neighbouring Uganda the Society had become caught up in controversy surrounding the deportation of Kabaka Mutesa II, hereditary ruler of the province of Buganda.[97] The crisis revealed to Warren the inability of local missions to respond effectively to political difficulty. '[I]f we are to walk wisely in this field', he informed Bewes, 'it is imperative that we should learn the rules of the game'.[98] Missionaries, it seemed, might even learn from Brockway, who in April 1954 helped set up the anti-imperialist Movement for Colonial Freedom, and attracted expressions of support not only from John Collins but also from British Methodist leader Donald Soper. This development seems to have caused Warren to ponder anew the relevance of the CMS to contemporary debates about colonial Africa. If African political parties were banned, and if Africans were detained without trial and subjected to official abuse, who with authority or influence might speak out for them: Beecher? Brockway? Who would assist the families of detainees: ICA? the

94. Steel, transcript of sermon, 9 Jan. 1955, *St Andrew's Journal*, Feb. (Nairobi, 1955), pp. 11-19.

95. Rev. David Steel, private papers in the possession of Lord Steel of Aikwood, Col. A. E. Young to Steel, 30 Dec. 1954.

96. Bodleian Library of Commonwealth and African Studies at Rhodes House, Oxford (hereafter RHL) MSS. Brit Emp s. 486/6/9/19, Young papers, Bewes to Young, 22 Dec. 1954.

97. Kevin Ward, 'The Church of Uganda and the Exile of Kabaka Mutesa II, 1953-55', *JRA* 28, no. 4 (1998): 411-49.

98. UBL, CMS, AFE/AD3/2, Warren to Bewes, 10 March 1954.

Christian Council? Where stood the CMS in these and other matters of national as well as colonial importance? Warren was immensely impressed by Steel's sermon, and he hoped that Young would condemn as iniquitous and hypocritical the attitude of the government in Nairobi. Young's unwillingness to do so prompted Warren to decide that CMS headquarters should renounce its vow of public silence on Kenya. It did so in emphatic fashion, by publishing on 25 January 1955 a pamphlet entitled *Kenya — Time for Action!*

The pamphlet was heavily influenced by Steel's sermon, to which it made explicit reference. The pamphlet also referred to the desperate situation of detainees, to 'recurrent evidence of abuse of power by some members of the forces of law and order', to Young's efforts to end this abuse and to the unsatisfactory circumstances surrounding his resignation. The Society did not call explicitly for Baring to be replaced, but it did so implicitly, with reference to the 'second-rate standards' of an African colony currently run by 'second-rate people'. The pamphlet urged British people to offer prayers and donations of service and money for Africans in Kenya. Voters should write to their MPs on the subject of Young's resignation. There was an echo of Steel's words in the pamphlet's assertion that '. . . condemnation of others is a luxury none of us can afford, particularly when we ourselves stand condemned'. The pamphlet concluded on a note of hope: that those reading it would be convinced 'that the need for high standards in Kenya cannot be separated from the need for high standards in this country, beginning with — YOU'.[99]

There had been no consultation between CMS headquarters and missions or diocese in Kenya. Beecher was stunned, and openly expressed bewilderment at the action of the CMS. He soon recovered his poise. The Colonial Office reacted adroitly to the pamphlet. First the undersecretary of state emphasised in Parliament the divergence of views between Beecher and the CMS. Then Alan Lennox-Boyd, Lyttelton's successor (since July 1954) as Conservative secretary of state, invited Warren, Bewes and Kenneth Grubb to meet with him. Where Lyttelton had been brusque and blunt Lennox-Boyd was on this occasion urbane, reassuring — and disarming. There was no question of Baring being transferred or sacked, but the Colonial Office was committed to an improvement in the security situation.[100] Lennox-Boyd agreed to arrange that the Colonial Office and the Crown Agents (the procurement agency for the colonies) would assist the Kenya Appeal organisers in recruiting personnel to work in the detention camps. He subsequently in-

99. Church Missionary Society, *Kenya — Time for Action!* (London, 1955).

100. UBL, CMS, A5/6/14, Warren, account of meeting with A. Lennox-Boyd, 28 March 1955.

structed the authorities in Nairobi to adopt a more helpful attitude towards missions. He also utilised his personal contacts in the City of London to privately raise £16,000 for welfare and other social work in Kenya.[101]

Steel's sermon and the CMS pamphlet together constituted a howl of British Christian protest at what was occurring in Kenya. It was born not just of indignation at the treatment of Kenyan Africans but also of frustration at the chronic failure of church and mission representatives to influence change in government attitudes or policies during the previous two years. Yet for all the attention they received at the time, neither sermon nor pamphlet proved successful in their aims. Baring would remain in post until 1960. Abuses of authority would continue, during the remainder of Steel's time in Africa and after his departure in April 1957. The CMS pamphlet's reference to 'standards' of colonial rule would be echoed five and a half years later in a much better-known British public pronouncement, on the illegal death of detainees at Hola Camp, by Conservative MP Enoch Powell.[102] That incident conclusively demonstrated how perverted by coercion and violence had become the rehabilitation project. Yet for all the attention it received, Powell's pronouncement may not have had significant impact upon colonial policy. Steel's protest and that of the CMS was in any case overshadowed by a far more influential event: the launching, on 17 February 1955, of the Kenya Appeal. Its impact would be considerable.

Months of planning had gone into the appeal. Lacey drew on her many contacts, built up over years of work with the YWCA and the YMCA in Britain and in postwar Germany, and then with ICA, of which she had become secretary in 1952. Money poured in, from Protestant churches and church organisations in Britain, the United States, Canada, Australia and New Zealand. Notable contributions also came from European countries such as Germany and the Netherlands. Charitable foundations contributed substantial amounts. Although undertaken on behalf of Christian organisations, the appeal was not aimed exclusively at a Christian or even religious constituency. In Britain the appeal benefitted from being designated 'The Week's Good Cause' by the BBC during March, and this generated £8,000 in contributions. By the end of the year the sum raised was £43,000, and Lacey made plans for another appeal, for 1956. Collated by ICA, with the assistance of the Conference of British Missionary Societies in London, funds were forwarded to Kenya, for disbursement

101. SOAS, Christian Aid papers, CA/A/2/5, O. Paynton to Lord Kilmaine, 2 Oct. 1956. The contributors included Barclays Bank, Lloyds Bank, Barings Bank, ICI and Union Castle Line.

101. UK House of Commons Debates, 610, 237-38, 27 July 1959.

by the Christian Council. Two-fifths of the total went to churches and missions, the remainder to other Christian organisations.[103]

The funding enabled religious groups in Kenya to give much greater attention than before to welfare and related social issues, especially in urban areas such as Nairobi where community centres were now set up. To Morrison the relief project was primarily intended to meet emergency human need. He envisaged that Christian workers from Britain would be taken on for a period not exceeding three years, by which time the situation in Kenya was expected to be more stable. The responsibilities of recruits from Britain might vary greatly. Those with suitable professional skills (say in teaching, or nursing or social work) were especially valued. Morrison did not expect such workers to engage in primary evangelism; but their presence would make it possible to free up missionaries for such work.[104] In the event, volunteers came not just from Britain but from many other countries also, bringing a wide range of experience and expertise. Some, such as Jocelyn Murray, were committed to mission from the outset. She travelled from Wellington, New Zealand, and worked for the CMS at Kahuhia, remaining in Kenya until 1967. Others, working for the Christian Council, used their time in Kenya to learn more about the Kikuyu and about Mau Mau. Over time they contributed to a less partial and more nuanced understanding of the movement than that provided by official advisors such as Leakey and Carothers.[105] Still others researched Kenyan society and economy, and published their findings.[106]

Eileen Fletcher travelled with three other Quaker volunteers from England to Kenya. An experienced social worker, she would initially undertake rehabilitation work at Kamiti. It was not her first visit to Africa; during the Second World War she had worked for the Friends Service Council at a camp for Polish refugees in Uganda. She was shocked by the conditions she encountered at Kamiti and at other camps. In May 1956 (having resigned her post the previous year and then later returned to England), she produced an account of her experiences, alleging that camp staff meted out inhumane and degrading treatment to inmates irrespective of age or gender. This account was initially published in the Quaker periodical *Peace News*. It attracted a great deal of attention, the more so when Fenner Brockway took up Fletcher's cause. Unfor-

103. RHL, MSS Micr. Afr. 642 CCK/R/1/3/3/214-17, Bostock papers, Lacey to Rev. P. G. Bostock, 28 Jan. 1957.

104. SOAS, CBMS, 577, 'Kenya Appeal' file, Morrison to Lacey, 6 Dec. 1954.

105. Gretha Kershaw, 'Mau Mau from Below: Fieldwork and Experience, 1955-57 and 1962', *Canadian Journal of African Studies* 25, no. 2 (1991): 274-97.

106. Marion W. Forrester, *Kenya Today: Social Prerequisites for Economic Development* (The Hague, 1962).

tunately her alliance with Brockway was to prove fatal to Fletcher's credibility. The Colonial Office exploited it. Fellow Quakers became wary of supporting her. Morrison (who had made representations to government about conditions in the camps) became coldly unsympathetic towards her. Lacey, who had encountered Fletcher's work during her visit to Kenya and described it as 'excellent', now concluded that she had a '"chip on her shoulder"'.[107]

Ultimately Fletcher's allegations made as little impact as the protests of Steel and of the CMS. They nevertheless reinforced doubts among some missionaries as to the nature of their involvement in the work being carried out in Kenya, be it of rehabilitation or of relief. Those doubts also owed something to theology. Rather than 'giving the cup of water in Christ's name', might not the Christian Council, Norman Goodall wondered, instead be 'sponsoring secular activity under Christian auspices'?[108] Warren meanwhile pondered how an overseas Christian worker on a two- or three-year contract could contribute substantially (as could a long-service missionary) to the ongoing life of the church.[109] A visit to Kenya during November 1955 caused Warren fresh doubt about the future. Notwithstanding the vigour of Revival (on which subject he had recently published a book), the missions seemed so far to have achieved worryingly little in combatting the effects of Mau Mau on the church. Warren's pessimism was deepened further by his suspicion that Baring, weary of Protestant mission criticism, was now in thrall to 'unscrupulous' Roman Catholic missionaries.[110]

This suspicion bespoke a not dissimilar weariness of Kenya in the CMS general secretary. During his visit Warren had looked for signs of African engagement with political discourse, and had drawn some (misplaced) encouragement from the activities of the Capricorn Africa Society. Curiously, it was not until some months after his return to London that he learned of a promising new name in Kenyan African politics: Tom Mboya (who would remain politically active and influential in Kenya until his murder in 1969). With the proscription of colony-wide African political parties, trade unions provided a platform from which Africans could articulate their grievances and their aspirations. Mboya worked as a trade union official. During 1955-56 he lived and studied in Britain. He also undertook a speaking tour of the United

107. SOAS, CBMS, 577, 'Kenya Appeal' file, Lacey, report on visit to Kenya; UBL, CMS, A5/6/3, Lacey to P. D. Sturge, 27 June 1956.

108. Norman Goodall, 'The Limits of Co-operation', *International Review of Missions* (hereafter *IRM*) 44, no. 176 (1955): 452-4.

109. Max Warren, 'Nationalism as an International Asset', *IRM* 44, no. 176 (1955): 388-9.

110. UBL, CMS, uncatalogued, Max Warren, journal of visit to Tanganyika and Kenya, Nov.-Dec. 1955, p. 478.

States. In May 1956 he spoke at a conference on Kenya organised by the Africa Bureau in London. He launched a swingeing attack on the half-hearted political reforms of 1954 and also on rehabilitation. Rather than being reformist in its intentions, Mboya argued, the rehabilitation project demonstrated instead that the state was determined to control the lives and livelihoods of all of Kenya's Africans. Frustration and political extremism, he warned, would be the inevitable outcome of such policies.[111] Bernard Nicholls, in attendance, reported the speech to Warren, noting also the tremendous impact it had made upon those present. To listen to Mboya, Nicholls wrote, 'was to become deeply fearful and gloomy about Kenya's future. . . . To them, "multiracialism" and "partnership" are concepts just about as congenial as "communism" or "nazism" [*sic*] are to us . . .' Africans, it seemed to Nicholls, would not long tolerate colonial rule: Kenya must undoubtedly become 'a primarily African state'.[112] Warren did not at all share Nicholl's gloominess. Mboya, he thought, had summed up the situation perfectly, not merely in relation to Kenyan Africans but, unwittingly, in relation to the church in Kenya as well. It was now vitally necessary, Warren confided to Bewes,

> . . . to try and wake people up to the fact that things are not going to stand still in Kenya; that the time is running out very fast, and that there is the most grave danger that the Church will be not so much neutral over political issues as hopelessly compromised by being tied to the Government's chariot wheels. The really alarming thing about Kenya is that all the people out there are both obsessed with rehabilitation under the pathetic illusion that Africa and the world are going to stand still while Kenya goes in for rehabilitation for the next twenty years. It is this frame of mind rather than anything else which is so terrifying.[113]

Mboya's voice was but one of many now raised against rehabilitation and against colonial rule in Kenya. There were other African voices, in the detention camps, of which Warren was unaware.[114] However, missionaries and other Christian workers in Kenya did not tend to perceive rehabilitation as inherently oppressive; for them it constituted part of a much broader project,

111. RHL MSS Afr. s. 1681/289/2, Africa Bureau papers, T. J. Mboya, address, from Africa Bureau, 'Report of Conference on Kenya', 12 May 1956.

112. UBL, CMS, AFg O1, Nicholls, notes on Africa Bureau conference, 12 May 1956.

113. UBL, CMS, AFg O1, Warren to Bewes, n.d., but June 1956. Warren and Mboya met in London in July 1957, but I have found no detailed account of the meeting.

114. Derek R. Peterson, 'Culture and Chronology in African History', *Historical Journal* 50, no. 2 (2007): 492-4.

encompassing work both within and outside detention camps and prisons. Such work might involve short-term relief of hardship. It might also include such things as 'agricultural training' for girls and women and instruction on 'health and hygiene in the home'.[115] As Cora Ann Presley and Marina E. Santoru among others have shown, the authorities believed that such activities would prove indirectly harmful to Mau Mau as well as having longer-term societal benefits.[116] Missionaries accorded with this view. In seeking financial support from the authorities, secular relief agencies such as the Save the Children Fund meanwhile emphasised how their work with women and children could have a 'softening' effect upon core support for Mau Mau.[117] Notwithstanding his unhappiness with rehabilitation's lack of opportunity for evangelism, Warren accepted that emergency conditions meant the state continuing to exercise a preponderant influence on Kenyan life. What, though, would be the extent of the state's role when emergency conditions were finally ended? As he had worried years before about the effect upon religious life of a 'Social Service State' in postwar Britain, now Warren pondered the implications for mission and church in Kenya, not only of African nationalism but also of a colonial state busy forming new relationships with secular agencies in the interests of rehabilitation and social change.

Even allowing for Lacey's avowed commitment to support for missions and churches in Kenya and Morrison's long record of CMS service, Warren mistrusted both ICA and the Christian Council, the former because of its place within the myriad mysterious bureaucracies of the World Council of Churches, the latter because its support of secular agencies risked diluting the Christian ethos it ostensibly represented. But neither Lacey nor Morrison — nor Beecher — envisaged rehabilitation as a long-term project. Nor did they consider it as the most important task in which they were engaged. Rehabilitation, Beecher admitted, might not even prove especially successful. He knew, as Warren did not, the extent to which detained Kikuyu were capable of subverting official rehabilitative activities. Beecher acknowledged this in an extremely critical review of his brother-in-law Louis Leakey's 1954 book, *Defeating Mau Mau* — '. . . a somewhat emotional and unfounded indictment of the Christian Church'. Beecher believed Leakey to be arguing for a dual, racially based standard of Christian morality in Kikuyu marriage and family

---

115. Dr. Mary Shannon, 'Rehabilitating the Kikuyu', *African Affairs* 54, no. 215 (1955): 129-37. Shannon was a Church of Scotland medical missionary.

116. Cora Ann Presley, *Kikuyu Women, the Mau Mau Rebellion and Social Change in Kenya* (Boulder, CO, 1992); Marina E. Santoru, 'The Colonial Idea of Women and Direct Intervention: The Mau Mau Case', *African Affairs* 95, no. 379 (1996): 253-67.

117. TNA: PRO, CO859/660, Brig. T. W. Boyce to Lennox-Boyd, 1 June 1955.

life. Leakey's argument suggested compromise, and insufficient recognition of those Kikuyu Christians who, Beecher averred, had chosen a martyr's death rather than 'a defection from the standards which they have voluntarily adopted in matters of faith and order, not because they are twentieth-century western European standards, but because they are fundamentally Christian'. The church in Kenya, Beecher argued in response to Leakey, would not compromise, nor would it condescend to Africans in communicating to them 'our most sacred faith'. He also criticised 'the older churches' in the West for their failure to respond sufficiently to the needs of what he described as 'the Christian frontier'.[118] Four years prior to the emergency Beecher had identified in his report on African education a pressing need for Christian workers. This had been acted upon in Britain only after diocesan pressure on the CMS. The Society had subsequently made funds available to the diocese, and of course it still sent missionaries to Kenya. But its resources were insufficient to the need precipitated by Mau Mau and by emergency conditions. This need could only be met by combining the efforts and resources of many agencies, as Beecher had by this time long acknowledged and accepted. The CMS would not play a leading role in such an arrangement; it would be one of many participants in a project primarily run not from the United Kingdom but from Kenya and under the auspices not of a missionary society but of a local ecumenical organisation, the Christian Council.

Complementing this shift of emphasis, from 1956 the relationship between mission and diocese in Kenya also began to alter, gradually but appreciably. African church leadership finally became more apparent. The previous year Fisher had visited Kenya, as part of a tour of Africa. He laid the foundation stone for a Church of the Martyrs at Fort Hall (Muranga), in the Central Province. He was accompanied by, among others, Obadiah Kariuki, one of two Kenyan Africans (the other being Festo Olang', rural dean for Central Nyanza) whom he had recently consecrated bishop at Namirembe Cathedral, Kampala, Uganda. During 1957, CMS Kenya discussed with diocesan representatives the future role of the mission in Kenya.[119] These developments were indicative of a subsequent, broader shift in the ecclesiastical 'centre of gravity' in east Africa, with local church leaders discussing future plans among themselves and with Fisher rather than with Warren and his CMS colleagues.[120] Increasingly, it would be churches in territories such as Kenya rather than a missionary soci-

---

118. Rt Rev. L. J. Beecher, 'After Mau Mau — What?', *IRM* 44, no. 174 (1955): 205-11.

119. UBL, CMS, A/2, CMS Kenya, executive board minutes, 25-29 Oct. 1957.

120. Caroline Howell, 'Church and State in Decolonisation: The Case of Buganda, 1939-62' (University of Oxford DPhil thesis, 2002), pp. 203-4, 228-9.

ety based in London that would decide where in Africa mission and church workers from the United Kingdom would be based, and for what purpose.

Even though Morrison worked for the Christian Council rather than for a particular church or mission, his activities and those of the Council also influenced the nature of overseas religious service in Kenya. During 1955-56 he was a ubiquitous presence. He worked at a tremendous pace. But he allowed himself to become distracted by the rehabilitation project, in part because of Fletcher's allegations. In July 1956 he visited London, to discuss matters with Lacey but also to refute (in letters to the press) the 'misleading' image of rehabilitation portrayed by Fletcher.[121] On 14 July he died suddenly and unexpectedly. Fletcher appears to have borne Morrison no ill will; she attended his memorial service, held in the CMS chapel at Church Mission House, London. The work of the Council continued. Lacey continued to fund-raise. New religious leadership in Kenya was provided by expatriate Anglican priests such as Stanley Booth-Clibborn (1924-96), who was appointed training secretary in 1956, and Andrew Hake (1925-2003), appointed industrial adviser in 1957. Unlike Morrison these younger men took an active interest in political affairs — and encouraged Africans to do likewise.[122] They even saw the Christian Council as a forum through which communication among politicians of different races in Kenya might be improved.[123]

For Warren, uneasy about excessive focus on rehabilitation and about the 'over-exuberance' of Morrison and ICA, these were belatedly welcome developments. They helped reassure him that the work of the Christian Council might not after all be inimical to missions and churches. Instead, the Council appeared by 1957 to be working towards a more equable set of relationships among religious and secular organisations committed variously to evangelism and to humanitarian activity.[124] Besides, the situation for mission in Kenya from 1957 had to be set against that in other parts of Africa. From the viewpoint of the CMS, Arab rather than African nationalism posed a potentially greater threat. In the aftermath of the Suez Crisis of late 1956 the government of Egypt deported CMS missionaries. The situation in Kenya differed in many respects from that in Egypt, where the level of indigenous hostility to Christian mission was much greater.[125] Ambivalent towards and even critical

121. *The Manchester Guardian*, 5 July 1956.

122. SOAS, Hake papers, 6:9, Rev. A. A. G. Hake to J. M. Murumbi, 2 Sept. 1957.

123. RHL, MSS Micr. Afr. 642, Bostock papers, CCK/R/1/7/99, A. D. McIver, report of meeting with Lennox-Boyd, 8 Nov. 1957.

124. UBL, CMS, A/5/4, Warren to Bewes, 25 Feb. 1957.

125. On Egypt, see Heather J. Sharkey, *American Evangelicals in Egypt: Missionary Encounters in an Age of Empire* (Princeton, and Oxford, 2008), pp. 96-148.

of British missions they might sometimes be, but Kenyan Africans had in the past derived material and spiritual benefit from religious organisations as they were now also deriving from work carried out under the auspices of the Christian Council. Not without misgivings Warren became reconciled to this new reality.

To 1960: 'missionaries from abroad may no longer be welcome . . .'

During the mid-1940s, as Warren contemplated the direction that CMS should take in the postwar world he reminded colleagues that 'as Evangelical Anglicans we have our own distinctive contribution to offer to the younger Churches'.[126] 'Our goal', he informed them, 'is to build a Christian Church which shall build a free Africa, India, China . . . which shall control its own institutions and have a deciding voice in its own destiny'.[127] There was no knowing how long that task might take: in the life of the church as in the political sphere African leaders, Warren observed in 1948, were 'still all too far behind to be likely to count, as they ought to do, for some years to come'.[128] For all his alertness to the growth of nationalism Warren could not of course foresee the developments that would ensue in Kenya and in the rest of Africa during the 1950s. Committed to the indigenisation of the overseas church he nevertheless envisaged a continuing role for the CMS. With fellow-Anglicans he vigorously asserted the CMS evangelical view of mission.[129] He insisted that the sending of missionaries from Britain was essential to the vitality of the overseas church, a view from which some other missionaries dissented; they believed that this would give the appearance of undue foreign influence in African church affairs.[130] Warren undoubtedly realised this; but he believed that Christian work in Africa undertaken by British men and women under mission auspices would engender in those men and women as could no other activity knowledge of and respect for Africa and its peoples. This knowledge and respect could then be fed back into British society by returned missionaries through domestic mission and church networks. In March 1959 he shared with colleagues his views on the responsibilities of the missionary society in a period of African nationalist and western imperial upheaval: 'A

126. UBL, CMS, G/AP1, Warren, draft memo, 'Our Society in the Calling of God', Sept. 1944.
127. UBL, CMS, G/AP1, Warren, memo, 'Rocks Ahead', 3 April 1944.
128. UBL, CMS, G/AP11, Warren to Carey, 4 May 1948.
129. UBL, CMS, G/O 3/5 (3), Warren to Canon J. McLeod Campbell, 22 June 1949.
130. UBL, CMS, G/APc: 4/1-7 (3), Goodall to Warren, 21 April 1950.

missionary society is being *responsible*', he wrote, 'when it is producing missionary-minded people for service at home and overseas and educating Church people generally about the Christian mission'.[131]

The main priority of the 'missionary-minded', Warren asserted, should be 'to set forth Christ's Gospel in Africa'. Yet as developments in Kenya since the launch of the appeal in 1955 had shown, it was not always easy to maintain a clear distinction between evangelism and the provision of aid and relief; and rehabilitation was a further complicating factor. In May 1957 Lacey launched the first Christian Aid Week. Its objective was very much broader than would have been any missionary society appeal of the time. It would ultimately become very successful. As for links to imperial authority, the CMS had not been able to distance itself successfully. Yet that did not prove unduly problematic. During 1959 both Alan Lennox-Boyd and his successor as Colonial Secretary, Iain Macleod, made use of the Society's connection with Kenya. Pressed by Opposition leader Hugh Gaitskell to ensure that official scrutiny of the deaths at Hola Camp had a suitably 'humanitarian' tenor, Lennox-Boyd secured the services of Cecil Bewes for the commission of enquiry.[132] At Macleod's request later that year the CMS organised a reception at their headquarters for African and other delegates to the constitutional conference on Kenya, held in London in January 1960.[133] Some political progress was made at the conference, and with large numbers of detainees by now having been released the state of emergency was ended that month. But independence for Kenya was still almost four years away. Meanwhile, ecclesiastical change was already occurring with implications for mission and for the CMS as a missionary society.

Inevitably, the Lambeth Conference of 1958 discussed the role to be played by Anglican overseas missions (Warren advised Fisher on the current situation in Kenya).[134] In Nairobi other discussions were already in progress, whereby a diocesan board of missions, supervised by the bishop, would in time assume authority for mission affairs previously exercised by CMS headquarters. Beecher described the process succinctly, as one of 'missionary realignment'.[135] In November 1959 Beecher and other bishops requested that Fisher proceed with plans for the creation of a new ecclesiastical province such as had first

131. SOAS, CBMS, 15, 'CMS' file, Warren, memo, 'An Appraisal of Situation Confronting the Church in Tropical Africa', 23 March 1959.

132. TNA: PRO, CO822/1269, Lennox-Boyd to Baring, 13 May 1959.

133. LPL, FP, 246, Warren to Fisher, 6 Jan. 1960.

134. J. G. H. Baker, 'The Anglican Communion and Its Missionary Task: Lambeth, 1958', *IRM* 47, no. 188 (1958): 451-3.

135. LPL, FP, 225, Beecher, personal newsletter, May 1959.

been mooted for east Africa some forty years earlier and which had already been carried out for west Africa and for central Africa. Subsequent developments culminated in Fisher's visit to Dar es Salaam, Tanganyika, in August 1960 to inaugurate the new province and to consecrate Beecher as its first archbishop. Warren had readied CMS missionaries for this eventuality, informing them the previous year that the church in east Africa would shortly be 'in charge of its own destiny'.[136] The Society would in the future offer missionaries to dioceses overseas rather than send them unbidden, an important consideration. Warren mused that 'the time may be approaching, perhaps sooner than we think, when missionaries from abroad may no longer be welcome in East Africa'.[137] Mission had to be seen to become the primary responsibility of the church rather than of the British-based voluntary society. And it was on behalf of the church in Africa that the CMS should therefore work most closely, while maintaining an equally close watch not only on political developments but also on the activities of overseas agencies committed to aid and relief. Those agencies might in time exert considerable influence throughout Africa, as by 1960 they already were in Kenya. What might be the future effect not only of African nationalism but also of western aid and development, on mission, on missionaries and on missionary societies?

136. UBL, CMS, A7/1/3, Warren, circular letter, 23 Oct. 1959.
137. UBL, CMS, A7/1/3, Warren, memo, 'CMS in the Service of the Church Overseas', Oct. 1959.

CHAPTER 6

Overseas Mission, Voluntary Service and the End of Empire in Africa, 1954-64

In April 1960 Archbishop of York Michael Ramsey (1904-88) undertook an official five-week tour of east and central Africa, to mark one hundred years of UMCA activity. 'This is not a political visit', Ramsey was reported as saying on his departure.[1] But he undoubtedly realised how politicised church and mission affairs in Africa had become, not least in the Central African Federation. In Nyasaland, Africans boycotted a reception in Ramsey's honour: word had been spread that he was a 'Federal Archbishop'.[2] For all that, Ramsey received a warm welcome almost everywhere he visited, and he returned to Britain convinced of the part that the church should play in Africa's future.

In the meantime ecclesiastical devolution continued to take place. In August 1960 at Dar es Salaam Geoffrey Fisher inaugurated the new Anglican Province of East Africa. This had entailed no little theological difficulty and compromise: the province would contain CMS missions as well as those of the UMCA, and the two organisations espoused different views on issues such as episcopal authority, ministerial training and church union. These differences contributed to the decision of the Bishop of Masasi (a diocese in southern Tanganyika) to resign his post. He would be succeeded in November 1960 by Trevor Huddleston. In a way, Huddleston's appointment was all too indicative of the dearth of suitably qualified African candidates for bishoprics. But Huddleston's open encouragement of African political aspirations

---

1. *The Times*, 20 April 1960. Ramsey succeeded Geoffrey Fisher as Archbishop of Canterbury in 1961.

2. John Poole, *Baptize the Nations: UMCA Review of 1960* (London, 1961), p. 13.

made him much more acceptable to local African clergy and laypeople than his more conservative predecessor.[3]

Devolution such as was marked formally at Dar es Salaam did not mean a clean break between overseas mission and local church. Missionaries would continue to play a role in African church affairs. As the case of Masasi demonstrated, however, matters of ecclesiastical succession now had to be handled with due attention to issues of race and politics. Of itself this was hardly a new phenomenon. What was different was the level of sensitivity required in relation to African opinion. Fisher was alive to these requirements, and he strove to ensure that the church was perceived, in Britain as well as in Africa, as being in the vanguard of change. Lambeth Palace publicised the Dar es Salaam ceremony as indicative of 'the contemporary movement towards ecclesiastical as well as political self-government'.[4] The implication was clear: although Africans might not yet be ready to lead the church in Africa, they soon would be, and would have the support and assistance of churches in the United Kingdom. Having visited Africa, Ramsey returned to England in June 1960. His biographer recounts him feeling that 'this was the most dangerous and the most creative moment in the history of Christianity' in Africa, 'and that the home Church ought to be much more aware of the needs than it seemed to be'.[5]

How aware was 'the home Church' of those needs? British public interest in the African colonies and in South Africa coincided with interest in other contemporary international and world problems, such as the threat of nuclear war. Still, the long-standing links of British missionary societies with Africa continued into the 1960s to provide a focus for Christian concern and activism. The missions' continuing presence in Africa, as in other parts of the non-western world, was by no means unproblematic. In July 1956 the government of Madhya Pradesh in central India published the Niyogi Committee Report. Widely publicised, it was extremely critical of foreign missions.[6] Four months later, writing in the aftermath of the Suez crisis, James Dougall informed Church of Scotland colleagues that 'it should not surprise us to note that the word "missionary" has come to be questioned in some quarters as out of date and embarrassing'.[7] In November 1958 the historian Roland Oli-

3. Frieder Ludwig, *Church and State in Tanzania: Aspects of a Changing Relationship, 1961-94* (Leiden, 1999), pp. 45-6.

4. Lambeth Palace Library, London, Fisher Papers, 241, Lambeth Palace, London, press release, n.d., but Aug. 1960.

5. Owen Chadwick, *Michael Ramsey: A Life* (Oxford, 1991), p. 240.

6. Sebastian C. H. Kim, *In Search of Identity: Debates on Religious Conversion in India* (New Delhi, 2003), pp. 60-73.

7. National Library of Scotland, Accession 7548, General Assembly of the Church of

ver, a member of the CMS Africa committee, summarised for the Society his impressions of a recent tour of the African continent. Anglicans, he wrote, might indeed attract most suspicion for their supposed links with empire; but 'it would be no good for Presbyterians to plead that they were Scottish nationalists, or Methodists that they abhorred the Establishment — in African eyes all alike were identified with those who bore rule'.[8]

Yet as events in Kenya perhaps most notably demonstrated, the situation was complicated: western interest and involvement in Africa was now widening greatly to include aid and development agencies and their workers. In the context of this phenomenon and of indigenous criticism of missions, western Christian thinkers worked to re-evaluate and re-define mission. Advocating fresh emphasis on 'the fundamentals of the Gospel' as well as re-acquaintance with the work of influential missionaries of the recent past such as Roland Allen, the Church of South India bishop and theologian Lesslie Newbigin (1909-98) posited in 1958 new ecumenical religious orders (possibly on Roman Catholic lines) in which lifetime vocation as well as short-term service might equally be accommodated, subject in every case to the wishes of indigenous churches.[9] This idea did not come to fruition, but it was indicative of, among other things, Newbigin's strong commitment to 'integration' of the International Missionary Council with the World Council of Churches, finally attained after much debate in 1961. This 'integration' may have represented for some British missionaries an achievement commensurate with contemporaneous arrangements in imperial policymaking whereby colonies having become independent nation states also became members of the Commonwealth. This had already occurred for Ghana and Nigeria as in December 1961 it would also for Tanganyika, as independent Tanzania. CMS general secretary Max Warren favoured Commonwealth membership for former British colonies. Conversely, he resolutely, but unsuccessfully, opposed 'integration' of the IMC with the WCC. Warren suspected, not without cause, that mission would become one of many potentially competing 'world church' priorities — another of which was inter-church aid. Yet the IMC was itself becoming a forum

---

Scotland Foreign Missions Committee Papers (hereafter NLS), B399, Rev. J. W. C. Dougall, circular letter, Nov. 1956.

8. University of Birmingham Library Special Collections (hereafter UBL), Church Missionary Society Papers (hereafter CMS), AFg O16/1, Africa Committee minutes, 28 Nov. 1958.

9. J. E. L. Newbigin, *One Body, One Gospel, One World: The Christian Mission Today* (London, 1958); Geoffrey Wainwright, *Lesslie Newbigin: A Theological Life* (New York, 2000), pp. 169-73. Probably the most influential written work of Roland Allen (1868-1947) is *The Spontaneous Expansion of the Church* (1927).

through which Asian and African Christians might increasingly express criticism of western mission. Only by shedding 'cultural "western" accretions', some Africans argued, could Christians from the West usefully contribute both to the church in Africa and to the universality of the Christian faith.[10]

Western missionaries responded as they could to the tumult in African church and colonial affairs during the period 1954-64. They committed greater resources to indigenous ministerial training. They refocused attention on western laypeople and on the role they might play in the church overseas. Missionaries also took increased heed of international non-governmental organisations and of government interest in overseas aid and development projects. In no significant sense did the period mark a culmination much less an end of missionary involvement in Africa. Rather it was a period in which missionaries from Britain attempted with varying degrees of success to adapt both to unprecedented change in colonial and imperial affairs and also to emerging African statehood. Unsurprisingly, missionaries acted in a variety of ways; some consulted with government ministers and civil servants in Whitehall; others forged strong personal links with African nationalist movements, political parties and their leaders. They increasingly agreed that overseas mission from the West could and should continue by arrangement with the indigenous church in Africa, whenever the end of empire might formally occur.

The Oversea Service Idea

The idea and practice of mission underwent no little change during the 1950s and 1960s, as innovations such as Oversea Service demonstrated. Beginning its activities in 1954, this organisation, which focussed on Christian lay workers, developed in response to the pressures of end of empire in Africa.

Sir Charles Jeffries was a career civil servant and an Anglican layman.[11] An active supporter of overseas missions, he was also a vice-president of the Society for the Propagation of the Gospel. During the 1940s he played an influential role in training and recruitment for the Colonial Service — the civil

---

10. K. A. Busia, 'Has the Christian Faith Been Adequately Presented?', *International Review of Missions* (hereafter *IRM*) 50, no. 197 (1961): 86-9. Busia, a Christian, an academic, and later a politician, had been involved with the All-Africa Church Conference, held at Ibadan, Nigeria, in January 1958.

11. This section is based in part on John Stuart, 'Overseas Mission, Voluntary Service and Aid to Africa: Max Warren, the Church Missionary Society and Kenya, 1945-63', *Journal of Imperial and Commonwealth History* 36, no. 3 (2008): 527-43.

service of the overseas colonies. In the early 1950s Jeffries was deputy under-secretary of state at the Colonial Office. The situation in colonial Africa was extremely unsettled, with racial tensions and racially motivated violence increasingly in evidence. Jeffries thought that new Colonial Service recruits might benefit from additional voluntary training, to better prepare them for the difficulties they would encounter overseas. He believed that churches and missionary societies might assist with the provision of this training. In February 1953 he contacted Geoffrey Fisher.[12] Coincidentally, on the day that Jeffries' letter arrived at Fisher's office Max Warren was chairing a meeting at the Conference of British Missionary Societies headquarters, also in London. The topic for discussion was lay Christian overseas work. In July of the previous year Warren had attended an important IMC meeting at Willingen, in Germany. It had been a mostly dispiriting experience for him: missions appeared unwilling or unable to adapt to present uncertainty or to plan for future exigency. Warren drew solace from the enthusiasm of certain European missionaries for greater lay participation in mission and church affairs.[13] He had long believed this participation to be vital to the life of the church both 'at home' and overseas, and after Willingen he exhorted colleagues to devise suitable plans.[14] At their London meeting in February 1953 British mission representatives contrasted decreasing missionary numbers with the increased number of western laypeople working abroad due in part to the expanding role of the United Nations, its subsidiary organisations and other agencies.[15] Warren had recently received a personal letter from an Edinburgh-based medical doctor recently returned from Pakistan. His name was Harry Holland (1911-96), and his father, Henry, had for more than four decades run a renowned CMS-supported eye hospital at Quetta, earning in the process the gratitude of locals, and also a knighthood.[16] Influenced by his family experiences, Holland wanted to foster a sense of Christian fellowship among British men and women going overseas to work. His ideas were similar to those of Jeffries, and to Warren they made good sense.

12. The National Archives of the UK: Public Record Office (hereafter TNA: PRO), CO859/248, Sir C. Jeffries to Most Rev. G. F. Fisher, 9 Feb. 1953.

13. Robert Kurtz, 'The Lay-Worker as a New Type of Missionary', IRM 42, no. 167 (1953): 308-17. Kurtz was an official of the Basel Mission.

14. Max Warren, 'The Role of the Missionary Society', in Norman Goodall, ed., Missions under the Cross (London, 1953), pp. 201-7.

15. School of Oriental and African Studies, London (hereafter SOAS), Conference of British Missionary Societies Papers (hereafter CBMS), 31, Edinburgh House meeting on lay overseas work, minutes, 10 Feb. 1953.

16. Sir Henry Holland, Frontier Doctor (London, 1958).

Holland was ambitious. He envisaged a non-profit-making organisation that would train employees not only of government but also of British businesses overseas. Warren and Jeffries supported this idea. So too did Fisher, with whom Holland and Jeffries met in November 1953. Holland also obtained administrative support from the British Council of Churches. From the Colonial Office Holland received assurance (negotiated by Jeffries) that its overseas personnel and those of the Crown Agents would have his training recommended to them.[17] Holland meanwhile canvassed the business community, securing agreement to use his services from, among others, Barclays Bank DCO (Dominions and Colonial Office), Booker Brothers, British Petroleum, Cable & Wireless, Imperial Chemical Industries and Shell Oil. These firms, along with the Colonial Office and the Crown Agents, would pay fees to the training organisation that Holland was now working to set up. Notwithstanding Jeffries' influence, Holland had little expectation of direct financial aid from the government. In the event, the government made available a series of small grants. Holland was successful in obtaining funds from interested philanthropic bodies such as the Cadbury Trust and the Nuffield Foundation. He aimed to further expand his business contacts and increase fee income to ensure financial viability by the end of an initial three-year period. A total of 115 men and women signed up for the first set of training courses, to begin in January 1954. These would be run by an organisation that Holland named Oversea Service. It would operate under the joint auspices of the Conference of British Missionary Societies and the British Council of Churches. Its slogan would be 'Training for Responsible Partnership Abroad'.

The courses would at first be held at two venues: the underused (and soon to be redundant) Imperial Institute in South Kensington, London, and Dunford House in West Sussex, birthplace of Richard Cobden, use of which Holland had negotiated with the current owners, the YMCA.[18] Each course lasted six days and focused on a certain geographic region. Holland secured the services of experienced lecturers and guest speakers who included colonial governor Sir Charles Arden-Clarke, social anthropologist Kenneth Kirkwood and development adviser Arthur Gaitskell. Themes and topics encompassed a wide range, from the workings of colonial administration to the necessities of personal health care in the tropics. Current events, such as those in Kenya, figured prominently: one lecture was on 'Social and Race Relations

17. TNA: PRO, CO 859/248, H. B. T. Holland to D. Bishop, 12 Dec. 1953.
18. Oversea Service subsequently leased premises for a time at Moor Park College, Farnham, Surrey.

in East Africa'; another was on 'Mau Mau — Cause and Effect'. Holland ensured that at least one session on each course had an overtly religious emphasis; this was typically led by a clergyman or an ordained missionary: Rev.
John V. Taylor of the CMS was one participant, as was Rev. Obadiah Kariuki,
visiting from the diocese of Mombasa.

Holland briefed these religious lecturers carefully. He requested that they
emphasise in their teaching Christian aspects of citizenship and 'community
service'. He insisted above all that participants in the training courses should
learn to become more sensitive to overseas cultures and also become able to
distinguish between 'Christian' ideas and values and those that might be considered 'western'. This mattered greatly to Holland; he regarded trainees
about to head overseas as unofficial ambassadors of their home country and
also as ambassadors of the church. 'The layman's witness overseas (and in this
country)', he wrote, 'is not merely incidental to the Christian Gospel. It is
unique. Without it "official" Christian presence of the Gospel is essentially in-
complete, because it is not incarnate'.[19]

Holland aimed to provide instruction of a kind not available elsewhere.
But his courses had to have sufficient practical content, so as to be attractive
to employers and employees alike. A strong emphasis upon religion might
not go down well, especially if the aim was to attract, in the interests of viability, what one civil servant described as 'non-Christians or luke-warm Christians'.[20] Arguably, employees who were already strongly Christian in their beliefs would gain least from the religious aspects of the training. Holland
nevertheless reported high levels of satisfaction among participants, but take-
up for the 1955 round of courses was disappointingly slow and small. Reporting to the British Council of Churches on the difficulties of what he
termed 'frontier' work in Britain, Holland lamented the 'baffling strength of
that familiar obstacle to the Church's work in this country — indifference'.[21]
He regretfully acknowledged that in order to survive, Oversea Service might
have to broaden its appeal, and reduce its already small but significant emphasis upon Christian teaching.

This was a potential outcome of regret to Warren and other missionaries,
who perceived the work of Oversea Service as complementary to that of the
missionary societies, which were experiencing difficulties of recruitment.
What use to the church might Oversea Service be, they wondered, if it became

19. H. B. T. Holland, 'Oversea Service: An Experiment in Lay Responsiblity', *IRM* 44,
no. 174 (1955): 188-91.

20. TNA: PRO, CO 859/248, Bishop, minutes, 24 June 1953.

21. SOAS, CBMS, 571, Holland, report to British Council of Churches, n.d., but April
1955.

'only vaguely Christian'?[22] Inter-Church Aid (ICA) secretary Janet Lacey was interested in Oversea Service. She had noted the response of Christian laypeople to the Kenya Appeal of 1955, and was determined to exploit this further. In 1959 Lacey provided Oversea Service with ICA funds to set up a subsidiary: an Overseas Appointments Information and Advisory Service that would act as a recruitment agency for ICA.[23] She also challenged British businesses to make more use of Oversea Service. To Lesslie Newbigin, now IMC general secretary, Lacey admitted having sometimes to deny to sceptical employers that Oversea Service was 'a sort of missionary breeding-ground'.[24] Even allowing for this, only through attenuation of its founding principles, it seemed, could the organisation that Holland had done so much to create be adapted to meet the needs of business people interested in making use of its services.

Supporting Oversea Service was but one of Lacey's many commitments. She made use of her contacts within international ecumenism to tap into sources of funding and expertise. It was vital, she confided to one missionary, to '. . . put up a good case and get in first'.[25] She was often successful. Three months earlier, in May 1957, she had organised the first Christian Aid Week. In mid-September she attended a London meeting of voluntary and other organisations under the auspices of the United Nations Association. The aim of the meeting was to devise methods whereby young people from Britain could undertake voluntary service in 'economically under-developed areas' overseas. These people would not primarily need to be religious, but they would certainly need to possess 'toughness, tolerance, reliability, humour and adaptability'.[26] This form of voluntary service owed much to the ideas and initiative of Alec Dickson and his wife Mora.[27] In 1958 the Dicksons set up what became VSO — Voluntary Service Overseas.

The early years of VSO were notable for growth, internal disagreement and financial difficulty; but it gradually garnered increasing levels of financial support from a wide range of unofficial agencies in Britain and from businesses and government also. VSO probably influenced the 1961 decision of US President John F. Kennedy to authorise the Peace Corps. In response to a colleague's

22. SOAS, CBMS (1961-70), 109, File 1, Rev. R. K. Orchard to Rev. N. Goodall, 15 March 1957.

23. This advisory service was wound up in 1965. There is a successor organisation: Christians Abroad.

24. SOAS, CBMS (1961-70), 107, File 1, J. Lacey to Rt Rev. J. E. L. Newbigin, 17 Nov. 1959.

25. SOAS, CBMS, 577, 'Kenya Appeal' file, Lacey to Rev. P. G. Bostock, 15 Aug. 1957.

26. SOAS, CBMS, 572, '1958' file, unsigned, 'Report of the Steering Committee', n.d.

27. Dick Bird, *Never the Same Again: A History of VSO* (Cambridge, 1998), pp. 15-40.

suggestion that new Peace Corps–type initiatives might render missions out of date, Max Warren chose to praise instead the difficult yet rewarding long-term nature of mission work. Decrying the 'starry-eyed romanticism' that he perceived might underpin Peace Corps–type recruitment, Warren wrote that 'the real need of . . . overseas communities cannot be met by tourists, however well-intentioned'.[28] For Warren the Peace Corps idea was not objectionable in itself; it seemed, however, symptomatic of broader, unfocussed western efforts to render assistance to non-western peoples without due consideration of the consequences for those peoples. Those efforts, Warren suspected, would emphasise 'aid' and 'development' rather than individual spiritual need. They would likely be characterised by waste, inefficiency and excess bureaucracy. Over the course of two decades Warren had striven, with some success, to rid the CMS of such characteristics. But were missions now about to be succeeded by bureaucratic aid agencies? Warren appears to have had a presentiment of this possibility in his dealings with Kenya and with Leonard Beecher. Forwarding large sums of money raised by CMS to Beecher for diocesan use, he cautioned against frittering away funds 'in introducing European personnel and providing them with cars'.[29] Warren was not alone in thinking this way. In 1959 the historian and Anglican layman Hugh Tinker considered the implications for non-western countries of over-reliance on expensive western aid. He argued that aid should be offered, not given, and that western technicians should live simply overseas, without refrigerators and air-conditioning, in conditions 'partially reminiscent of the life of a settlement officer in the old Indian Civil Service or of a pioneer Christian missionary.'[30]

The Changing Nature of Overseas Mission

If conditions for mission in Africa were undergoing great change so too were expectations of mission as career and vocation. Over the course of a ten-year period Dorothea Lehmann worked with the LMS mission in Mufulira, Northern Rhodesia, on loan from the Berlin Missionary Society. It was a very rewarding experience in many ways, but Lehmann continually fretted about money. She remitted what she could afford from her allowance to her mother in Germany. She attempted without success to obtain a pension from the

28. SOAS, CBMS (1961-70), 107, 1, Canon M. A. C. Warren to Rev. R. M. Bennett, 21 April 1961.

29. UBL, CMS, A5/6/1, Warren to Rt Rev. L. J. Beecher, 24 Sept. 1953.

30. Hugh Tinker, 'The Name and Nature of Foreign Aid', *International Affairs* 35, no. 1 (1959): 43-52.

BMS, with which she had been a probationer in the late 1930s. The opportunity in 1957-58 to work with John V. Taylor on the IMC-sponsored project on Christian and church life in the Copperbelt was to prove tremendously beneficial to Lehmann. She was able to put her research skills to full use, and, eventually, to contemplate a new career. After several years she was able to fulfil her ambition of becoming a teacher and researcher. Having left the LMS in 1959, Lehmann worked as a welfare official in Chingola. In 1966 she took up a post at the African Studies Department at the University of Zambia.[31]

Lehmann had only been able to take up the Copperbelt research post because the IMC agreed in effect to pay the LMS for her services. The Society was in considerable financial difficulty. In 1950 it had raised salaries and allowances in response to entreaties from missionaries in Africa about the high cost of living.[32] This response had little or no effect on the clamour, which continued much as before. The LMS forbade missionary wives from undertaking paid work. In 1952 several married male missionaries formally requested of the Society that their wives be permitted to take paid employment as a means of supplementing family incomes. This presented the LMS with a dilemma: some families might benefit more than others from such a scheme. There was also a risk of compromising a fundamental tenet of LMS mission life: Africa Secretary Ronald Orchard reminded missionaries of 'the importance of voluntary service — something which we are so constantly emphasising to the Younger Churches'.[33] At Orchard's recommendation, it was arranged that missionary wives' earnings should in future be paid into a central fund upon which mission families could draw to cover certain justifiable expenses. This arrangement appears to have been accepted for a time, but by the end of the decade it was proving unworkable: missionary wives insisted that they should be allowed to work — and to earn much-needed income, for children's education costs and other expenses.[34] Seeking guidance on what had become a difficult and delicate problem, Orchard's successor Rev. Frank Griffiths contacted his Church of Scotland missions' counterpart. He discovered that the Scots dealt with such cases as they arose, relying on a less than satisfactory 'rule of thumb'. Rev. John Watt of the Foreign Missions Committee admitted to Griffiths that the consequences of this ad hoc arrangement were some 'flagrant anomalies'.[35]

31. Much later Lehmann returned to Germany, where she died in 1982.

32. SOAS, Council for World Mission Archive, London Missionary Society Papers (hereafter CWM), AF/25/22, Rev. A. J. Haile to Orchard, 23 Sept. 1950.

33. SOAS, CWM AF/10H, Orchard, LMS confidential memo, July 1952.

34. SOAS, CWM, AF/15P, H. A. B. Packer to Rev. A. F. Griffiths, 3 Jan. 1960.

35. NLS, B399, Rev. J. A. R. Watt to Griffiths, 17 Jan. 1957.

Missions were by no means unaffected by or immune from contemporary debate in Britain about employment equality.[36] But they were slow to adapt to changing expectations of work, especially among women. As Watt conceded, the Scottish attitude to missionary wives in the mid-1950s remained in many respects 'somewhat Victorian'.[37] Both the LMS and the Scottish missions did adapt, however, mainly in response to action initiated by male missionaries and their wives (with the Scots also granting equal pay to single women missionaries). That this issue did not become more of a problem was partly due to expansion of British missions' denominational links during the 1950s: in central Africa LMS and Church of Scotland missions and churches benefitted in terms of Canadian funds and personnel, supplied by the United Church of Canada. Not all Christian workers from the West were willing or, because of family commitments, able to follow Hugh Tinker's suggestion of living like a pioneer, and missionary societies could not hope to match pay and conditions offered by aid agencies. There were also other, more troublesome discrepancies of pay and conditions: between European and African clergy. These gave rise to disquiet and complaint; but the effects may have been offset to some extent by funds now being made available to churches in Africa through international ecumenical agencies, notably in Kenya and Northern Rhodesia.[38]

From the late 1950s ecumenical institutions assumed increasing importance in that regard. They also assumed a more varied international character. The Mindolo Ecumenical Foundation (MEF), based at Kitwe in Northern Rhodesia, had as its first executive secretary the 'whirlwind'-like Australian Congregationalist minister Peter Mathews.[39] He negotiated with the World Council of Churches, with local Christian organisations and with business concerns, African trade unions and political parties to set up forums for debate and training on citizenship and social affairs, years in advance of Zambian independence.[40] The MEF facilitated interracial dialogue during a period of great uncertainty in Northern Rhodesia and the Central African Federation. In so doing it took on a broader role that missions for various reasons had been unable or unwilling to perform. In Kenya, the Swiss-born

36. On this debate, see Gerry Holloway, *Women and Work in Britain since 1840* (London and New York, 2005), pp. 195-201.

37. NLS, B398, Watt to Rev. E. H. Johnson, 6 April 1955.

38. SOAS, CWM, AF27/16, Rev. E. A. Read to Griffiths, 19 June 1962.

39. SOAS, CWM, AF26/29, Griffiths to Rev. M. O. Janes, 12 May 1961.

40. Loretta Kreider Andrews and Herbert D. Andrews, 'The Church and the Birth of a Nation: The Mindolo Ecumenical Foundation and Zambia', *Journal of Church and State* 17 (1975): 191-216.

Moravian clergyman Paul Fueter, for a time secretary of the Christian Council, acknowledged in 1960 the failure of missions and colonial state alike to invest adequately in African expertise.[41] He pledged that the Council would seek to remedy that deficiency, in part through training of Africans by skilled westerners. But Fueter was intent that the Council should also educate westerners in the ways of the church in Africa. In 1960 VSO sent seven volunteers to Kenya. Two worked with the Christian Council, the others with church-related organisations such as the YWCA. Sir Patrick Renison, appointed governor of Kenya the previous year in succession to Sir Evelyn Baring, reported on this development to the Colonial Office. Volunteers placed with church groups, he noted, 'must be prepared to work within the framework of the African Church'.[42]

Christians in Britain interested in overseas mission work also had to take account of other changes. In 1961 the British government devised new ways to render technical assistance to 'developing' countries in Africa and other parts of the world. It set up a Department of Technical Co-operation, which drew on expertise and experience gained over the course of two decades' administration of colonial welfare and development policies. Sir Charles Jeffries had retired five years before, which allowed him time to unofficially promote the interests of the SPG and other organisations, among them the now struggling Oversea Service. Through personal contacts and persistent lobbying Jeffries secured in 1961 an acknowledgement from government that Oversea Service might now fulfil a larger role in the training of workers going abroad on officially sponsored aid and development projects. Government would provide financial assistance for its move to new premises, a former bishop's palace at Farnham, in Surrey.[43] This financial commitment owed nothing whatever to religious considerations; it was motivated by official concern that overseas workers be properly trained. In the same year, government also agreed to make funds available (mainly from colonial development and welfare resources) to VSO.[44] For years Harry Holland had met with only limited success in his efforts to attract financial support for Oversea Service from philanthropic bodies in Britain, Europe and North America. Prospective business and commercial clients meanwhile suspected it of being too religious in its orientation. Many missionaries, conversely, thought it was insufficiently

41. P. S. Fueter, 'A Christian Council in Africa: The Christian Council of Kenya', *IRM* 49, no. 195 (1960): 292.

42. TNA: PRO, CO 859/1445, Sir P. Renison to C. Y. Carstairs, 24 Aug. 1960.

43. TNA: PRO, OD 8/4, Dept. of Technical Co-operation, memo, 'Oversea Service', n.d., but *c.* Dec. 1961.

44. TNA: PRO, CO 859/1446, Sir A. Cohen, minutes, 19 July 1961.

mission-oriented. Holland persisted in his endeavours until 1964. He left England that year, returning to Pakistan to resume a medical career. In 1966 he would be ordained priest in the diocese of Lahore.

Oversea Service became for a time the Oversea Service College and subsequently Farnham Castle, a business currently committed to 'intercultural' training for business and government. Ultimately, Oversea Service failed to realise its potential as a Christian agency; it was not viable on such terms. In consequence, missionaries deemed it advisable to liaise more closely with certain secular organisations that might be sympathetic to Christian humanitarianism. One such organisation was the Overseas Development Institute (ODI), a 'think tank' set up in London in late 1960 with funding from the Ford Foundation and other bodies. Its first director, William Clark, favoured western volunteers being made available to African countries, to help smooth their transition from colonial to independent status.[45] Clark was also open to informal discussion with British religious representatives on imperial affairs, about which he was knowledgeable and well informed.[46] Clark considered that the ODI could become a coordinating agency for voluntary organisations in Britain, with which missions might have informal links.[47] Missionaries for their part felt they could ill afford *not* to associate, on an informal basis at least, with the ODI.[48] CMS president Sir Kenneth Grubb became a member of its council.[49] Grubb believed that while retaining their distinct identity as agencies of evangelisation and overseas church growth, missionary societies should not hesitate to participate in discourse on matters relating to aid and development.[50]

Inevitably, perhaps, missionaries were not of one mind on these issues. A multiplicity of organisations was now focussing western public attention on overseas aid and development. A great deal of discussion on Africa was taking place very far away from Africa, without African involvement. In such circumstances missionaries strove to retain focus on mission and to emphasise its importance. There were after all still British men and women who wished to serve

45. William Clark, 'After Independence in East Africa,' *African Affairs* 61, no. 243 (1962): 126-37.

46. Church of England Record Centre, London, British Council of Churches Papers, 5/2/2ix, Rev. A. Keighley to W. C. Clark, 25 June 1959. Clark had been a foreign and diplomatic correspondent for *The Observer* and also, for a time, press secretary to Prime Minister Anthony Eden.

47. TNA: PRO, CO 859/1449, W. H. Chinn, minutes, 14 June 1961.

48. SOAS, CBMS, (1961-70), 107, File 1, Rev. J. V. Taylor to Rev. F. Short, 25 Jan. 1961.

49. Grubb was knighted in 1953.

50. SOAS, CBMS (1961-70), 77, File 8, Sir K. Grubb to Short, 6 Feb. 1961.

the overseas church in a primarily religious rather than exclusively professional or technical capacity. In March 1961 the IMC sponsored a consultation at its London office, Edinburgh House, on candidacy for mission. From this event it appeared that young candidates presenting for service were realistic about what they might achieve and what might be expected of them. They seemed open-minded and knowledgeable (to an extent that some of their predecessors of an earlier generation might not have been) about cultures and societies outside the West. They seemed aware of shortcomings in western cultures and societies. They seemed to think that there was a continuing need for overseas Christian mission.[51] How well equipped were missionary societies in the early 1960s to help these candidates realise their aspirations and ambitions to serve overseas? If British missionary societies faced challenge on one front from African nationalism and African Christian independency, they also faced other challenges within the United Kingdom, not least that of attracting and retaining overseas workers for the church in parts of Africa.

Many of those candidates in the early 1960s might have read Trevor Huddleston's book, *Naught for Your Comfort*, published in 1956. It was an intensely personal and movingly written account of Huddleston's work in South Africa and of his struggle against apartheid. It brought him international renown. His biographer has commented that readers might learn from it 'that religious, social and political commitment could . . . call forth dormant qualities of self-sacrifice in unlikely places, could change lives'.[52] Deciding, also in 1956, to take up a post in Northern Rhodesia, the Methodist minister Colin Morris (b. 1929) brought with him from England a copy of *Naught for Your Comfort*, by which he had been inspired. For all its virtues he found it a poor guide to the complexities and ambiguities of racial and political life in a British central African colony.[53] As many clerical visitors to the region from Britain (such as George MacLeod and John V. Taylor) would also discover, Morris found that a disconcertingly large number of resident Europeans accepted racial discrimination as a fact of life. Morris decided to work from the premise that discrimination was wrong and objectionable. He made forays into politics that proved ultimately unsuccessful, in electoral terms at least. The outcome of the 1962 Northern Rhodesia General Election resulted in the colony's first black government, which took office in December of that

---

51. SOAS, CBMS, (1961-70), 107, File 1, P. Löffler, memo, on Edinburgh House consultation, 24 March 1961. Also, Paul Löffler, *The Layman Abroad in the Mission of the Church: A Decade of Discussion and Experiment* (London, 1962).

52. Robin Denniston, *Trevor Huddleston: A Life* (London, 1999), p. 70.

53. Colin M. Morris, *The Hour after Midnight: A Missionary's Experience of the Racial and Political Struggle in Northern Rhodesia* (London, 1961), pp. 2-15.

year. Reflecting on this transformative event, Morris thought it absurd that a European (and especially, perhaps, a European clergyman) could any longer represent African political interests. As in the world of politics, so also in the church: European clergy, Morris insisted in his writings, should work with and for the indigenous church, securing from the 'Mother Church' in the United Kingdom whatever assistance Africans might request.[54] However ambivalent some African Christians might be about missions and about British imperialism, they might well require some assistance from Britain: it would matter greatly to the future of the church in Africa that such assistance be offered and accepted in good spirit. It followed that missionaries from Britain should know when *not* to offer assistance. This realisation did not prevent certain missionaries and a small number of other Britons in east and central Africa from becoming involved in the politics of 'multiracialism' in the early 1960s, in an attempt to encourage European support for racial and political equality. Outside of Southern Rhodesia, most Europeans in the central African colonies, including missionaries, came to accept the rightness of black self-government and political independence.

Missions, the 'African Revolution' and the End of Empire

From Nyasaland to Kenya, the road to African political autonomy was uncertain and unpredictable. In Nyasaland, the Malawi Congress Party was increasingly intolerant of criticism. The Church of Central Africa Presbyterian had close links with Congress. What effect might all this have on the church's readiness to criticise the party? Scottish-born clergymen in the CCAP such as Andrew Doig hoped that Hastings Banda would exercise a moderating influence on Congress, and especially on the increasingly 'terrifying' antics of the Malawi Youth League.[55] Banda's power, and that of the party, continued to grow. After a sweeping victory for the MCP in the general election of August 1961 Banda became de facto prime minister (being formally recognised as such in February 1963). In December 1962 the government in London acceded to his demand that Nyasaland be allowed to secede from the Central African Federation. Banda could charm British politicians; conversely, former Scottish missionaries who had previously supported him were now uneasy about the impact upon church and society in Nyasaland of his authoritarian tendencies.

After thirty-five years of service in Africa and in Britain, James Dougall

---

54. Colin M. Morris, *Nothing to Defend* (London, 1963), pp. 32-6.
55. NLS, B418, Rev. A. B. Doig, circular letter, 2 Feb. 1961.

retired in 1960. He was alarmed by events in Nyasaland. Invited to contribute to a series of lectures at the University of Edinburgh in memory of the nineteenth Scottish missionary to India, Alexander Duff, Dougall chose as one of his themes the 'interaction of politics and mission'. Central Africa provided timely examples of this phenomenon. Dougall argued that in their active defence of 'backward and underprivileged peoples' missionaries had long undertaken work with 'political' overtones. Now they had to accept and welcome the long-suppressed right of such peoples to order their own affairs. In so doing, missionaries should not, he thought, abnegate their continuing political responsibilities: 'social and political witness', according to Dougall, was 'inseparable from evangelism'. But Nyasaland presented peculiar difficulties in this regard: events in the colony since 1959 had contributed to racial division in the church notwithstanding the assimilation of English-speaking congregations at Blantyre and Zomba into the CCAP and the appointment of Jonathan Sangaya as synod general secretary, both in 1962. Dougall insisted that the indigenous church 'has to correct the idolatry of the nation and the Utopian pretensions of political propaganda. To do this will mean taking risks. It is not characteristic of new nations to be tolerant of criticism'.[56] With his experience and knowledge of colonial Africa and with the case of South Africa undoubtedly in mind, Dougall knew how useless and even counterproductive might be criticism emanating from the United Kingdom. The church there might help its counterpart in Africa best by assisting it to make its own way. He was certain that Scots would continue to play a role in the Christian world mission, and would also be accepted in an independent Africa 'once we rid ourselves of any colonial or imperial overtones . . .'[57]

This was far from a straightforward matter, least of all in Nyasaland. To Congress the presence of European church workers might indeed be indicative of residual colonialism. Any sympathy on the part of those workers for Banda's political opponents would in a short time suffice to attract the sinister attentions of MCP activists. Within months of Malawian independence, Scots and other westerners would flee the country.[58] Andrew Ross, a staunch supporter of Banda and of Congress (and an unsuccessful electoral candidate in 1961), fled Malawi with his family in May 1965.[59] Scottish missionaries took pride in their readiness to subject political authority to scrutiny and overt

56. J. W. C. Dougall, *Christians in the African Revolution: The Duff Missionary Lectures, 1962* (Edinburgh, 1963), pp. 46, 52.

57. Dougall, *Christians in the African Revolution*, p. 93.

58. Colin Baker, *Revolt of the Ministers: The Malawi Cabinet Crisis, 1964-65* (London, 2001), pp. 202-3.

59. Baker, *Revolt of the Ministers*, pp. 251-7.

criticism. But in Nyasaland such actions became ever more complicated and more dangerous, not only for the Scots but for Africans also. In Scotland, meanwhile, home support for radical missionary activity in Nyasaland dissipated quickly after 1959. The General Assembly of the Church of Scotland's Special Committee Anent Central Africa became ever more divided against itself following George MacLeod's 1961 resignation as convenor. Its subsequent deliberations degenerated into factionalism, recrimination and eventual irrelevancy. It was dissolved in 1963.

MacLeod and the Iona Community had set great store by the Special Committee, through which, they hoped, the Kirk, and Scotland, might be reenergised by events in Nyasaland and Northern Rhodesia. For them missionary work had always been 'intimately related to the evangelistic task at home'.[60] So political was the Special Committee's remit, however, that it could not but attract the opprobrium of those within and outside the Kirk who opposed mission identification with African nationalism. Yet the influence of the missions on Scotland was also made felt in other small but significant ways at this time: tutors at St. Colm's Missionary College, Edinburgh, such as Rev. Kenneth Mackenzie alerted trainees to the complexities of mission, church, empire and nationalism in central Africa. But Scots were never entirely in agreement as to missionary methods. In October 1962 Andrew Doig left Nyasaland of his own volition to return to work in Scotland. The previous year Doig had written to the assistant secretary of the Women's Foreign Missions Committee, reiterating in a new context an age-old Protestant missionary worry: 'I wonder if Scotland appreciates how badly we are losing out these days to the Roman Church. They are far outstripping us in education, medical and social welfare work. We have earned a reputation for outspokenness on public issues but we are open to serious criticism when it comes to getting on with our special services to body and soul'.[61] Some of Doig's compatriots working in Nyasaland would doubtless have argued that these ostensibly different responsibilities were intertwined and indivisible. The troubling question remained all the same, as to what might be the missionary task after the end of empire in Africa.

Would there even be a place in independent Africa for missionaries from Britain? In the early 1960s missionaries were hopeful, even optimistic on this score, without ever being certain about the impact on their work of political developments. The situation varied from one part of sub-Saharan Africa to

60. NLS, 9084, 195, 'The Church of Scotland Report of the Iona Community Board' (May, 1955), p. 7.

61. NLS, B418, Doig to Miss B. G. R. Reid, 21 Sept. 1961.

another. In 1961 LMS secretary Frank Griffiths undertook an official tour of the Society's work. It proved to be a sobering experience. Griffiths (1902-75) was taken aback by how much influence missionaries still wielded in church affairs. In some ways this was to be expected: European clergy still outnumbered their African counterparts. But higher-level church business was still invariably conducted in English, and Griffiths was disappointed by missionaries' tendency to privilege their mother tongue over those of their African colleagues. Unless corrected the effects of this practise, Griffiths thought, were sure to prove insidious, the more so given current African dissatisfaction over matters such as clerical stipends. African ministers earned a great deal less than their European counterparts and their compatriots in other careers such as teaching. Griffiths resolved to petition the Society to increase stipends as soon as possible. The issue prompted further difficult questions: Could the church in Africa afford in terms of financial cost and potential for ill-will continuing missionary involvement? Griffiths concluded that the weakness of the indigenous church in LMS areas of operation would undoubtedly necessitate continuing missionary involvement.[62] Besides, 1961 was proving a bountiful year for recruitment: the Society accepted seventeen men and women for overseas work, mainly as clergymen, teachers, doctors and nurses: ten would go to Africa.

As for so long in the past, so also in the future by such means as teaching and medical work would missionaries from Britain continue to occupy a place in the life of late colonial and independent Africa. Inevitably, though, there were still complicated political issues with which to contend also. As Griffiths visited LMS churches, missions and their associated institutions in Northern Rhodesia, Southern Rhodesia, the Bechuanaland Protectorate and South Africa, he constantly bore in mind the troubled state of relations between government in Pretoria and in London. In March 1961 South African prime minster Hendrik Verwoerd announced that South Africa would leave the Commonwealth. On 31 May South Africa became a republic. Griffiths anticipated further difficulties for churches in southern Africa: members of LMS church councils who resided in South Africa might in future be prohibited from attending council meetings outside its borders. Not only would this have a detrimental effect on church unity in the region, it might also lead to increased reliance by the church in Africa on resources from overseas.[63]

White intransigence was not of course confined to South Africa. The European inhabitants of Southern Rhodesia had viewed with alarm and anger

---

62. SOAS, CWM, AF26/29, Griffiths, report on visit to Africa, May-July 1961, pp. 9-10.
63. SOAS, CWM, AF26/29, Griffiths, report on visit to Africa, May-July 1961, p. 10.

the growth of African nationalism and the supine (as it seemed) attitude of Conservative politicians such as Harold Macmillan and Iain Macleod in Britain. Concessions to Banda and Kaunda galled white Rhodesians and drove them temperamentally towards extremism.[64] With the Central African Federation a lost cause by the end of 1962 and finally dissolved on 31 December 1963, they increasingly asserted their own right to independence. Opinion within churches and missionary societies in Southern Rhodesia was divided, but only to a degree; few missionaries spoke out either against the government or in favour of African majority rule. Those who did might be transferred back to Britain by their churches, as happened to the Methodist clergyman Whitfield Foy in 1960. In 1964 the government of Southern Rhodesia declared the American Methodist bishop Ralph Dodge 'PI', and deported him.[65]

These deportations continued a pattern apparent from 1959, with the prohibition from the Central African Federation of the Scottish clergyman Tom Colvin and the detention in Southern Rhodesia of the British-born activist Guy Clutton-Brock. Government in Salisbury was not only opposed to majority rule, it was also intolerant of dissent from whatever source. On 11 December 1965 Rhodesian Prime Minister Ian Smith would declare unilateral independence (UDI), ostensibly in the interests of justice, civilisation and Christianity. That assertion would be contested by local church leaders and by the Christian Council of Rhodesia (which had been set up in 1964), but opinion in Rhodesian churches would remain divided for a long time to come.[66] That devolution by Britain of political authority in east and central Africa (Southern Rhodesia aside) up to 1964 proved relatively peaceful was nonetheless a relief to missionaries, some of whom as late as 1961 still feared 'racial war' in the Rhodesias.[67] The case of Southern Rhodesia would serve, especially after UDI, as a troubling reminder of what might ensue from settler intransigence and failures in British imperial policymaking.

States of emergency, suspension of civil liberties, maltreatment and unjustifiable deaths of detainees all contributed during the 1950s and early 1960s to the final, fatal weakening of empire in Britain's African colonies. Even so,

---

64. R. F. Holland, *European Decolonization, 1918-1981* (Basingstoke, 1985), p. 233.

65. W. R. Peaden, 'Aspects of the Church and Its Political Involvement in Southern Rhodesia, 1959-1972', *Zambezia* 7, no. 2 (1979): 191-210.

66. Chengetai J. Zvobgo, 'Church and State in Rhodesia: From the Unilateral Declaration of Independence to the Pearce Commission, 1965-72', *Journal of Southern Africa Studies* 31, no. 2 (2005): 381-402.

67. SOAS, CBMS, 570, 'Federation Group' file, Central Africa Group, minutes, 13 July 1961.

the actions of Conservative governments during the period 1960-64 appeared to missionaries immeasurably more reasonable and more progressive than the actions of governments in Salisbury and in Pretoria. British decolonisation in Africa compared favourably with that of other European powers, notably Belgium in relation to Congo. In September 1961 the Conference of British Missionary Societies and the British Council of Churches jointly stated their approval of government policy for Africa. This earned public rebuke from none other than the Marquess of Salisbury, most die-hard Tory opponent of imperial retrenchment. He described the statement as 'a classic example of muddled thinking' on the part of people he regarded as political amateurs.[68] There was some truth in Salisbury's assertion. Missionaries had attempted in vain to keep pace with developments in imperial policymaking. Their efforts to elicit meaningful information from government came almost to nothing. They remained uncertain and uneasy about African nationalism. Their public statements had negligible influence on the government. In a sense none of this mattered unduly. The churches had somehow to bear witness. To British church leaders it remained vital that people in Britain, whether Christian or not, were kept aware of Africa and of the church's work there, now and in time to come.

The Future for Overseas Mission

In 1962, in response to a request for information from the Overseas Development Institute, Edinburgh House estimated the number of Protestant missionaries working overseas from the United Kingdom at 4,475.[69] That amount contrasts with a figure of approximately 9,300 calculated just prior to the outbreak of the Second World War.[70] Numbers can tell us only so much. And numbers do not equate with influence. All the same, it is possible to see the decline in missionary numbers over this period as in some ways indicative of decline both in British Christian vocation and also in British overseas influence. However, we should not think of the period as one of absolute decline for British missions, especially where Africa is concerned. The loss of China to missions at the beginning of the 1950s meant redeployment of personnel to many other places, including parts of Africa. For those in-

---

68. UK House of Lords Debates, 235, c. 65, 1 Nov. 1961.

69. SOAS, CBMS (1961-70), 77, 8, information for ODI, n.d., but late 1962.

70. TNA: PRO, INF 1/413, MOI, Publicity Division, memo, 'Protestant Missions', 16 Aug. 1939.

volved, adaptation to this new environment was anything but easy, but the overall effect was probably beneficial to mission in Africa. The number of British missionaries should in any case be viewed against the number from North America. In 1938 the number of foreign missionaries from North America (of whom the vast majority were from the United States) was 12,136. By 1960 the number had grown to 29,380.[71] By that time American influence on Protestant overseas mission was also being felt in other ways: in greater suspicion of western imperial authority in Africa and Asia and in greater receptivity towards and support for indigenous churches and indigenous church leadership.[72] British missionaries were hardly less worried about communism than their American counterparts; but they were often ambivalent about the American presence in Africa, be it in the form of missionaries or of Peace Corps volunteers who arrived in British colonies (such as Tanganyika) and former colonies (such as Ghana) from 1961 onwards. By dint of its scale the American presence could appear overbearing, but it brought benefit to many religious organisations. In his work with the Christian Council of Kenya Andrew Hake was able to take advantage of IMC and WCC initiatives backed by American church and philanthropic resources. These initiatives helped the CCK devise theologically based programmes of urban assistance and renewal in cities such as Nairobi.[73]

Beneficial to mission as such programmes undoubtedly were, they did not rely for administration upon missionaries from Britain in particular. This marked a change, of sorts. Over the course of a century and a half, from the early 1800s to the 1960s, Protestant missionaries journeyed from Britain to work in Africa. There they established a multiplicity of relationships: with indigenous peoples, colonial authority, European settlers and missionaries from other western countries. Over time those relationships underwent great change. Similarly the extent of the British missionary presence in Africa waxed and then waned: in numerical terms its apogee was probably the period 1900-1914. It endured far beyond 1914 nevertheless. It encompassed men and women of many different backgrounds and denominations, many recruited via the missions' links with local churches and with other Christian organisations in England, Scotland, Wales and Ireland. An entire history

71. Julie Hearn, 'The "Invisible" NGO: US Evangelical Missions in Kenya', *Journal of Religion in Africa* 32, no. 1 (2002): 37.

72. John Coventry Smith, *From Colonialism to World Community: The Church's Pilgrimage* (Philadelphia, 1982), pp. 150-72.

73. SOAS, PP MS 46 ADD 1:1, Hake additional papers, CCK, 'The Mission of the Church in Urban Areas: Report of an East African Regional Consultation', 13-15 March 1961.

might be written about the regional, class, family, educational and religious background of missionaries from Britain during the period 1939-64.

Change in the 'supply' of overseas missionaries from Britain to Africa and other parts of the world during that period was influenced by many factors, not least the changing nature of missionary vocation and of the churches' role in British society. But British attitudes to overseas mission were also influenced by imperial affairs. In many ways this was as true of the period of end of empire as it was of the 1890s when, famously (or notoriously), Uganda became a missionary *cause célèbre*. Events in late colonial Africa, from the banishment of Seretse Khama and the establishment of the Central African Federation to states of emergency in Kenya and Nyasaland, focussed Christian as well as wider public attention in Britain on the continent (as also of course did events in South Africa). From the late 1950s the evangelistic impulse might become confused or on occasion even conflated with the impulse to provide overseas aid and development. In time Christian dissatisfaction in the West with the potential for confusion between overseas aid and evangelism would contribute to a renewed evangelical focus on overseas mission, one effect of which would be a late twentieth-century 'surge' in evangelical mission from Britain.[74] As during the period 1939-64, Africa continued long after the end of empire to influence ideas and practices in British missionary activity.

74. Jeffrey Cox, *The British Missionary Enterprise since 1700* (London, 2006), p. 259.

Conclusion

The independence of virtually all Britain's colonial territories in Africa by the mid-1960s has been described as the culmination of a 'long and inevitable process', shaped variously by international pressures, British politics and, not least, African political nationalism.[1] Everywhere attitudes towards empire changed after 1945, through the growth of indigenous nationalist movements, through the indirect and sometimes oblique influence of the United Nations and also through the dissemination of ideas about human rights. Missionaries were cognisant of these developments: for the Anglo-Catholic general secretary of the UMCA as for the Congregationalist Africa secretary of the LMS, concern for 'human rights' readily accorded with overseas missionary vocation.[2] In the aftermath of the Second World War, missionaries still perceived Britain as a guarantor of such rights for the peoples of its African colonies. The commitment of the South African government to apartheid in 1948 confirmed and strengthened this perception and helped reconcile missionaries in the early 1950s to the Central African Federation: British policies appeared enlightened in comparison with those of South Africa. For a time the actions of D. F. Malan and his successors helped grant the Federation a spuri-

---

1. Wm. Roger Louis, 'The Dissolution of the British Empire', in Louis and Judith M. Brown, eds., *The Oxford History of the British Empire, Volume IV: The Twentieth Century* (Oxford, 1999), p. 354.

2. Bodleian Library of Commonwealth and African Studies at Rhodes House, Oxford (hereafter RHL), Universities' Mission to Central Africa Papers (hereafter UMCA), SF115, Canon G. W. Broomfield to bishops of east and central Africa, 5 Sept. 1945; School of Oriental and African Studies, Council for World Mission Archive, London Missionary Society Papers, AF40/80A, Rev. R. K. Orchard to Rev. N. Goodall, 21 March 1949.

ous legitimacy. During the mid-1950s missionary attitudes altered. Correspondence and reports from Northern Rhodesia, from Nyasaland and also from Kenya evinced dismay, disillusion and anger with British colonialism. All that took time to emerge in public form, and missionaries in the mid-1950s could treat very shabbily indeed someone like Eileen Fletcher who had their interests at heart. But disapproval of colonialism emerged more openly at the end of the 1950s, in the witness of Colin Morris and Merfyn Temple, in the writings of John V. Taylor and in the less well-known and less acknowledged work of many other missionaries in British colonies. It is nevertheless fair to assert that the moral vocabulary and rhetoric of British overseas mission was a good deal less relevant at the end of empire than it had been at the height of empire's 'civilising mission' for Africa in the late nineteenth century.[3] Missionaries' roles, responsibilities and ideas about empire had altered greatly.

Missionaries no longer served as they had in the 1920s and 1930s as interlocutors between empire and indigenous peoples. Many other Africans besides Seretse Khama found that they had much more in common with British anti-colonialists such as Fenner Brockway than with missionaries. No longer did missionaries speak for Africans; Africans spoke for themselves. To British politicians such as Iain Macleod, meanwhile, missionaries were but one of many means to larger political ends. Colonial authorities, for their part, exerted ever greater authority over Christian educational and medical facilities as, subsequently also, would governments of independent African states. From the mid-1950s NGOs posed a new and different sort of challenge to missions and to the missionary vocation.

For all that, there still remained the church in Africa, and African Christianity. Missionaries worried that the greatly increased pace of imperial decolonisation from 1960 would leave churches unready, because of inadequately trained clergy and laity and inadequate local funding, to withstand the pressures of political change: anti-colonial nationalism might redound to damaging effect upon the church. The situation was more complicated than missionaries realised. As David Maxwell has noted, anti-colonialism did not always engender opposition to the ideals and principles of western institutions, including Christianity. And nationalism might not always constitute a mass movement. It was nevertheless the case that Christianity helped equip Africans to challenge western imperialism. Political leaders and ordinary people alike drew upon the Bible and upon evangelical language 'to sanctify colo-

---

3. Brian Stanley, 'Christianity and the End of Empire', in Brian Stanley, ed., *Missions, Nationalism, and the End of Empire* (Grand Rapids, MI, and Cambridge, 2003), p. 2.

nial politics and justify their activism'.[4] As ever, Christianity found new uses and new outlets in a rapidly changing world.

'. . . the era of the Missionary Society is at an end'

In 1961 Leonard Beecher attended an ecumenical gathering in Tanganyika. Afterwards he circulated details to Anglican colleagues in Africa and in Britain. 'In one sense', Beecher wrote, 'the era of the Missionary Society is at an end'.[5] He did not intend to imply the end of overseas mission from Britain and the West. Instead he was asserting the entitlement of the indigenous church to decide how and where foreign missionaries might be deployed, in east Africa and elsewhere. In his dealings as a bishop with the Church Missionary Society, Beecher had never been less than assertive; he had exerted considerable influence on mission as well as on local church affairs in Kenya and the diocese of Mombasa. Now primate of an autonomous ecclesiastical province, he was determined that the advance of the church in the region should continue to match that of African self-determination in Kenya and Tanganyika. Reflecting on recent elections held in Kenya, Beecher was 'quietly optimistic' about the colony's political situation. At this time Kenyan independence was still more than two and a half years away. In August 1961, however, Jomo Kenyatta was released from imprisonment. In October he joined the Kenya Africa National Union, the party he would lead to power as Kenya's first independent government in December 1963. Beecher, along with other church leaders both Protestant and Roman Catholic, would be an official participant in the independence celebrations. In a sense, then, the formal end of the colonial era, in Kenya at least, approximately coincided with what might indeed be termed the end of 'the era of the Missionary Society'.

Strong-willed and well-connected, Beecher was a religious leader of substance. Kenyatta recognised this, as he also recognised the value to the new state of church-run educational facilities. Furthermore, Kenyatta publicly announced that the Anglican Church, with other churches, would have an important role to play in fostering unity in the new nation.[6] Kenyatta had little desire to dwell, publicly at least, on Kenyan suffering during the emergency. The ambi-

---

4. David Maxwell, 'Decolonization', in Norman Etherington, ed., *Missions and Empire* (Oxford, 2005), pp. 298-9.

5. RHL, UMCA, SF102, Rt Rev. L. J. Beecher, circular letter, encl. with Rt Rev. F. O. Thorne to Broomfield, 17 March 1961.

6. Galia Sabar, *Church, State and Society in Kenya: From Mediation to Opposition, 1963-93* (London, 2002), pp. 65-6.

guities of that period in Kenya's history have not yet been fully resolved by either state or church.[7] In any case, the formal ending of empire in Kenya did not mean a sundering of links with Britain. Quite the contrary — one set of official relationships gave way to another: Kenya joined the Commonwealth. Also, prior to independence the Treasury in London made grants and loans for land resettlement available to government in Nairobi. The World Bank also gave loans. For its part, the Anglican Church in Kenya would continue to rely on the services of the CMS and other external Anglican agencies for recruits, training, publicity and funds. To a greater or lesser extent the same was true of other indigenous African churches of British mission origin. Tensions might ensue, as David H. S. Lyon has noted in relation to the Scottish mission presence: financial inequality would cause difficulties between 'younger' and 'older' partners that would take much time and effort to resolve.[8] Missionaries meanwhile acknowledged that they might become the object of suspicion concerning neo-colonialism.[9] Nevertheless, many missionaries rejoiced at the coming of African independence; for some it was an answer to their prayers.

That this was so strikingly the case in relation to certain missionaries connected with Nyasaland is indicative of how ambiguous might be the missionary relationship with colonial authority and with African nationalism alike. In the aftermath of Frank Thorne's resignation as bishop, officials of the Diocese of Nyasaland and of the Province of Central Africa struggled to formulate a response to the African clamour that Michael Scott be appointed as his successor. They were terrified that the unpredictable and 'so unsuitable' Scott might respond by putting his name forward. Archbishop of Central Africa James Hughes requested of Trevor Huddleston that he try to dissuade Scott from doing so.[10] In the event (and probably irrespective of Huddleston's intervention), Scott professed no interest in the post. Almost as quickly as it had arisen the crisis passed, to the relief of all concerned. This development coincided with the success of Hastings Banda and the Malawi Congress Party in the Legislative Council election of 1961, an outcome that in both Anglican provincial and diocesan circles appeared to guarantee stability in Nyasaland after two years of

7. Daniel Branch, *Defeating Mau Mau, Creating Kenya: Counterinsurgency, Civil War, and Decolonization* (Cambridge, 2009), pp. 209-12.

8. David H. S. Lyon, *In Pursuit of a Vision: The Story of the Church of Scotland's Developing Relationship with the Churches Emerging from the Missionary Movement in the Twenty-five Years from 1947 to 1972* (Edinburgh, 1998), pp. 274-7.

9. Max Warren, *The Missionary Movement from Britain in Modern History* (London, 1965), pp. 165-66.

10. RHL, MSS Huddleston, 4, Rt Rev. W. J. Hughes to Rt Rev. E. U. T. Huddleston, 8 June 1961.

unrest and uncertainty. Now 'the difficulties for the Church will disappear', Hughes confidently assured Huddleston.[11] A similar mood of optimism pervaded UMCA headquarters. A year earlier there had been great apprehension about constitutional discussions in London between Iain Macleod and Banda. But the success of that conference, which would set Nyasaland on the road to independence in July 1964, was to missionaries as welcome as it was unexpected. To Gerald Broomfield, who, with others, had anticipated a bloody aftermath to Banda's release from detention four months earlier, the outcome of the constitutional talks was nothing less than 'a miracle'.[12]

Although Banda had divided Scottish missionary opinion, he continued to enjoy, for some time after 1959, strong support from that quarter. The missionaries of the UMCA were more generally wary of him. By 1961 he had done much to win them over with his promises of an independent Nyasaland that would be stable and tolerant if not necessarily prosperous (poverty was preferable to oppression, Banda would declaim). Thorne was among those who would reserve judgement on those promises. He had come to know the Congress leader quite well since his (Banda's) return to Nyasaland in 1958. Thorne had also come to know, from the denigration to which he had been subjected for having professed belief in a Congress murder plot in 1959, that there were apparently 'two Dr Bandas': one charming, one ruthless.[13] Under Thorne's successor, Donald Arden, the Anglican Church would encounter difficulty in discerning Banda's true attitude to the church. As in Kenya and other decolonising British territories, government in independent Malawi would rely upon church educational and medical facilities as, also, on external aid and development funds. But the church might continue to find itself caught up in politics: in late 1964 Arden would assist in aiding the family of one of Banda's former lieutenants and now sworn enemy, Henry Chipembere, son of Archdeacon Habil Chipembere. Once Banda consolidated his power in the aftermath of the Malawian 'cabinet crisis' of 1964-65, churches of all denominations would find it difficult to criticise much less defy party, leader or state.[14]

Ultimately, the early 1960s seemed a time of promise. John McCracken has suggested, though, that Scots might too easily overlook and fail to adequately criticise nationalist tendencies towards authoritarianism evident even at that time.[15] In Nyasaland this oversight was an unfortunate corollary of

11. RHL, MSS Huddleston, 4, Hughes to Huddleston, 17 Aug. 1961.

12. RHL, UMCA, SF29xv, Broomfield to Thorne, 18 Aug. 1960.

13. RHL, UMCA, SF29xv, Thorne to Broomfield, 28 May 1960.

14. Colin Baker, *Revolt of the Ministers: The Malawi Cabinet Crisis, 1964-1965* (London, 2001), pp. 205-8.

15. John McCracken, 'Church & State in Malawi: The Role of the Scottish Presbyterian

well-intentioned Scottish missionary 'anti-imperialism'. Yet British imperial policymakers set the pace. They balanced pragmatism with expediency. They identified nationalists with whom they could collaborate and to whom they could devolve authority at the formal ending of empire. Too frequently, however, collaborative arrangements took insufficient account of ethnic and political diversity. To the chosen collaborators, in time democratically elected to government, would accrue benefits of power too good to relinquish: later, one-party states would emerge in Malawi, in Kenya, in Zambia, in Tanzania and even (in benign form) in Botswana, which became independent in 1966. This might have serious consequences for any African churches deemed subversive of party, and thereby state authority. Nothing in the early 1960s was more illustrative of this possibility than the violent suppression by Kenneth Kaunda's government-in-waiting of the Lumpa Church of Alice Lenshina in 1964, the year of Zambian independence.[16] Some months earlier, in a presidential statement for the synod of the United Church of Central Africa, Rhodesia, Colin Morris had contemplated the emergence of a 'national' church in Northern Rhodesia and the future relationship it might have with the state. 'We must always judge the state cautiously', he advised, 'lest we condemn out of hand the unfamiliar and strange as defective'. It would be the responsibility of the church, as an institution representative of all the people, he asserted, to always be vigilant lest the state degenerate into tyranny.[17] Vigilant the church might seek to be, but its influence on the state in independent Zambia (as in Malawi) would be variable: the state was more likely to influence the church. In Zambia as in other former British colonies, church-state relations would become extremely complicated.[18]

1939-64: The Period in Context

The history of British Protestant missionaries in east, central and southern Africa during the period 1939-64 forms part of many other longer and larger

---

Missions, 1875-1965', in I. Phiri, K. Ross and J. L. Cox, eds., *The Role of Christianity in Development, Peace, and Reconstruction: Southern African Perspectives* (Nairobi, 1996), pp. 188-9.

16. David M. Gordon, 'Rebellion or Massacre?: The UNIP-Lumpa Conflict Revisited', in Jan-Bart Gewald, Marja Hinfelaar and Giacomo Macola, eds., *One Zambia, Many Histories* (Leiden, 2008), pp. 45-76.

17. Colin M. Morris, statement by president of synod, UCCAR, 'Towards a National Church in an Independent Northern Rhodesia', 1 Sept. 1963.

18. R. Drew Smith, 'Missionaries, Church Movements and the Shifting Religious Significance of the State in Zambia', *Journal of Church and State* 41, no. 3 (1999): 525-50.

histories, of Christianity and the church in Africa and of western involvement in the continent. The missionary activity that took place during that period did not reach some sort of 'end' in 1964. It was part of a much larger and longer endeavour from Britain begun, essentially, during the final decade of the eighteenth century and continuing still into the twenty-first. The year 1964 is a suitable terminal date for this particular history, for several reasons. It is the year of Malawian and Zambian independence. It is also the year in which Inter-Church Aid changed its name — to Christian Aid. Finally, on 31 December 1964 the British overseas mission agency that identified itself most explicitly and exclusively with Africa — the UMCA — ceased to exist as a separate entity; it merged with the SPG, thus creating the United Society for the Propagation of the Gospel.

As Jeffrey Cox has written, it is 'a paradox of mission history in Africa that on the continent where mission work probably had its greatest influence, the missionary role in African history has been so minimised' of late.[19] The formal ending of European empires in the 1960s sparked an understandable and necessary explosion of interest in African national histories in which missions only sometimes featured. Most historians of European imperialism in Africa evinced little interest in missions. The effect of all this on mission history, according to Cox, has been to leave it stranded 'between national histories, and marginal to the histories of both sending and receiving nations'.[20] This book has sought to redress that imbalance, in part by arguing that during the period 1939-64, missionary activity was important both in its own right and also as a means through which broader historical phenomena such as the expansion of Christianity and the ending of European empires may be studied anew and perhaps better understood.

During the period covered by this book long-term historical trends emerged in the life of the church and also in the religious life of the West and of Africa. Theological trends that originated during the late colonial era are still in the process of development and change.[21] The propensity of religion and religious organisations for flux may at times appear self-evident, but is worth noting, and especially for British Protestant missionaries and their relationships with empire and with African nationalism. That missionaries in the

19. Jeffrey Cox, *The British Missionary Enterprise since 1700* (London, 2008), p. 252.
20. Cox, *British Missionary Enterprise*, p. 252.
21. On Africa, see Tite Tiénou, 'Evangelical Theology in African Contexts', in Timothy Larsen and Daniel J. Treier, eds., *Cambridge Companion to Evangelical Theology* (Cambridge, 2007), pp. 216-18. On changing western attitudes to mission in the 1960s, see William R. Hutchison, *Errand to the World: American Protestant Thought and Foreign Missions* (Chicago, 1987), pp. 183-6.

late 1950s and early 1960s hoped, prayed and in some cases worked actively for African self-determination and by implication also the end of empire could not have been foreseen in 1939, or 1945. We should be wary nonetheless of ascribing to British missionaries any crusading zeal for African advancement after 1945. Attitudes to Africans during the late colonial period might still range from paternalism through ambivalence to suspicion and even hostility. Missionaries might be racist, but also anti-racist, as they might at times be imperialistic and at other times resolutely anti-imperialist. In retrospect the 'decolonisation' of the church in colonial Africa may have the appearance of planning and forethought, but this was seldom actually the case. In its sometimes ad hoc nature, ecclesiastic devolution might not be so very different from transfers of political authority to independent African states.[22] The end of empire in Africa owed something to metropolitan policymaking, but it owed a great deal also to a combination of international and local African pressures, economic, social and political. Missionaries felt these pressures and responded as they could. But the 'revolutionary' change advocated for the church by Bishop Stephen Neill in 1947 did not come from within the missionary societies, it came, partly at least, in reaction to missions, notably through independent, Pentecostal and other African churches. Although British missionaries in colonial Africa during the period 1939-64 were not active in the instigation of Christian 'revolution', this was a development of which many were supportive. From the sidelines, as it were, retired missionary leaders such as James Dougall and Max Warren offered in the early 1960s advice for the future on mission in contemporary imperial and world affairs.[23] Christianity in independent Africa was by this time already acquiring new momentum.

Missionaries proved less able to adapt to changing circumstances than either the government in London or nationalists in Africa. Their faith, though, compelled them to continually hope and pray for and strive towards better things. In 1957 Gerald Broomfield published a short book celebrating the centenary of the UMCA. There he noted the crippling effect of staff shortages upon the mission's current work. This was all the more unfortunate, he wrote, given that 'a new phase of the struggle' for Christ in Africa had now been reached.[24] That phase was one of many, past, present and future. The work was never-ending.

22. On the rationale of transfers of power, see John Darwin, *The End of the British Empire: The Historical Debate* (Oxford, 1991).

23. J. W. C. Dougall, *Christians in the African Revolution* (Edinburgh, 1963); M. A. C. Warren, 'Christian Missions in the Contemporary Revolution', in Warren, *The Missionary Movement from Britain in Modern History* (London, 1965), pp. 160-80.

24. Gerald W. Broomfield, *Towards Freedom* (London, 1957), p. 133.

Malawi, 1970-71

During 1970-71 discussions took place in the Anglican Province of Central Africa as to how the huge diocese of Nyasaland might be administered more effectively. In 1936, when Frank Thorne became bishop, the diocese covered an area of some 250,000 square kilometres encompassing the colony of Nyasaland and also parts of Tanganyika and Portuguese East Africa (Mozambique). Travelling via an inadequate network of roads, Thorne could hope to visit every church and mission station only once every two years. The creation out of the diocese of Nyasaland in 1952 of a new diocese, of South-West Tanganyika, eased the bishop's burden slightly. Likoma Island was no longer the geographical 'centre' of the diocese, and this influenced Thorne's decision to move his administrative base southward and closer to the colonial capital, Zomba. These arrangements remained in place until 1971. In that year out of the diocese now of Malawi were formed two new units: the dioceses of Southern Malawi and of Lake Malawi. Bishop Donald Arden would retain responsibility for Southern Malawi. The new Bishop of Lake Malawi would be Josiah Mtekateka (1903-96), a suffragan since 1965. Following the inauguration of his new diocese at All Saints' Church, Nkhotakota, on the eastern shore of Lake Malawi, Mtekateka journeyed to Likoma Island for his enthronement at St Peter's Cathedral as the first Malawian-born diocesan bishop. The event had an international aspect, for among those present were the Bishop of Birmingham and the Suffragan Bishop of Texas, testifying to the links between the Anglican Church in Malawi and other parts of the world-wide Anglican Communion.

Mtekateka had been ordained deacon more than thirty years earlier, by none other than Frank Thorne. Thorne was not at Likoma that day. He had retired to Liuli, also on the eastern shore of Lake Malawi, but in Tanzania. He did, however, attend the enthronement of another African bishop in 1971, for the new diocese of Ruvuma. He did so as an ecclesiastical envoy, representing the successor organisation to the UMCA, the United Society for the Propagation of the Gospel. Thorne had originally intended to retire as Bishop of Nyasaland in 1959 but he changed his mind. It was a decision he would regret. Congress attacks on his character wounded him deeply, and he saw out the final year of his long episcopate in an agony of self-reproach, for having admitted to the possible existence of a Congress murder plot. 'Each day that passes deepens my sense of failure,' he confided to Gerald Broomfield; '. . . my episcopate will end with my being like that king of Israel — I can never remember which one — who died "no man regretting him"'.[1] He retired in 1961, sustained in part thereafter by his faith, in part by friendships, with Africans and with Europeans such as Trevor Huddleston.[2] He died in 1981.

Hastings Banda and the Malawi Congress Party undoubtedly caused many other people in late colonial Nyasaland and independent Malawi a great deal more sorrow than they caused Frank Thorne. But his experiences help to show how difficult and even painful it may have been for adherents of one British missionary tradition, steeped not merely in Anglo-Catholicism but also to some degree in African language and custom, to come to terms with radical nationalism and the phenomenon with which it became for a time intertwined: the end of empire in Africa.

1. Bodleian Library of Commonwealth and African Studies at Rhodes House, Oxford (hereafter RHL), Universities' Mission to Central Africa Papers, SF29xv, Rt Rev. F. O. Thorne to Canon G. W. Broomfield, 27 Nov., and 28 May 1960.

2. RHL, MSS Huddleston, 9, Thorne to Rt Rev. E. U. T. Huddleston, 8 July 1968.

Bibliography

PRIMARY SOURCES

1. Government Papers

The National Archives of the UK, London

COLONIAL OFFICE PAPERS
CO 323: Colonies, General: Original Correspondence
CO 533: Kenya Original Correspondence
CO 537: Confidential General and Confidential Original Correspondence
CO 795: Northern Rhodesia: Original Correspondence
CO 822: East Africa: Original Correspondence
CO 847: Recognition of Missionary Societies
CO 859: Social Services Department
CO 1015: Central Africa and Aden: Original Correspondence
CO 1027: Information Department

DOMINIONS OFFICE AND COMMONWEALTH RELATIONS OFFICE PAPERS
DO 35: Original Correspondence

MINISTRY OF INFORMATION PAPERS
INF/1: Ministry of Information Records, 1939-46

DEPARTMENT OF TECHNICAL CO-OPERATION PAPERS
OD/8: Recruitment and Staffing Departments

2. Archival Collections

Bodleian Library of Commonwealth and African Studies at Rhodes House, Oxford

Africa Bureau Papers: MSS. Afr. s. 1681
Anti-Slavery Society Papers: MSS. Brit. Emp. s. 19, 22, 23
Sir Robert Perceval Armitage Papers: MSS Afr. s. 2204
Sir Michael Blundell Papers: MSS. Afr. s. 746
Canon Peter Geoffrey Bostock Papers: Micr. Afr. 642
1959 Nyasaland (Devlin) Commission of Enquiry Papers
Fabian Colonial Bureau Papers: MSS. Brit. Emp. s. 365
Trevor Huddleston Papers
Dame Margery Freda Perham Papers: MSS. Perham
Michael Scott Papers
United Society for the Propagation of the Gospel in Foreign Parts Papers, including
    Universities' Mission to Central Africa Papers
Sir Roy Welensky Papers: MSS. Welensky
Sir Arthur Edwin Young Papers: MSS. Brit. Emp. s. 846

Church of England Record Centre, London
British Council of Churches Papers
Missionary Council of the Church Assembly Minutes and Papers

Lambeth Palace Library, London
Geoffrey Francis Fisher Papers
Cosmo Gordon Lang Papers
Michael Ramsey Papers
William Temple Papers

National Archives of Scotland, Edinburgh
Reports to the General Assembly of the Church of Scotland
General Assembly of the Church of Scotland Church and Nation Committee: Minute
    Books

National Library of Scotland, Edinburgh
General Assembly of the Church of Scotland Foreign Missions Committee: Papers:
    Accession 7548 and 9638
General Assembly of the Church of Scotland Foreign Missions Committee: Minute
    Books: Deposit 298
MacLeod of Fuinary and Iona Papers: Accession 9084

Mission Studies Library, Partnership House, London
(now Crowther Mission Education Centre Library, Oxford)
Church Missionary Society: Annual Reports
Church Missionary Outlook
CMS News-Letter

School of Oriental and African Studies Library, London:
Archives and Special Collections
Christian Aid Papers
Conference of British Missionary Societies Papers
Council for World Mission Papers (for London Missionary Society)
Rev. Andrew Augustus Gordon Hake Papers
International Missionary Council/Conference of British Missionary Societies Papers
Methodist Missionary Society Papers

University of Birmingham Library: Special Collections
Church Missionary Society Papers
Canon Max Warren: Travel Journals

University of Edinburgh Library: Centre for Research Collections
Rev. Kenneth Mackenzie Papers: Gen. 1871
Scottish Council on African Questions Papers: MS. 2495

3. United Kingdom Parliamentary Reports
House of Commons: Official Report
House of Lords: Official Report

4. Official Publications
Cmd. 5949 (1939): *Rhodesia-Nyasaland Royal Commission Report*
Cmd. 6175 (1940): *Statement of Policy on Colonial Development and Welfare*
Col. No. 186 (1943): *Mass Education in African Society*
Col. No. 216 (1948) *Education for Citizenship in Africa*
Kenya Colony and Protectorate, *African Education in Kenya* (Nairobi, 1949)
Cmd. 8233 (1951): *Central African Territories: Report of Conference on Closer Association: London, March 1951*
Cmd. 8411 (1951): *Closer Association in Central Africa: Statement by His Majesty's Government in the United Kingdom, 21 November 1951*
Cmd. 8573 (1952): *Southern Rhodesia, Northern Rhodesia and Nyasaland: Draft Federal Scheme: prepared by a Conference held in London in April and May 1952*
Cmd. 9081 (1954): *Report to the Secretary of State for Colonies by the Parliamentary Delegation to Kenya, January 1954*
Cmnd. 814 (1959): *Report of the Nyasaland Commission of Enquiry*

Cmnd. 815 (1959): *Nyasaland: Despatch of the Governor relating to the Report of the Nyasaland Commission of Enquiry*

Cmnd. 1030 (1960): *Historical Survey of the Origins and Growth of Mau Mau*

Cmnd. 1148 (1960): *Report of the Advisory Commission on the Review of the Constitution of Rhodesia and Nyasaland*

5. Interviews and Correspondence

Rt Rev. Donald Arden

Professor Colin Baker

James Foster

Professor Richard Gray

Rt Rev. Dr. Graham Kings

Dr. Gordon Mungeam

Dr. Andrew Ross

Professor George Shepperson

Lord Steel of Aikwood

Rev. Vernon Stone

6. Books

Abrecht, Paul, *The Churches and Rapid Social Change* (London, 1961).

Beveridge, Lord, *Voluntary Action: A Report on Methods of Social Advance* (London, 1948).

Bewes, T. F. C., *Kikuyu Conflict: Mau Mau and the Christian Witness* (London, 1953).

Broomfield G. W., *Colour Conflict: Race Relations in Africa* (London, 1943).

————, *Towards Freedom* (London, 1957).

Carothers, Dr. J. C., *The Psychology of Mau Mau* (Nairobi, 1954).

Cole, Keith, *Kenya: Hanging in the Middle Way* (London, 1959).

Collins, Lewis John, *Faith under Fire* (London, 1966).

Davis, J. Merle, *Modern Industry and the African* (London, 1933).

————, *New Buildings on Old Foundations* (New York and London, 1945).

Dougall, J. W. C., *Christians in the African Revolution: The Duff Missionary Lectures, 1962* (Edinburgh, 1963).

Forrester, Marion W., *Kenya Today: Social Prerequisites for Economic Development* (The Hague, 1962).

Goodall, Norman, ed., *Missions under the Cross* (London, 1953).

Gray, Richard, *The Two Nations: Aspects of the Development of Race Relations in the Rhodesias and Nyasaland* (London, 1960).

Hailey, Lord, *An African Survey: A Study of Problems Arising in Africa South of the Sahara*, 2nd ed. (London, 1945).

Hinden, Rita, *Fabian Colonial Essays* (London, 1945).

Hodgkin, Thomas, *Nationalism in Colonial Africa* (London, 1956).

Holland, Sir Henry, *Frontier Doctor* (London, 1958).

Huddleston, Trevor, *Naught for Your Comfort* (London, 1956).

Kariuki, J. M., '*Mau Mau' Detainee: The Account by a Kenyan African of his Experiences in Detention Camps, 1953-60* (London, 1963).

Kaunda, Kenneth, and Colin Morris, *Black Government?* (Lusaka, 1960).

Leakey, L. S. B., *Mau Mau and the Kikuyu* (London, 1952).

———, *Defeating Mau Mau* (London, 1954).

Leys, Colin, and Cranford Pratt, *A New Deal in Central Africa* (London, 1960).

Little, Kenneth L., *Negroes in Britain: A Study of Racial Relations in English Society* (London, 1947).

Löffler, Paul, *The Layman Abroad in the Mission of the Church: A Decade of Discussion and Experiment* (London, 1962).

MacLeod, George F., *Only One Way Left: Church Prospect* (Glasgow, 1956).

Mason, Philip, *Year of Decision: Rhodesia and Nyasaland in 1960* (London, 1960).

Morgan, E. R., and Roger Lloyd, *The Mission of the Anglican Communion* (London, 1948).

Morris, Colin M., *The Hour after Midnight: A Missionary's Experiences of the Racial and Political Struggle in Northern Rhodesia* (London, 1961).

———, *Nothing to Defend* (London, 1963).

Newbigin, J. E. L., *One Body, One Gospel, One World: The Christian Mission Today* (London, 1958).

Oldham, J. H., *New Hope in Africa* (London, 1955).

Paton, David M., *Christian Missions and the Judgment of God* (London, 1953).

Ranson, C. W., ed., *Renewal and Advance: Christian Witness in a Revolutionary World* (London, 1948).

Sanger, Clyde, *Central African Emergency* (London, 1960).

Scott, Michael, *A Time to Speak* (London, 1958).

Sundkler, Bengt G. M., *Bantu Prophets in South Africa* (London, 1948).

———, *Church of South India: The Movement towards Union, 1900-47* (London, 1954).

———, *Bantu Prophets in South Africa*, 2nd ed. (London, 1960).

———, *The Christian Ministry in Africa* (London, 1960).

Taylor, J. V., *Christianity and Politics in Africa* (Harmondsworth, 1957).

———, *The Primal Vision: Christian Presence amid African Religion* (London, 1963).

Taylor, John V., and Dorothea Lehmann, *Christians of the Copperbelt: The Growth of the Church in Northern Rhodesia* (London, 1961).

Warren, Max, *Revival — An Enquiry* (London, 1954).

———, *Caesar, the Beloved Enemy: Three Studies in the Relation of Church and State* (London, 1955).

———, *The Missionary Movement from Britain in Modern History* (London, 1965).

Welbourn, F. B., *East African Rebels: A Study of Some Independent Churches* (London, 1961).

Wiseman, E. M., *Kikuyu Martyrs* (London, 1959).

7. Journal Articles and Book Chapters

A China Missionary, 'First Thoughts on the Debacle of Christian Missions in China', *International Review of Missions* (hereafter *IRM*) 40, no. 160 (1951): 411-20.

Baxter, J. G. H., 'The Anglican Communion and Its Missionary Task: Lambeth 1958', *IRM* 47, no. 188 (1958): 445-53.

Beattie, John, 'Willingen 1952', *IRM* 41, no. 164 (1952): 433-43.

Beecher, Rt Rev. L. J., 'After Mau Mau — What?', *IRM* 44, no. 174 (1955): 205-11.

Bewes, T. F. C., 'The Work of the Christian Church among the Kikuyu', *International Affairs* 29, no. 3 (1953): 316-25.

Busia, K. A., 'Has the Christian Faith Been Adequately Presented?', *IRM* 50, no. 197 (1961): 86-9.

Clark, William, 'After Independence in East Africa', *African Affairs* (hereafter *AA*) 61, no. 243 (1962): 126-37.

Davis, J. Merle, 'Principles of Missions in a New Age', *IRM* 32, no. 127 (1943): 264-71.

————, 'Mission Strategy in the New Age', *IRM* 35, no. 139 (1946): 303-13.

Dougall, J. W. C., 'Colonial Policy and the Christian Conscience', *IRM* 30, no. 120 (1941): 477-92.

Freytag, Walter, 'Changes in the Patterns of Western Missions', *IRM* 47, no. 186 (1958): 163-70.

Fueter, Paul S., 'A Christian Council in Action: The Christian Council of Kenya', *IRM* 49, no. 195 (1960): 201-300.

Goodall, Norman, 'Editorial', *IRM* 38, no. 151 (1949): 273-5.

————, 'First Principles', *IRM* 39, no. 155 (1950): 257-62.

————, 'Towards Willingen', *IRM* 41, no. 162 (1952): 129-38.

————, 'The Limits of Co-Operation', *IRM* 44, no. 176 (1955): 447-54.

Green-Wilkinson, Most Rev. F. O., 'Christianity in Central Africa', *AA* 62, no. 247 (1963): 114-24.

High, Stanley, 'The Mau Mau's Unexpected Enemy', *Reader's Digest* 64, no. 385 (1954): 57-9.

Holland, H. B. T., 'Oversea Service: An Experiment in Lay Responsibility', *IRM* 44, no. 174 (1955): 187-92.

Kurtz, Robert, 'The Lay-Worker as a New Type of Missionary', *IRM* 42, no. 167 (1953): 308-17.

Kydd, A. S., 'The Missionary Situation and the Need of Renewal', *IRM* 23, no. 92 (1934): 555-61.

Langford-Smith, N., 'Mass Education and Rural Africa', *IRM* 34, no. 134 (1945): 121-35.

Latourette, Kenneth S., 'The Church in the Anglo-American World: The Post-War Situation', *IRM* 36, no. 142 (1947): 232-52.

Lehmann, Dorothea, 'Alice Lenshina Mulenga and the Lumpa Church', in John V. Taylor and Dorothea Lehmann, *Christians of the Copperbelt: The Growth of the Church in Northern Rhodesia* (London, 1961), pp. 248-68.

Mackenzie, Kenneth, 'The Struggle for Power in Central Africa', *Other Lands* 33, no. 2 (1952).

Neill, Stephen C., 'A Revolutionary Church', in C. W. Ranson, ed., *Renewal and Advance: Christian Witness in a Revolutionary World* (London, 1948), pp. 62-84.

Oldham, J. H. 'After Twenty-five Years', *IRM* 24, no. 95 (1935): 297-313.

————, 'Fifty Years After', *IRM* 49, no. 195 (1960): 257-72.

Paton, William, 'The International Missionary Council and the Future', *IRM* 25, no. 97 (1936): 106-15.

————, 'The Meeting of the International Missionary Council at Tambaram, Madras', *IRM* 28, no. 110 (1939): 161-73.

————, 'Christianity and Civilisation', *IRM* 29, no. 116 (1940): 486-96.

————, 'The Future of the Missionary Enterprise', *IRM* 31, no. 124 (1942): 385-93.

Shannon, Mary, 'Rehabilitating the Kikuyu', *AA* 54, no. 215 (1955): 129-37.

————, 'Rebuilding the Social Life of the Kikuyu', *AA* 56, no. 225 (1957): 276-84.

Shepherd, R. H. W., 'The Separatist Churches of South Africa', *IRM* 26, no. 104 (1937): 453-63.

Stevenson, J. W., 'A Liberating Church in Africa?: The Effects of African Politics on the Church', *Other Lands* 34, no. 3 (1953).

Taylor, J. V., 'The Church in the Smelter', *Central Africa* 77, nos. 920-21 (1959): 120-7.

Tinker, Hugh, 'The Name and Nature of Foreign Aid', *International Affairs* 35, no. 1 (1959): 45-52.

van Randwijck, S. C., 'Inter-Church Aid: A Challenge to Missions', *IRM* 50, no. 200 (1961): 385-9.

Warren, M. A. C., 'The Missionary Obligation of the Church in the Present Historical Situation — With Consideration of the Radical New Relationships between East and West', *IRM* 39, no. 156 (1950): 393-408.

————, 'The Role of the Missionary Society', in Norman Goodall, ed., *Missions under the Cross* (1953), pp. 201-7.

————, 'Nationalism as an International Asset', *IRM* 44, no. 176 (1955): 385-93.

————, '. . . Your Attention to Africa', *IRM* 46, no. 182 (1957): 129-35.

Wrong, Margaret, 'Colonial Development and Welfare', *IRM* 29, no. 116 (1940): 470-6.

————, 'The Church's Task in Africa South of the Sahara', *IRM* 36, no. 142 (1947): 206-31.

8. Pamphlets, Reports and Public Statements
(unless noted, the place of publication is London)

Banda, Hastings K., and Harry Nkumbula, *Federation in Central Africa* (1949).

British Council of Churches, *Human Rights and Religious Freedom* (1947).

————, *Human Rights: The Universal Declaration* (1949).

————, *Africa — A Time for Christian Advance* (1955).

Broomfield, G. W., *The Federation of Rhodesia and Nyasaland: A Survey of the Situation* (1959).

————, *1960: Last Chance in the Federation* (1960).

Campbell, Canon J. McLeod, *Our American Partners: The Life and Activities of the Episcopal Church in America* (1941).

Carey, Bishop Walter, *Crisis in Kenya: Christian Common Sense on Mau Mau and the Colour-Bar* (1953).

Church Missionary Society, *Mau Mau — What Is It?* (1952).

————, *Kenya — Time for Action!* (1955).

Church of Scotland Foreign Missions Committee, *Mau Mau and the Church* (Edinburgh, 1953).

Conference of British Missionary Societies, *Conference of Missionary Societies in Great Britain and Ireland to Lord Lloyd, Secretary of State for Colonies: A Memorandum Inspired by a Statement of Policy on Colonial Development and Welfare, Cmd. 6175* (1941).

————, *The Colour Bar and Race: Policy of British Missionary Societies* (1945).

————, *African National Movements* (1949).

General Assembly of the Church of Scotland Special Committee Anent Central Africa, *Report* (Edinburgh, 1959).

Greaves, L. B., *Central Africa Federation* (1953).

————, *Everyman's Concern: The Rhodesias and Nyasaland* (1959).

High Commission of the Federation of Rhodesia and Nyasaland, *Why Not Be Fair?* (1959).

International Missionary Council, *The Witness of a Revolutionary Church* (New York and London, 1948).

International Missionary Council and Department of Inter-Church Aid and Services to Refugees of the World Council of Churches, *A Report of a Conference on Arab Refugee Problems, Beirut, Lebanon, May 4-8, 1951* (Geneva, 1951).

Keighley, D. A., *Review in Central Africa* (1960).

Latourette, Kenneth S., and William Richey Hogg, *World Christian Community in Action: The Story of World War II and Orphaned Missions* (New York and London, 1949).

Macpherson, Fergus, 'Notes on the Beginning of the Movement', International Missionary Council Research Department: Department of Missionary Studies, *Occasional Papers* 1, no. 1 (1958).

Methodist Church of Great Britain, *A Declaration by the Methodist Church of Great Britain on Racial Policy in the Territories of Southern Africa* (1950).

Morris, Colin M., *Anything but This: The Challenge of Race in Central Africa* (1958).

Oliver, Roland, *How Christian Is Africa?* (1956).

Poole, John, *Baptize the Nations: UMCA Review of 1960* (1961).

Rhodesia and Nyasaland Committee, *The Kirk's New Face in Nyasaland* (1959).

Richards, C. G., *Archdeacon Owen of Kavirondo: A Memoir* (Nairobi, 1947).

Stone, W. V., 'The Church as the People of God', IMC Research Department: Department of Missionary Studies, *Occasional Papers* 1, no. 1 (1958).

————, 'The "Alice Movement" in 1958', IMC Research Department: Department of Missionary Studies, *Occasional Papers* 1, no. 1 (1958).

9. Mission and Church Periodicals

Central Africa (UMCA)
Chronicle (LMS)
Church Missionary Outlook
CMS News-Letter
International Review of Missions
Life and Work (Church of Scotland)
Nyasaland Diocesan Chronicle
Other Lands (Church of Scotland)
St Andrew's Journal (St Andrew's Church, Nairobi)

10. Newspapers and Newsmagazines

British Weekly
Church of England Newspaper
Church Times
East Africa and Rhodesia
The Economist
The Economist Foreign Report
The Glasgow Herald
Manchester Guardian
The New Statesman and Nation
The Observer
Reader's Digest
The Scotsman
Time
The Times

SECONDARY SOURCES

1. Books

Adi, Hakim, *West Africans in Britain, 1900-60: Nationalism, Pan-Africanism and Communism* (London, 1998).

Adi, Hakim, and Marika Sherwood, *The 1945 Manchester Pan-African Conference Revisited* (London, 1995).

Ajayi, J. F. Ade, and J. D. Y. Peel, eds., *People and Empires in African History: Essays in Memory of Michael Crowder* (Harlow, 1992).

Anderson, David, *Histories of the Hanged: Britain's Dirty War in Kenya and the End of the Empire* (London, 2005).

Anderson, David, and David Killingray, eds., *Policing and Decolonisation: Politics, Nationalism and the Police, 1917-65* (Manchester, 1992).

Ashton, S. R., and S. E. Stockwell, eds., *Imperial Policy and Colonial Practice, 1925-45:*

Metropolitan Reorganisation, Defence and International Relations, Political Change and Constitutional Reform (London, 1996).

Askwith, Tom, *From Mau Mau to Harambee: Memoirs and Memoranda of Colonial Kenya* (Cambridge, 1995).

Baker, Colin, *Development Governor: A Biography of Sir Geoffrey Colby* (London, 1994).

————, *State of Emergency: Crisis in Central Africa, Nyasaland* (London, 1997).

————, *Retreat from Empire: Sir Robert Armitage in Africa and Cyprus* (London, 1997).

————, *Sir Glyn Jones: A Proconsul in Africa* (London, 2000).

————, *Revolt of the Ministers: The Malawi Cabinet Crisis, 1964-1965* (London, 2001).

Baker, Derek, ed., *Church, Society and Politics* (Oxford, 1975).

Barber, James, *South Africa's Foreign Policy, 1945-70* (London, 1973).

Bates, Stephen, *A Church at War: Anglicans and Homosexuality* (London, 2004).

Beales, Derek, and Geoffrey Best, eds., *History, Society and the Churches: Essays in Honour of Owen Chadwick* (Cambridge, 1985).

Bebbington, D. W., *Evangelicalism in Modern Britain: A History from the 1730s to the 1980s* (London, 1989).

Bediako, Kwame, *Christianity in Africa: The Renewal of a Non-Western Religion* (Edinburgh, 1995).

Bennett, George, *Kenya, A Political History: The Colonial Period* (London, 1963).

————, *The Kenyatta Election: Kenya, 1960-61* (London, 1961).

Benson, Mary, *Tshekedi Khama* (London, 1960).

Berger, Elena L., *Labour, Race and Colonial Rule: The Copperbelt from 1924 to Independence* (Oxford, 1974).

Berman, Bruce, *Control and Crisis in Colonial Kenya: The Dialectic of Domination* (London, 1990).

Berman, Bruce, and John Lonsdale, *Unhappy Valley: Conflict in Kenya and Africa, Book One: State and Class* (Oxford, 1992).

————, *Unhappy Valley: Conflict in Kenya and Africa, Book Two: Violence and Ethnicity* (Oxford, 1992).

Bevir, Mark, and Frank Trentmann, eds., *Critiques of Capital in Modern Britain and America: Transatlantic Exchanges, 1800 to the Present Day* (Basingstoke, 2002).

Bickers, Robert A., and Rosemary Seton, eds., *Missionary Encounters: Sources and Issues* (Richmond, 1996).

Bird, Dick, *Never the Same Again: A History of VSO* (Cambridge, 1998).

Birn, Donald S., *The League of Nations Union, 1918-45* (Oxford, 1981).

Blake, Robert, *A History of Rhodesia* (London, 1977).

Blood, A. G., *The History of the Universities' Mission to Central Africa, Vol. II: 1907-32* (London, 1957).

————, *The History of the Universities' Mission to Central Africa, Vol. III: 1933-57* (London, 1962).

Blundell, Sir Michael, *So Rough a Wind: The Kenya Memoirs of Sir Michael Blundell* (London, 1964).

Bolink, Peter, *Towards Church Union in Zambia: A Study of Missionary Co-operation and Church-Union Efforts in Central Africa* (Franeker, 1967).

Bosch, David J., *Witness to the World: The Christian Mission in Theological Perspective* (London, 1980).

Brake, George Thompson, *Policy and Politics in British Methodism, 1932-82* (London, 1984).

Branch, Daniel, *Defeating Mau Mau, Creating Kenya: Counterinsurgency, Civil War, and Decolonization* (Cambridge, 2009).

Bredekamp, Henry, and Robert Ross, eds., *Missions and Christianity in South African History* (Johannesburg, 1995).

Brockway, Fenner, *Towards Tomorrow: The Autobiography of Fenner Brockway* (London, 1977).

Brouwer, Ruth Compton, *Modern Women Modernizing Men: The Changing Missions of Three Professional Women in Asia and Africa, 1902-69* (Vancouver, BC, 2002).

Brown, Callum G., *The Social History of Religion in Scotland since 1730* (London, 1987).

———, *Religion and Society in Scotland since 1707* (Edinburgh, 1997).

———, *The Death of Christian Britain: Understanding Secularisation, 1800-2000* (New York, 2001).

Brown, Judith M., and Wm. Roger Louis, eds., *The Oxford History of the British Empire, Vol. IV: The Twentieth Century* (Oxford, 1999).

Burton, Antoinette, ed., *After the Imperial Turn: Thinking With and Through the Nation* (Durham, NC, 2003).

Bush, Barbara, *Imperialism, Race and Resistance: Africa and Britain, 1919-45* (London and New York, 1999).

Butler, L. J., *Copper Empire: Mining and the Colonial State in Northern Rhodesia, c.1930-64* (Basingstoke, 2007).

Calder, Angus, *The People's War: Britain, 1939-45* (London, 1999).

Carey, Hilary M., ed., *Empires of Religion* (Basingstoke, 2008).

Carpenter, Edward, *Archbishop Fisher: His Life and Times* (Norwich, 1991).

Carruthers, Susan L., *Winning Hearts and Minds: British Governments, the Media and Colonial Counter-Insurgency, 1944-60* (London, 1995).

Ceadel, Martin, *Semi-Detached Idealists: The British Peace Movement and International Relations, 1854-1945* (Oxford, 2000).

Cell, John W., *Hailey: A Study in British Imperialism, 1872-1969* (Cambridge, 1992).

Chadwick, Owen, *Michael Ramsey: A Life* (Oxford, 1991).

Chanock, Martin, *Unconsummated Union: Britain, Rhodesia and South Africa, 1900-45* (Manchester, 1977).

Chepkwony, Agnes, *The Role of Non-Governmental Organisations in Development: A Study of the National Christian Council of Kenya (NCCK), 1963-78* (Uppsala, 1987).

Church, J. E., *Quest for the Highest: An Autobiographical Account of the East African Revival* (Exeter, 1981).

Clements, Keith, *Faith on the Frontier: A Life of J. H. Oldham* (Edinburgh, 1999).

Cockram, Gail-Maryse, *South West African Mandate* (Wynberg, 1976).

Comaroff, Jean, and John Comaroff, *Of Revelation and Revolution: Christianity, Colonialism and Consciousness in South Africa* (Chicago, 1991).

Constantine, Stephen, *The Making of British Colonial Development Policy, 1914-40* (London, 1984).

Cooper, Frederick, *Africa since 1940: The Past of the Present* (Cambridge, 2002).

Cox, Jeffrey, *Imperial Fault Lines: Christianity and Colonial Power in India, 1818-1940* (Stanford, CA, 2002).

————, *The British Missionary Enterprise since 1700* (London, 2008).

Crouch, Margaret, ed., *A Vision of Christian Mission: Reflections on the Great Commission in Kenya, 1943-93* (Nairobi, 1993).

Crowder, Michael, *The Flogging of Phinehas McIntosh: A Tale of Colonial Folly and Injustice, Bechuanaland, 1933* (New Haven, CT, 1988).

————, ed., *The Cambridge History of Africa, Vol. 8: From c. 1940 to c. 1975* (Cambridge, 1984).

Cull, Nicholas J., *Selling War: The British Propaganda Campaign against American 'Neutrality' in World War II* (New York, 1995).

Darch, John H., *Missionary Imperialists?: Missionaries, Government and the Growth of the British Empire in the Tropics, 1860-85* (Eugene, OR, 2009).

Darwin, John, *Britain and Decolonisation: The Retreat from Empire in the Post-War World* (Basingstoke, 1988).

————, *The End of the British Empire: The Historical Debate* (Oxford, 1991).

Davenport, T. R. H., and Christopher Saunders, *South Africa: A Modern History* (Basingstoke, 2000).

Davis, J. Merle, ed., *Modern Industry and the African* (London, 1933).

de Gruchy, John W., *The Church Struggle in South Africa* (Grand Rapids, MI, 1986).

Denniston, Robin, *Trevor Huddleston: A Life* (London, 1999).

Dillistone, F. W., *Into All the World: A Biography of Max Warren* (London, 1980).

Doig, The Very Reverend Dr Andrew B., *It's People That Count* (Bishop Auckland, 1997).

Douglas-Home, Charles, *Evelyn Baring: The Last Proconsul* (London, 1978).

Dubow, Saul, and Alan Jeeves, eds., *South Africa's 1940s: Worlds of Possibilities* (Cape Town, 2005).

Dutfield, Michael, *A Marriage of Inconvenience: The Persecution of Ruth and Seretse Khama* (London, 1990).

Elkins, Caroline, *Britain's Gulag: The Brutal End of Empire in Kenya* (London, 2005).

Elphick, Richard, and Rodney Davenport, eds., *Christianity in South Africa: A Political, Social and Cultural History* (Berkeley, CA, 1997).

Etherington, Norman, ed., *Missions and Empire* (Oxford, 2005).

Falola, Toyin, ed., *African Historiography: Essays in Honour of Jacob Ade Ajayi* (Harlow, 1993).

Fasholé-Luke, Edward, Richard Gray, Adrian Hastings and Godwin Tasie, eds., *Christianity in Independent Africa* (London, 1978).

Ferguson, Ronald, *George MacLeod: Founder of the Iona Community* (London, 1990).

———, *Chasing the Wild Goose: The Story of the Iona Community* (Glasgow, 1998).

Fey, Harold E., ed., *The Ecumenical Advance: A History of the Ecumenical Movement, Vol. 2: 1948-68* (London, 1970).

Frost, Richard, *Race against Time: Human Relations and Politics in Kenya before Independence* (London, 1978).

Furedi, Frank, *The Mau Mau War in Perspective* (London, 1989).

———, *Colonial Wars and the Politics of Third World Nationalism* (London, 1994).

———, *The Silent War: Imperialism and the Changing Perception of Race* (London, 1998).

Gann, L. H., *A History of Northern Rhodesia: Early Days to 1953* (London, 1964).

Garnett, Jane, Matthew Grimley, Alana Harris, William Whyte and Sarah Williams, eds., *Redefining Christian Britain: Post-1945 Perspectives* (London, 2007).

Geiss, Imanuel, *The Pan-African Movement: A History of Pan-Africanism in America, Europe and Africa* (London, 1974).

Gewald, Jan-Bart, Marja Hinfelaar and Giacomo Macola, eds., *One Zambia, Many Histories* (Leiden, 2008).

Gish, Steven D., *Alfred B. Xuma: African, American, South African* (Basingstoke, 2000).

Goldsworthy, David, *Colonial Issues in British Politics, 1945-61: From 'Colonial Development' to 'Wind of Change'* (Oxford, 1971).

———, *Tom Mboya: The Man Kenya Wanted to Forget* (Nairobi, 1982).

———, ed., *The Conservative Government and the End of Empire, 1951-57, Part I: International Relations* (London, 1994).

Good, Charles M., Jr, *The Steamer Parish: The Rise and Fall of Missionary Medicine on an African Frontier* (Chicago and London, 2004).

Goodall, Norman, *A History of the London Missionary Society, 1895-1945* (London, 1954).

———, *Second Fiddle: Recollections and Reflections* (London, 1979).

Grant, Kevin, Philippa Levine and Frank Trentmann, eds., *Beyond Sovereignty: Britain, Empire and Transnationalism, c.1860-1950* (Basingstoke, 2007).

Gray, Richard, *Black Christians and White Missionaries* (New Haven, CT, 1990).

Green, S. J. D., and R. C. Whiting, eds., *The Boundaries of the State in Modern Britain* (Cambridge, 1996).

Greenlee, James G., and Charles M. Johnston, *Good Citizens: British Missionaries and Imperial States, 1870-1918* (Montreal, 1999).

Groves, C. P., *The Planting of Christianity in Africa, Vol. IV: 1914-54* (London, 1958).

Grubb, Sir Kenneth, *A Layman Looks at the Church* (London, 1964).

———, *Crypts of Power: An Autobiography* (London, 1971).

Gupta, Partha Sarathi, *Imperialism and the British Labour Movement, 1914-64* (New Delhi, 2002).

Hake, Andrew, *African Metropolis: Nairobi's Self-Help City* (London, 1977).

Hansen, Holger Bernt, and Michael Twaddle, eds., *Religion and Politics in East Africa: The Period since Independence* (London, 1995).

——, *Christian Missionaries and the State in the Third World* (Oxford and Athens, OH, 2002).

Hardyman, J. T., and R. K. Orchard, *Two Minutes from Sloane Square: A Brief History of the Conference of Missionary Societies of Great Britain and Ireland* (London, 1977).

Hargreaves, John D., *Decolonisation in Africa* (London, 1996).

Harvie, Christopher, *Scotland and Nationalism: Scottish Society and Politics, 1707 to the Present Day* (London and New York, 1998).

Hastings, Adrian, *A History of African Christianity, 1950-75* (Cambridge, 1979).

——, *The Church in Africa, 1450-1950* (Oxford, 1994).

——, *A History of English Christianity, 1920-2000* (London, 2001).

——, *The Construction of Nationhood: Ethnicity, Religion, and Nationalism* (Cambridge, 1997).

Havinden, Michael, and David Meredith, *Colonialism and Development: Britain and Its Tropical Colonies, 1850-1960* (London, 1993).

Hein, David, *Geoffrey Fisher, Archbishop of Canterbury, 1945-61* (Eugene, OR, 2008).

Heinlein, Frank, *British Government Policy and Decolonisation, 1945-63: Scrutinising the Official Mind* (London, 2002).

Hetherington, Penelope, *British Paternalism in Africa, 1920-40* (London, 1978).

Hewat, Elizabeth G. K., *Vision and Achievement, 1796-1956: A History of the Churches United in the Church of Scotland* (Edinburgh, 1960).

Hewitt, Gordon, *The Problems of Success: A History of the Church Missionary Society, 1910-42: Vol. One* (London, 1971).

Hinchliff, Peter, *The Church in South Africa* (London, 1968).

Hogg, William Richey, *Ecumenical Foundations: A History of the International Missionary Council and Its Nineteenth Century Background* (New York, 1952).

Holland, Robert F., *European Decolonization, 1918-81: An Introductory Survey* (Basingstoke, 1985).

——, ed., *Emergencies and Disorder in the European Empires after 1945* (London, 1994).

Holloway, Gerry, *Women and Work in Britain since 1840* (London and New York, 2005).

Holtrop, Pieter N., and Hugh McLeod, eds., *Missions and Missionaries* (Woodbridge, 2000).

Horne, Alistair, *Macmillan, 1957-86* (London, 1989).

Howe, Stephen, *Anticolonialism in British Politics: The Left and the End of Empire, 1918-64* (Oxford, 1993).

Hudson, Darril, *The Ecumenical Movement in World Affairs* (London, 1969).

——, *The World Council of Churches in World Affairs* (Leighton Buzzard, 1977).

Hughes, Richard, *Capricorn: David Stirling's Second African Campaign* (London, 2003).

Hutchison, William R., *Errand to the World: American Protestant Thought and Foreign Missions* (Chicago, 1987).

Hyam, Ronald, *The Failure of South African Expansionism, 1908-48* (London, 1972).

———, ed., *The Labour Government and the End of Empire, 1945-51, Part I: High Policy and Administration* (London, 1992).

———, *Britain's Declining Empire: The Road to Decolonisation, 1918-68* (Cambridge, 2006).

Hyam, Ronald, and Wm. R. Louis, eds., *The Conservative Government and the End of Empire, 1957-64, Part I: High Policy, Political and Constitutional Change* (London, 2000).

Hyam, Ronald, and Peter Henshaw, *The Lion and the Springbok: Britain and South Africa since the Boer War* (Cambridge, 2003).

Ipenburg, At, *'All Good Men': The Development of Lubwa Mission, Chinsali, Zambia, 1905-67* (Frankfurt am Main, 1992).

Isichei, Elizabeth, *A History of Christianity in Africa from Antiquity to the Present* (London, 1995).

Jackson, Ashley, *Botswana, 1939-45: An African Country at War* (Oxford, 1999).

Jackson, Bill, *Send Us Friends* (private publication, n.d.).

Jackson, Eleanor M., *Red Tape and the Gospel: A Study of the Significance of the Ecumenical Missionary Struggle of William Paton (1886-1943)* (Birmingham, 1980).

Jenkins, Philip, *The Next Christendom: The Coming of Global Christianity* (New York, 2002).

Johnson, Anna, *Missionary Writing and Empire, 1800-1860* (Cambridge, 2003).

Johnson, M. Glen, and Janusz Symonides, *The Universal Declaration of Human Rights: A History of Its Creation and Implementation* (Paris, 1998).

Jones, R. Tudur, *Congregationalism in England, 1662-1962* (London, 1962).

Kalu, Ogbu, and Alaine Low, eds., *Interpreting Contemporary Christianity: Global Processes and Local Identities* (Grand Rapids, MI, and Cambridge, 2008).

Kanogo, Tabitha, *Squatters and the Roots of Mau Mau, 1905-63* (London, 1987).

Kendall, Elliott, *The End of an Era: Africa and the Missionary* (London, 1978).

Kennedy, Dane, *Islands of White: Settler Society and Culture in Kenya and Southern Rhodesia, 1890-1939* (Durham, NC, 1987).

Kent, John, *William Temple: Church, State and Society in Britain, 1880-1950* (Cambridge, 1992).

Kershaw, Greet, *Mau Mau from Below* (Oxford, 1997).

Killingray, David, ed., *Africans in Britain* (London, 1994).

———, *Fighting for Britain: African Soldiers in the Second World War* (Woodbridge, 2010).

Killingray, David, and Richard Rathbone, eds., *Africa and the Second World War* (Basingstoke, 1986).

Kim, Sebastian C. H., *In Search of Identity: Debates on Religious Conversion in India* (New Delhi, 2003).

King, Paul S., ed., *Missions in Southern Rhodesia* (Cape Town, 1959).

Kings, Graham, *Christianity Connected: Hindus, Muslims and the World in the Letters of Max Warren and Roger Hooker* (Zoetermeer, 2002).

Kirk-Greene, Anthony, ed., *On Crown Service: A History of HM Colonial and Overseas Civil Services, 1837-1997* (London, 1999).

Korey, William, *NGOs and the Universal Declaration of Human Rights: 'A Curious Grapevine'* (New York, 1998).

Küster, Sybille, *African Education in Colonial Zimbabwe, Zambia and Malawi: Government Control, Settler Antagonism and African Agency, 1890-1964* (Hamburg, 1999).

Kyle, Keith, *The Politics of the Independence of Kenya* (Basingstoke, 1999).

————, *Suez: Britain's End of Empire in the Middle East* (London, 2003).

Lacey, Janet, *A Cup of Water: The Story of Christian Aid* (London, 1970).

Landau, Paul S., *The Realm of the Word: Language, Gender and Christianity in a Southern African Kingdom* (London, 1995).

Larsen, Timothy, and Daniel J. Treier, eds., *The Cambridge Companion to Evangelical Theology* (Cambridge, 2007).

Lee, J. M., *Colonial Development and Good Government: A Study of the Ideas expressed by the British Official Classes in Planning Decolonisation, 1939-64* (Oxford, 1967).

Lee, J. M., and Martin Petter, *The Colonial Office, War and Development Policy: Organisation and the Planning of a Metropolitan Initiative, 1939-45* (London, 1982).

Lester, Alan, *Imperial Networks: Creating Identities in Nineteenth Century South Africa and Britain* (London and New York, 2001).

Lewis, Joanna, *Empire State-Building: War and Welfare in Kenya, 1925-52* (Oxford, 2000).

Ling, Oi Ki, *The Changing Role of the British Protestant Missionaries in China, 1945-52* (Madison, NJ, 1999).

Lloyd, Roger, *The Church of England, 1900-65* (London, 1966).

Louis, Wm. Roger, *Imperialism at Bay, 1941-45: The United States and the Decolonisation of the British Empire* (Oxford, 1977).

Low, D. A., and Alison Smith, eds., *History of East Africa: Vol. III* (Oxford, 1976).

Ludwig, Frieder, *Church and State in Tanzania: Aspects of a Changing Relationship, 1961-94* (Leiden, 1999).

Lyon, David H. S., *In Pursuit of a Vision: The Story of the Church of Scotland's Developing Relationship with the Churches Emerging from the Missionary Movement in the Twenty-five Years from 1947 to 1972* (Edinburgh, 1998).

Macmillan, Hugh, and Shula Marks, eds., *Africa and Empire: W. M. Macmillan, Historian and Social Critic* (Aldershot, 1989).

Macpherson, Fergus, *North of the Zambezi: A Modern Missionary Memoir* (Edinburgh, 1998).

Macpherson, Robert, *The Presbyterian Church in Kenya: An Account of the Origins and Growth of the Presbyterian Church of East Africa* (Nairobi, 1970).

Makulu, Henry F., *Education, Development and Nation-Building in Independent Africa* (London, 1971).

Maloba, Wunyabari O., *Mau Mau and Kenya: An Analysis of a Peasant Revolt* (Bloomington, 1993).

Markovitz, Irving L., ed., *African Politics and Society: Basic Issues and Problems of Government and Development* (New York, 1970).

Maxwell, David, with Ingrid Lawrie, eds., *Christianity and the African Imagination: Essays in Honour of Adrian Hastings* (Leiden, 2002).

McCracken, John, *Politics and Christianity in Malawi, 1875-1940: The Impact of the Livingstonia Mission in the Northern Province* (Cambridge, 1977).

McLaine, Ian, *Ministry of Morale: Home Front Morale and the Ministry of Information in World War II* (London, 1979).

Moodie, T. Dunbar, *The Rise of Afrikanerdom: Power, Apartheid and the Afrikaner Civil Religion* (Berkeley, CA, 1975).

M'Passou, Denis, *Mindolo: A Story of the Ecumenical Movement in Africa* (Lusaka, 1983).

Mulford, David C., *The Northern Rhodesia General Election, 1962* (Nairobi, 1964).

———, *Zambia: The Politics of Independence, 1957-64* (Oxford, 1967).

Murphy, E. Jefferson, *Creative Philanthropy: Carnegie Corporation and Africa, 1953-73* (New York and London, 1976).

Murphy, Philip, *Party Politics and Decolonization: The Conservative Party and British Colonial Policy in Tropical Africa* (Oxford, 1995).

———, *Alan Lennox-Boyd: A Biography* (London, 1999).

———, ed., *Central Africa: Closer Association, 1945-58* (London, 2005).

———, *Central Africa: Crisis and Dissolution, 1959-65* (London, 2005).

Murray, Jocelyn, *Proclaim the Good News: A Short History of the Church Missionary Society* (London, 1985).

Murray-Brown, Jeremy, *Kenyatta* (London, 1972).

Ncozana, Silas S., *Sangaya: A Leader in the Synod of Blantyre, Church of Central Africa Presbyterian* (Blantyre, 1996).

Neill, Stephen, *Colonialism and Christian Missions* (London, 1966).

———, *A History of Christian Missions*, 2nd ed. (Harmondsworth, 1986).

Norman, Edward R., *Church and Society in England, 1770-1970: A Historical Survey* (Oxford, 1976).

Nurser, John, *For All Peoples and All Nations: Christian Churches and Human Rights* (Geneva, 2005).

O'Connor, Daniel, and others, *Three Centuries of Mission: The United Society for the Propagation of the Gospel, 1701-2000* (London and New York, 2000).

Odhiambo, E. S. Atieno, and John Lonsdale, eds., *Mau Mau and Nationhood: Arms, Authority and Narration* (Oxford, 2003).

Ogot, B. A., and W. R. Ochieng', eds., *Decolonization and Independence in Kenya, 1940-93* (Oxford, 1995).

Oliver, Roland, *The Missionary Factor in East Africa*, 2nd ed. (London, 1965).

———, *In the Realms of Gold: Pioneering in African History* (London, 1997).

Oosthuizen, G. C., *Shepherd of Lovedale* (Johannesburg, 1970).

Paton, Alan, *Apartheid and the Archbishop: The Life and Times of Geoffrey Clayton, Archbishop of Cape Town* (Cape Town, 1973).

Payne, Ernest A., *Thirty Years of the British Council of Churches, 1942-1972* (London, 1972).

Pearce, R. D., *The Turning Point in Africa: British Colonial Policy, 1938-48* (London, 1982).

Perham, Margery, *Colonial Sequence, 1949 to 1969: A Chronological Commentary upon British Colonial Policy in Africa* (London, 1970).

Peterson, Derek R., *Creative Writing: Translation, Bookkeeping and the Work of Imagination in Colonial Kenya* (Portsmouth, NH, 2004).

Peterson, Derek R., and Giacomo Macola (eds.), *Recasting the Past: History Writing and Political Work in Modern Africa* (Athens, OH, 2009).

Pickering, W. S. F., *Anglo-Catholicism: A Study in Religious Ambiguity* (London and New York, 1989).

Porter, Andrew, ed., *The Oxford History of the British Empire, Volume III: The Nineteenth Century* (Oxford, 1999).

————, *Religion versus Empire?: British Protestant Missionaries and Overseas Expansion, 1700-1914* (Manchester, 2004).

Porter, A. N., and A. J. Stockwell, eds., *British Imperial Policy and Decolonisation, 1938-64: Vol. 1, 1938-51* (Basingstoke, 1987).

————, *British Imperial Policy and Decolonisation, 1938-64: Vol. 2, 1951-64* (Basingstoke, 1989).

Presley, Cora Ann, *Kikuyu Women, the Mau Mau Rebellion and Social Change in Kenya* (Boulder, CO, 1992).

Prochaska, Frank, *Christianity and Social Service in Modern Britain: The Disinherited Spirit* (Oxford, 2006).

Purcell, William, *Fisher of Lambeth: A Portrait from Life* (London, 1969).

Ranger, T. O. and John Weller, eds., *Themes in the Christian History of Central Africa* (Berkeley and Los Angeles, 1975).

Redfern, John, *Ruth and Seretse: 'A Very Disreputable Transaction'* (London, 1955).

Regehr, Ernie, *Perceptions of Apartheid: The Churches and Political Change in South Africa* (Scottdale, PA, 1979).

Rich, Paul B., *Race and Empire in British Politics,* 2nd ed. (Cambridge, 1990).

Roberts, Andrew D., *The Lumpa Church of Alice Lenshina* (Lusaka, 1972); originally published in Robert I. Rotberg and Ali A. Mazrui, eds., *Protest and Power in Black Africa* (New York, 1970), pp. 513-68.

————, ed., *The Cambridge History of Africa Vol. 7: From 1905 to 1940* (Cambridge, 1986).

Robinson, Kenneth, *The Dilemmas of Trusteeship: Aspects of British Colonial Policy between the Wars* (London, 1965).

Robinson, Kenneth, and Frederick Madden, eds., *Essays in Imperial Government presented to Margery Perham* (Oxford, 1963).

Roelker, Jack R., *Mathu of Kenya: A Political Study* (Stanford, CA, 1976).

Rosberg, Carl G., Jr, and John Nottingham, *The Myth of 'Mau Mau': Nationalism in Kenya* (Stanford, CA, 1966).

Rose, Sonya O., *Which People's War?: National Identity and Citizenship in Britain, 1939-45* (Oxford, 2003).

Ross, Andrew C., *Blantyre Mission and the Making of Modern Malawi* (Blantyre, 1996).

————, *Colonialism to Cabinet Crisis: A Political History of Malawi* (Zomba, 2009).

Rotberg, Robert I., *Christian Missionaries and the Creation of Northern Rhodesia, 1880-1924* (Princeton, 1965).

————, *The Rise of Nationalism in Central Africa: The Making of Malawi and Zambia, 1873-1964* (Cambridge, MA, 1966).

Rotberg, Robert I., and Ali A. Mazrui, eds., *Protest and Power in Black Africa* (New York, 1970).

Rouse, Ruth, and Stephen Charles Neill, eds., *A History of the Ecumenical Movement, 1517-1948,* 2nd ed. (London, 1967).

Sabar, Galia, *Church, State and Society in Kenya: From Mediation to Opposition, 1963-93* (London, 2002).

Sachs, William L., *The Transformation of Anglicanism: From State Church to Global Communion* (Cambridge, 1993).

Said, Edward W., *Culture and Imperialism* (London, 1993).

Sandgren, David P., *Christianity and the Kikuyu: Religious Divisions and Social Conflict* (New York, 1989).

Seager, Alan, *In the Shadow of a Great Rock* (Connah's Quay, 2005).

Semple, Rhonda, *Missionary Women: Gender, Professionalism and the Victorian Idea of Christian Mission* (Woodbridge, 2002).

Sharkey, Heather J., *American Evangelicals in Egypt: Missionary Encounters in an Age of Empire* (Princeton, 2008).

Sheils, W. J., ed., *The Church and War* (Oxford, 1983).

Shepherd, Robert, *Iain Macleod: A Biography* (London, 1994).

Shipway, Martin, *Decolonization and Its Impact: A Comparative Approach to the End of the Colonial Empires* (Malden, MA, and Oxford, 2008).

Short, Philip, *Banda* (London, 1974).

Simpson, A. W. B., *Human Rights and the End of Empire: Britain and the Genesis of the European Convention* (New York, 2001).

Sinclair, Georgina, *At the End of the Line: Colonial Policing and the Imperial Endgame, 1945-80* (Manchester, 2006).

Sivonen, Seppo, *White Collar or Hoe Handle?: African Education under British Colonial Policy, 1920-45* (Helsinki, 1995).

Slack, Kenneth, ed., *Hope in the Desert: The Churches' United Response to Human Need, 1944-84* (Geneva, 1986).

Smith, Alison, and Mary Bull, eds., *Margery Perham and British Rule in Africa* (London, 1991).

Smith, John Coventry, *From Colonialism to World Community: The Church's Pilgrimage* (Philadelphia, 1982).

Smith, Graham, *When Jim Crow Met John Bull: Black American Soldiers in World War II Britain* (London, 1987).

Smith, Harold L., ed., *War and Social Change: British Society in the Second World War* (Manchester, 1986).

Sorrensen, M. P. K., *Land Reform in the Kikuyu Country: A Study in Government Policy* (Nairobi, 1967).

Spencer, John, *The Kenya Africa Union* (London, 1985).

Spencer, Stephen, *William Temple: A Calling to Prophecy* (London, 2001).

Stanley, Brian, *The Bible and the Flag: Protestant Missions and British Imperialism in the Nineteenth and Twentieth Centuries* (Leicester, 1990).

————, ed., *Missions, Nationalism, and the End of Empire* (Grand Rapids, and Cambridge, 2003).

Stockwell, Sarah, ed., *The British Empire: Themes and Perspectives* (Oxford and Malden, MA, 2008).

Strayer, Robert W., *The Making of Mission Communities in East Africa: Anglicans and Africans in Colonial Kenya, 1875-1935* (London, 1978).

Studdert-Kennedy, Gerald, *Providence and the Raj: Imperial Mission and Missionary Imperialism* (New Delhi, 1998).

Sundkler, Bengt, and Christopher Steed, *A History of the Church in Africa* (Cambridge, 2000).

Temple, Merfyn, *Zambia Stole My Heart* (London, 2010).

Ter Haar, Gerrie, *Halfway to Paradise: African Christians in Europe* (Cardiff, 1998).

Thomas, David, *Christ Divided: Liberalism, Ecumenism and Race in South Africa* (Pretoria, 2002).

Thompson, Andrew, *The Empire Strikes Back?: The Impact of Imperialism on Britain from the Mid-Nineteenth Century* (Harlow, 2005).

Thorogood, Bernard, ed., *Gales of Change. Responding to a Shifting Missionary Context: The Story of the London Missionary Society, 1945-77* (Geneva, 1994).

Throup, David, *Economic and Social Origins of Mau Mau, 1945-53* (London, 1987).

Tignor, Robert L., *The Colonial Transformation of Kenya: The Kamba, Kikuyu, and Maasai from 1900 to 1939* (Princeton, 1976).

Tinker, Hugh, *Race, Conflict and the International Order: From Empire to United Nations* (London, 1977).

Tlou, Thomas, Neil Parsons and Willie Henderson, *Seretse Khama, 1921-80* (Gaborone, 1995).

van Binsbergen, Wim M. J., *Religious Change in Zambia: Exploratory Studies* (London and Boston, 1981).

Vaughan, David A., *Negro Victory: The Life Story of Dr Harold Moody* (London, 1950).

Veldman, Meredith, *Fantasy, the Bomb, and the Greening of Britain: Romantic Protest, 1945-80* (Cambridge, 1994).

Villa-Vicencio, Charles, *Trapped in Apartheid: A Socio-Theological History of the English-Speaking Churches* (Maryknoll, NY, 1988).

Visser 't Hooft, W. A., *The Genesis and Foundation of the World Council of Churches* (Geneva, 1987).

Wainwright, Geoffrey, *Lesslie Newbigin: A Theological Life* (New York, 2000).

Walls, Andrew F., *The Missionary Movement in Christian History: Studies in the Transmission of Faith* (Edinburgh, 1996).

Ward, Kevin, *A History of Global Anglicanism* (Cambridge, 2006).

Ward, Kevin, and Brian Stanley, eds., *The Church Mission Society and World Christianity, 1799-1999* (Grand Rapids, MI, and Richmond, Surrey, 2000).

Warren, Max, *Social History and Christian Mission* (London, 1967).

———, *Crowded Canvas: Some Experiences of a Life-time* (London, 1974).

Wasserman, Gary, *Politics of Decolonisation: Kenya Europeans and the Land Issue, 1960-65* (Cambridge, 1976).

Weight, Richard, *Patriots: National Identity in Britain, 1940-2000* (London, 2003).

Welsby, Paul A., *A History of the Church of England, 1945-80* (Oxford, 1984).

White, Luise, *Speaking with Vampires: Rumor and History in Colonial Africa* (Berkeley and Los Angeles, 2000).

Williams, C. Peter, *The Ideal of the Self-Governing Church: A Study in Victorian Missionary Strategy* (Leiden, 1990).

Williams, Susan, *Colour Bar: The Triumph of Seretse Khama and His Nation* (London, 2006).

Wingate, Andrew, Kevin Ward, Carrie Pemberton and Wilson Sitshebo, eds., *Anglicanism: A Global Communion* (London, 1998).

Winks, Robin W., ed., *The Oxford History of the British Empire, Volume V: Historiography* (Oxford, 1999).

Wolffe, John, *God and Greater Britain: Religion and National Life in Britain and Ireland, 1843-1945* (London, 1994).

Wolton, Suke, *Lord Hailey, the Colonial Office and the Politics of Race and Empire in the Second World War: The Loss of White Prestige* (Basingstoke, 2000).

Wood, David, *Poet, Priest and Prophet: The Life and Thought of Bishop John V. Taylor* (London, 2002).

Wood, J. R. T., *The Welensky Papers: A History of the Federation of Rhodesia and Nyasaland* (Durban, 1983).

Worsnip, Michael E., *Between the Two Fires: The Anglican Church and Apartheid, 1948-57* (Pietermaritzburg, 1991).

Wylie, Diana, *A Little God: The Twilight of Patriarchy in a Southern African Chiefdom* (Hanover, NH, 1990).

Yates, Ann, and Lewis Chester, *The Troublemaker: Michael Scott and His Lonely Struggle against Injustice* (London, 2006).

Yates, Timothy E., *Venn and Victorian Bishops Abroad: The Missionary Policies of Henry Venn and their Repercussions upon the Anglican Episcopate of the Colonial Period, 1841-72* (Uppsala and London, 1978).

———, *Christian Mission in the Twentieth Century* (Cambridge, 1994).

2. Journal Articles and Book Chapters

Andrews, Loretta Kreider, and Herbert D. Andrews, 'The Church and the Birth of a

Nation: The Mindolo Ecumenical Foundation and Zambia', *Journal of Church and State* (hereafter *JCS*) 17 (1975): 191-216.

Bediako, Kwame, 'Africa and Christianity on the Threshold of the Third Millennium: The Religious Dimension', *African Affairs* (hereafter *AA*) 99, no. 395 (2000): 303-23.

Bennett, George, 'Imperial Paternalism: The Representation of African Interests in the Kenya Legislative Council', in Kenneth Robinson and Frederick Madden, eds., *Essays in Imperial Government presented to Margery Perham* (Oxford, 1963), pp. 141-69.

Boobyer, Philip, 'Moral Re-Armament in Africa in the Era of Decolonization', in Brian Stanley, ed., *Missions, Nationalism, and the End of Empire* (Grand Rapids, MI, and Cambridge, 2003), pp. 212-36.

Brock, Peggy, 'New Christians as Evangelists', in Norman Etherington, ed., *Missions and Empire* (Oxford, 2005), pp. 132-52.

Carter, David, 'The Ecumenical Movement in Its Early Years', *Journal of Ecclesiastical History* 49, no. 3 (1998): 465-85.

Casson, John, 'Mission Archives and New Directions in Mission History', *Bulletin of the Association of British Theological and Philosophical Libraries* 4, no. 1 (1997): 13-19.

————, 'Missionaries, Mau Mau and the Christian Frontier', in Pieter N. Holtrop and Hugh McLeod, eds., *Missions and Missionaries* (Woodbridge, 2000), pp. 200-15.

Clark, John, 'CMS and Mission in Britain: The Evolution of a Policy', in Kevin Ward and Brian Stanley, eds., *The Church Mission Society and World Christianity, 1799-1999* (Grand Rapids, MI, and Richmond, Surrey, 2000), pp. 319-43.

Cleary, A. S., 'The Myth of Mau Mau in Its International Context', *AA* 89, no. 355 (1990): 227-45.

Cook, David J., 'The Influence of Livingstonia Mission upon the Formation of Welfare Associations in Zambia, 1912-31', in T. O. Ranger and John Weller, eds., *Themes in the Christian History of Central Africa* (Berkeley and Los Angeles, 1975), pp. 98-134.

Cooper, Frederick, 'Mau Mau and the Discourses of Decolonisation', *Journal of African History* (hereafter *JAH*) 29, no. 2 (1988): 313-20.

Crowder, Michael, 'Tshekedi Khama, Smuts and South West Africa', *Journal of Modern African Studies* 25, no. 1 (1987): 25-42.

Dachs, Anthony J., 'Missionary Imperialism: The Case of Bechuanaland', *JAH* 12, no. 4 (1972): 647-58.

Darwin, John, 'Imperialism in Decline? Tendencies in British Imperial Policy between the Wars', *The Historical Journal* (hereafter *HJ*) 23, no. 3 (1980): 657-79.

————, 'British Decolonisation since 1945: A Pattern or a Puzzle', *Journal of Imperial and Commonwealth History* (hereafter *JICH*) 12, no. 2 (1984): 187-209.

————, 'The Central African Emergency, 1959', in Robert F. Holland, ed., *Emergencies and Disorder in the European Empires after 1945* (London, 1994), pp. 217-34.

Ekechi, Felix K., 'Studies on Missions in Africa', in Toyin Falola, ed., *African Historiography: Essays in Honour of Jacob Ade Ajayi* (Harlow, 1993), pp. 145-65.

Elphick, Richard, 'The Benevolent Empire and the Social Gospel: Missionaries and South African Christians in the Age of Segregation', in Richard Elphick and Rodney Davenport, eds., *Christianity in South Africa: A Political, Social and Cultural History* (Berkeley, CA, 1997), pp. 347-69.

Elkins, Caroline, 'The Struggle for Mau Mau Rehabilitation in Late Colonial Kenya', *International Journal of African Historical Studies* (hereafter *IJAHS*) 33, no. 1 (2000): 25-57.

———, 'Detention, Rehabilitation and the Destruction of Kikuyu Society', in E. S. Atieno Odhiambo and John Lonsdale, eds., *Mau Mau and Nationhood: Arms, Authority and Narration* (Oxford, 2003), pp. 191-226.

Etherington, Norman, 'Missions and Empire', in Robin W. Winks, ed., *The Oxford History of the British Empire, Volume V: Historiography* (Oxford, 1999), pp. 303-14.

Finlay, Richard J., '"For or Against?": Scottish Nationalists and the British Empire, 1919-39', *Scottish Historical Review* 71, no. 1, 2: 191/2 (1992): 184-206.

Fyfe, Christopher, 'Race, Empire and the Historians', *Race and Class* 33, no. 4 (1992): 15-30.

Gifford, Paul, 'Some Recent Developments in African Christianity', *AA* 93, no. 173 (1994): 524-8.

Gordon, David M., 'Rebellion or Massacre?: The UNIP-Lumpa Conflict Revisited', in Jan-Bart Gewald, Marja Hinfelaar and Giacomo Macola, eds., *One Zambia, Many Histories* (Leiden, 2008), pp. 45-76.

Grant, Kevin, 'Trust and Self-Determination: Anglo-American Ethics of Empire and International Government', in Mark Bevir and Frank Trentmann, eds., *Critiques of Capital in Modern Britain and America: Transatlantic Exchanges, 1800 to the Present Day* (Basingstoke, 2002), pp. 151-73.

Gray, Richard, 'Christianity', in Andrew D. Roberts, ed., *The Cambridge History of Africa, Vol. 7: From 1905 to 1940* (Cambridge, 1986), pp. 140-90.

Hastings, Adrian, 'The Clash of Nationalism and Universalism within Twentieth Century Missionary Christianity', in Brian Stanley, ed., *Missions, Nationalism, and the End of Empire* (Grand Rapids, MI, and Cambridge, 2003), pp. 15-33.

Heaney, Robert S., 'Coloniality and Theological Method in Africa', *Journal of Anglican Studies* 7, no. 1 (2009): 1-11.

Hearn, Julie, 'The "Invisible" NGO: US Evangelical Missions in Kenya', *Journal of Religion in Africa* (hereafter *JRA*) 32, no. 1 (2002): 32-60.

Henderson, Ian, 'The Origins of Nationalism in East and Central Africa: The Zambian Case', *JAH* 11, no. 4 (1970): 591-603.

———, 'The Limits of Colonial Power: Race and Labour Problems in Colonial Zambia, 1900-53', *JICH* 2, no. 3 (1974): 294-307.

Henshaw, Peter J., 'Britain and South Africa at the United Nations: "South West Africa", "Treatment of Indians" and "Race Conflict", 1946-61', *South African Historical Journal* 31, no. 1 (1994): 80-102.

Hinfelaar, Hugo, 'Women's Revolt: The Lumpa Church of Lenshina Mulenga in the 1950s', *JRA* 21, no. 2 (1991): 99-129.

Holland, R. F., 'The Imperial Factor in British Strategies from Attlee to Macmillan, 1945-63', *JICH* 12, no. 2 (1984): 165-86.

Hopkins, A. G., 'Back to the Future: From National History to Imperial History', *Past & Present* 164 (1999): 198-243.

Howe, Stephen, 'The Slow Death and Strange Rebirths of Imperial History', *JICH* 29, no. 2 (2001): 131-41.

Hyam, Ronald, 'The Political Consequences of Seretse Khama: Britain, the Bangwato and South Africa, 1948-1952', *HJ* 29, no. 4 (1986): 921-47.

————, 'The Geopolitical Origins of the Central African Federation: Britain, Rhodesia and South Africa, 1948-1953', *HJ* 30, no. 1 (1987): 145-72.

————, 'Africa and the Labour Government, 1945-51', *JICH* 16, no. 3 (1988): 148-72.

————, 'The Parting of the Ways: Britain and South Africa's Departure from the Commonwealth, 1951-61', *JICH* 26, no. 2 (1998): 157-75.

————, 'Bureaucracy and "Trusteeship" in the Colonial Empire', in Judith M. Brown and Wm. Roger Louis, eds., *The Oxford History of the British Empire, Vol. IV: The Twentieth Century* (Oxford, 1999), pp. 255-79.

Jackson, Ashley, 'Motivation and Mobilisation for War: Recruitment for the British Army in the Bechuanaland Protectorate, 1941-42', *AA* 96, no. 384 (1997): 399-417.

Kennedy, Dane, 'Constructing the Colonial Myth of Mau Mau', *IJAHS* 25, no. 2 (1992): 241-60.

Kershaw, Gretha, 'Mau Mau from Below: Fieldwork and Experience, 1955-57 and 1962', *Canadian Journal of African Studies* 25, no. 2 (1991): 274-97.

Kinghorn, Johann, 'Modernisation and Apartheid: The Afrikaner Churches', in Richard Elphick and Rodney Davenport, eds., *Christianity in South Africa: A Political, Social and Cultural History* (Berkeley, CA, 1997), pp. 135-44.

Kirby, Dianne, 'The Church of England and "Religions Division" during the Second World War: Church-State Relations and the Anglo-Soviet Alliance', *Electronic Journal of International History* 4 (2000), at http://www.history.ac.uk/resources/e-journal-international-history/kirby-paper.

————, '"Divinely Sanctioned": The Anglo-American Cold War Alliance and the Defence of Western Civilisation and Christianity, 1945-48', *Journal of Contemporary History* 35, no. 3 (2000): 385-412.

Kiyaga-Mulindwa, David, 'The Bechuanaland Protectorate and the Second World War', *JICH* 12, no. 3 (1984): 33-53.

Lloyd, Lorna, '"A Family Quarrel": The Development of the Dispute over the Indians in South Africa', *HJ* 34, no. 3 (1991): 703-25.

————, '"A Most Auspicious Beginning": The 1946 General Assembly and the Question of the Treatment of Indians in South Africa', *Review of International Studies* 16, no. 2 (1990): 131-53.

Lonsdale, John M., 'European Attitudes and African Pressures: Missions and Government in Kenya between the Wars', *Race* 10, no. 1 (1968): 141-51.

————, 'The Depression and the Second World War in the Transformation of Kenya', in David Killingray and Richard Rathbone, eds., *Africa and the Second World War* (Basingstoke, 1986), pp. 97-142.

————, 'Mau Maus of the Mind: Making Mau Mau and Remaking Kenya', *JAH* 31, no. 3 (1990): 393-421.

————, 'Kikuyu Christianities', *JRA* 29, no. 2 (1999): 206-29.

————, 'Mission Christianity and Settler Colonialism in East Africa', in Holger Bernt Hansen and Michael Twaddle, eds., *Christian Missionaries and the State in the Third World* (Oxford and Athens, OH, 2002), pp. 194-211.

————, 'Kikuyu Christianities: A History of Intimate Diversity', in David Maxwell with Ingrid Lawrie, eds., *Christianity and the African Imagination: Essays in Honour of Adrian Hastings* (Leiden, 2002), pp. 157-98.

Lonsdale, John, Stanley Booth-Clibborn and Andrew Hake, 'The Emerging Pattern of Church and State Co-operation in Kenya', in Edward Fasholé-Luke, Richard Gray, Adrian Hastings and Godwin Tasie, eds., *Christianity in Independent Africa* (London, 1978), pp. 267-84.

Louis, Wm. Roger, 'The Dissolution of the British Empire', in Judith M. Brown and Wm. Roger Louis, eds., *The Oxford History of the British Empire, Vol. IV: The Twentieth Century* (Oxford, 1999), pp. 329-56.

Low, D. A., and John M. Lonsdale, 'Introduction: Towards the New Order, 1945-63', in D. A. Low and Alison Smith, eds., *History of East Africa: Vol. III* (Oxford, 1976), pp. 1-63.

Macdonald, Roderick J., 'Dr. Harold Arundel Moody and the League of Coloured Peoples, 1931-47: A Retrospective View', *Race* 14, no. 3 (1973): 291-310.

MacKenzie, John M., 'Essay and Reflection: On Scotland and the Empire', *International History Review* 15, no. 4 (1993): 714-39.

————, 'Empire and National Identities: The Case of Scotland', *Transactions of the Royal Historical Society* Sixth Series, 8 (1998): 215-31.

Marshall, P. J., 'Imperial Britain', *JICH* 23, no. 3 (1995): 379-94.

Maxwell, David, 'Decolonization', in Norman Etherington, ed., *Missions and Empire* (Oxford, 2005), pp. 285-306.

McCracken, John, 'Democracy and Nationalism in Historical Perspective: The Case of Malawi', *AA* 97, no. 387 (1998): 231-49.

————, 'Church and State in Malawi: The Role of the Scottish Presbyterian Missions, 1875-1965', in I. Phiri, K. Ross and J. L. Cox, eds., *The Role of Christianity in Development, Peace, and Reconstruction: Southern African Perspectives* (Nairobi, 1996), pp. 188-9.

Nolde, O. F., 'Ecumenical Action in International Affairs', in Harold E. Fey, ed., *The Ecumenical Advance: A History of the Ecumenical Movement, Vol. 2: 1948-68* (London, 1970), pp. 263-85.

Ogot, B. A., 'The Decisive Years, 1956-63', in B. A. Ogot and W. R. Ochieng', eds., *Decolonization and Independence in Kenya, 1940-93* (London, 1995), pp. 48-79.

Ovendale, Ritchie, 'The South African Policy of the British Labour Government, 1947-51', *International Affairs* 59, no. 1 (1983): 41-58.

———, 'Macmillan and the Wind of Change in Africa, 1957-60', *HJ* 38, no. 2 (1995): 455-77.

Owen, Nicholas, 'Critics of Empire in Britain', in Judith M. Brown and Wm. Roger Louis, eds., *Oxford History of the British Empire, Vol. IV: The Twentieth Century* (Oxford, 1999), pp. 188-211.

Palmer, Robin, 'European Resistance to African Majority Rule: The Settlers' and Residents' Association of Nyasaland, 1960-63', *AA* 72, no. 288 (1973): 256-72.

Parsons, Neil, 'Colonel Rey and the Colonial Rulers of Botswana: Mercenary and Missionary Traditions in Bechuanaland, 1884-1955', in J. F. Ade Ajayi and J. D. Y. Peel, eds., *People and Empires in African History: Essays in Memory of Michael Crowder* (Harlow, 1992), pp. 197-216.

———, 'The Impact of Seretse Khama on British Public Opinion, 1948-56 and 1978', in David Killingray, ed., *Africans in Britain* (London, 1994), pp. 195-219.

Peaden, W. R., 'Aspects of the Church and its Political Involvement in Southern Rhodesia, 1959-72', *Zambezia* 7, no. 2 (1979): 191-210.

Peterson, Derek R., 'Culture and Chronology in African History', *HJ* 50, no. 2 (2007): 483-97.

Phiri, Bizeck Jube, 'The Capricorn Africa Society Revisited: The Impact of Liberalism in Zambia's Colonial History, 1949-63', *IJAHS* 24, no. 1 (1991): 65-83.

Porter, Andrew, 'Iain Macleod, Decolonisation in Kenya, and Tradition in British Colonial Policy', *Journal for Contemporary History* 2 (1977): 37-59.

———, 'Margery Perham, Christian Missions and Indirect Rule', *JICH* 19, no. 3 (1991): 83-99.

———, 'War, Colonialism and the British Experience: The Redefinition of Christian Missionary Policy, 1938-52', *Kirchliche Zeitgeschichte* 5, no. 2 (1992): 269-88.

———, 'The Universities' Mission to Central Africa: Anglo-Catholicism and the Twentieth Century Colonial Encounter', in Brian Stanley, ed., *Missions, Nationalism, and the End of Empire* (Grand Rapids, MI, and Cambridge, 2003), pp. 79-107.

———, '"Cultural Imperialism" and Protestant Missionary Enterprise, 1780-1914', *JICH* 25, no. 3 (1997): 367-91.

———, 'Religion, Missionary Enthusiasm, and Empire', in Andrew Porter, ed., *The Oxford History of the British Empire, Volume III: The Nineteenth Century* (Oxford, 1999), pp. 222-46.

———, 'Church History, History of Christianity, Religious History: Some Reflections on British Missionary Enterprise since the Late Eighteenth Century', *Church History* 71, no. 3 (2002): 555-84.

Proctor, J. H., 'The Church of Scotland and British Colonialism in Africa', *JCS* 29, no. 3 (1987): 475-93.

Ranger, Terence, 'Christian Mission, Capitalism and Empire: The State of the Debate', *Social Sciences and Missions* 17 (2005): 153-9.

Robbins, Keith, 'Britain, 1940 and "Christian Civilisation"', in Derek Beales and Geoffrey Best, eds., *History, Society and the Churches: Essays in Honour of Owen Chadwick* (Cambridge, 1985), pp. 279-99.

Robert, Dana L., 'The First Globalization?: The Internationalization of the Protestant Missionary Movement Between the World Wars', in Ogbu Kalu and Alaine Low, eds., *Interpreting Contemporary Christianity: Global Processes and Local Identities* (Grand Rapids, MI, and Cambridge, 2008), pp. 93-130.

Robinson, Ronald, 'The Moral Disarmament of African Empire 1919-47', *JICH* 8, no. 1 (1979): 86-104.

———, 'Imperial Theory and the Question of Imperialism after Empire', *JICH* 12, no. 2 (1984): 42-54.

Rose, Sonya O., 'Race, Empire and British Wartime National Identity, 1939-45', *Historical Research* 74, no. 184 (2001): 220-37.

Ross, Kenneth R., 'James Dougall, 1896-1980: Architect of Post-War Scottish Foreign Mission Policy', *Records of the Scottish Church History Society* 37 (2007): 183-206.

Rush, Anne Spry, 'Imperial Identity in Colonial Minds: Harold Moody and the League of Coloured Peoples, 1931-50', *20th Century British History* 13, no. 4 (2002): 356-83.

Santoru, Marina, 'The Colonial Idea of Women and Direct Intervention: The Mau Mau Case', *AA* 95, no. 379 (1996): 253-67.

Shepperson, George A., 'External Factors in the Development of African Nationalism, with Particular Reference to British Central Africa', in Irving L. Markovitz, ed., *African Politics and Society: Basic Issues and Problems of Government and Development* (New York, 1970), pp. 179-98.

Sherwood, Marika, 'Kwame Nkrumah: The London Years, 1945-47', in David Killingray, ed., *Africans in Britain* (London, 1994), pp. 164-94.

Short, Frank, 'National Councils of Churches', in Harold E. Fey, ed., *The Ecumenical Advance: A History of the Ecumenical Movement, Vol. 2: 1948-68* (London, 1970), pp. 95-113.

Simpson, Brian, 'The Devlin Commission (1959): Colonialism, Emergencies and the Rule of Law', *Oxford Journal of Legal Studies* 22, no. 1 (2002): 17-52.

Skinner, Robert, 'Christian Reconstruction, Secular Politics: Michael Scott and the Campaign for Right and Justice, 1943-45', in Saul Dubow and Alan Jeeves, eds., *South Africa's 1940s: Worlds of Possibilities* (Cape Town, 2005), pp. 246-66.

Smith, R. Drew, 'Missionaries, Church Movements and the Shifting Religious Significance of the State in Zambia', *JCS* 41, no. 3 (1999): 525-50.

Spencer, Ian, 'Settler Dominance, Agricultural Production and the Second World War in Kenya', *JAH* 21, no. 4 (1980): 497-514.

Spencer, Leon P., 'Christianity and Colonial Protest: Perceptions of W. E. Owen, Archdeacon of Kavirondo', *JRA* 13, no. 1 (1982): 47-60.

Stanley, Brian, 'Introduction: Christianity and the End of Empire', in Brian Stanley, ed., *Missions, Nationalism, and the End of Empire* (Grand Rapids, MI, and Cambridge, 2003), pp. 1-11.

Stockwell, Sarah, 'Ends of Empire', in Sarah Stockwell, ed., *The British Empire: Themes and Perspectives* (Oxford and Malden, MA, 2008), pp. 269-93.

————, '"Splendidly Leading the Way"? Archbishop Fisher and Decolonisation in British Colonial Africa', *JICH* 36, no. 3 (2008): 545-64.

Stuart, John, 'Scottish Missionaries and the End of Empire: The Case of Nyasaland', *Historical Research* 76, no. 193 (2003): 411-30.

————, '"Speaking for the Unvoiced"? British Missionaries and Aspects of African Nationalism, 1949-59', in Brian Stanley, ed., *Missions, Nationalism, and the End of Empire* (Grand Rapids, MI, and Cambridge, 2003), pp. 183-93.

————, 'Beyond Sovereignty?: Protestant Missions, Empire and Transnationalism, 1890-1950', in Kevin Grant, Philippa Levine and Frank Trentmann, eds., *Beyond Sovereignty: Britain, Empire and Transnationalism, c.1860-1950* (Basingstoke, 2007), pp. 103-25.

————, 'Empire and Religion in Colonial Botswana: The Seretse Khama Controversy, 1948-56', in Hilary M. Carey, ed., *Empires of Religion* (Basingstoke, 2008), pp. 311-32.

————, 'Overseas Mission, Voluntary Service and Aid to Africa: Max Warren, the Church Missionary Society and Kenya', *JICH* 36, no. 3 (2008): 527-43.

Tengatenga, James, 'The Good Being the Enemy of the Best: The Politics of Bishop Frank Oswald Thorne in Nyasaland and the Federation, 1936-61', *Religion in Malawi* 6 (1996): 20-9.

Throup, David, 'Crime, Politics and the Police in Colonial Kenya, 1939-63', in David Anderson and David Killingray, eds., *Policing and Decolonisation: Politics, Nationalism and the Police, 1917-65* (Manchester, 1992), pp. 127-57.

Tiénou, Tite, 'Evangelical Theory in African Contexts', in Timothy Larsen and Daniel J. Treier, eds., *The Cambridge Companion to Evangelical Theology* (Cambridge, 2007), pp. 213-24.

Tomlinson, B. R., 'The Contraction of England: National Decline and the Loss of Empire', *JICH* 11, no. 1 (1982): 58-72.

Ward, Kevin, 'The Church of Uganda and the Exile of Kabaka Mutesa II, 1953-55', *JRA* 28, no. 4 (1998): 411-49.

————, '"Taking Stock": The Church Missionary Society and Its Historians', in Kevin Ward and Brian Stanley, eds., *The Church Missionary Society and World Christianity, 1799-1999* (Grand Rapids, MI, and Richmond, Surrey, 2000), pp. 15-42.

Weller, John, 'The Influence on National Affairs of Alston May, Bishop of Northern Rhodesia, 1914-40', in T. O. Ranger and John Weller, eds., *Themes in the Christian History of Central Africa* (Berkeley and Los Angeles, 1975), pp. 195-211.

Westcott, N. J., 'Closer Union and the Future of East Africa, 1939-48: A Case Study on the "Official Mind of Imperialism"', *JICH* 10, no. 1 (1981): 67-88.

Whitehead, Clive, 'The Historiography of British Imperial Education Policy, Part II: Africa and the Rest of the Colonial Empire', *History of Education* 34, no. 4 (2005): 441-54.

Willis, Justin, 'The Nature of a Mission Community: The Universities' Mission to Central Africa in Bonde', *Past & Present* 140 (1993): 127-54.

Zvobgo, Chengetai J., 'Church and State in Rhodesia: From the Unilateral Declaration of Independence to the Pearce Commission, 1965-72', *Journal of Southern African Studies* 31, no. 2 (2005): 381-402.

3. Theses

Ditchburn, Pamela J., 'The History of Tiger Kloof, 1904-56: A London Missionary Society Educational Institution in Southern Africa', University of London PhD thesis (2008).

Howell, Caroline, 'Church and State in Decolonisation: The Case of Buganda, 1939-62', University of Oxford DPhil thesis (2002).

Kumwenda, Linda B., 'Healing, Conflict and Conversion: Medical Missions in Northern Rhodesia, 1880s-1954', University of London PhD thesis (2005).

Overy, Neil, '"These Difficult Days": Mission Church Reactions to Bantu Education in South Africa', University of London PhD thesis (2002).

Robins, Catherine E., 'Tukutendereza: A Study of Social Change and Sectarian Revival in the Balokole Revival of Uganda', Columbia University PhD thesis (1975).

Ross, Gavin A., 'European Support for and Opposition to Closer Union of the Rhodesias and Nyasaland, with Special Reference to the Period 1945-53', University of Edinburgh MLitt thesis (1988).

Skinner, Robert, 'The Roots of Solidarity: Race, Religion and the Foundation of British Anti-Apartheid Activism, 1946-58', University of Sussex DPhil thesis (2003).

Stuart, John, 'Race, Politics and Evangelisation: British Protestant Missionaries and African Colonial Affairs, 1940-63', University of London PhD thesis (2004).

4. Position Paper

Weber, Charles, 'Christianity and West African Decolonisation, 1945-60', North Atlantic Missiology Project, Position Paper No. 80 (1997).

5. Websites

Mundus: Gateway to Missionary Collections in the United Kingdom http://www.mundus.ac.uk/.

'Towards 2010: Roots and Fruits: Retrieving Scotland's Missionary Heritage' http://www.towards2010.org.uk/roots_and_fruits.

Index